The Miles Davis Lost Quintet
and Other Revolutionary
Ensembles

The Miles Davis Lost Quintet and Other Revolutionary Ensembles

Bob Gluck

The University of Chicago Press

Chicago and London

Bob Gluck is a pianist, composer, and jazz historian, as well as associate professor of music and director of the Electronic Music Studio at the State University of New York, Albany. He is the author of *You'll Know When You Get There: Herbie Hancock and the Mwandishi Band*, also published by the University of Chicago Press.

The University of Chicago Press, Chicago 60637
The University of Chicago Press, Ltd., London
© 2016 by The University of Chicago
All rights reserved. Published 2016.
Printed in the United States of America

25 24 23 22 21 20 19 18 17 16   1 2 3 4 5

ISBN-13: 978-0-226-18076-2 (cloth)
ISBN-13: 978-0-226-30339-0 (e-book)
DOI: 10.7208/chicago/9780226303390.001.0001

Library of Congress Cataloging-in-Publication Data

Gluck, Bob, author.
   The Miles Davis Lost Quintet and other revolutionary ensembles / Bob Gluck.
      pages cm
   Includes bibliographical references and index.
      ISBN 978-0-226-18076-2 (cloth: alkaline paper) — ISBN 978-0-226-30339-0 (e-book)
1. Davis, Miles. 2. Jazz — 1961 – 1970 — History and criticism. 3. Jazz — 1971 – 1980 —
History and criticism. 4. Jazz musicians — United States — Biography. I. Title.
   ML419.D39G58 2016
   785'.32195165 — dc23   2015019938

♾ This paper meets the requirements of ANSI/NISO Z39.48-1992 (Permanence of Paper).

In loving memory:

Jim Richard Wilson

Don Funes

CONTENTS

PREFACE

I was introduced to Miles Davis's *Bitches Brew* in 1970 by my family's rabbi, Chaim Stern. At the time, I was a student at Juilliard's Preparatory Division. Having just begun to broaden my exposure to music beyond what I was experiencing at the conservatory, that recording was a jolt to my system. The inspiration to write this book, the companion piece to my previous work, *You'll Know When You Get There: Herbie Hancock and the Mwandishi Band*, dates to experiences I had four years after that first encounter with Davis, when I entered college.

The phenomenal creative cauldron that was the Crane School of Music at the State University of New York at Potsdam allowed me to make sense of *Bitches Brew* and introduced me to Herbie Hancock's Mwandishi recordings. I joined a circle of friends there, mostly musicians and artists who were clustered around a charismatic young professor named Donald J. Funes. Don's nonjudgmental embrace of every conceivable musical form and culture afforded me the space to explore new musical possibilities. We listened to

John Coltrane's *A Love Supreme* and the entire Wagner *Ring* cycle in his apartment. Don's Live/Electronic Ensemble introduced me to the kind of open improvisation that I had found so baffling about *Bitches Brew*, and I have been thinking about this music ever since. I have Don to thank for so much.

In addition to the profound broadening of my musical sensibilities that Don encouraged, another life-changing experience for me in Potsdam was my friendship with Jim Richard Wilson, then an art history student. Jim, two years my senior, was one of the few non-musicians in our circle. He brought a deep intellectual and artistic curiosity and acuity to the group, and in turn was able to cultivate his lifelong deep appreciation of music in its myriad forms. Jim was a much-appreciated supporter of our collective and often wild musical and multimedia endeavors.

After leaving Potsdam, Jim and I went our separate ways. Some years later, having recently moved to the Albany, New York, area to attend a graduate program in electronic arts, I discovered his name in the regional arts council newsletter, and we renewed our friendship. Jim was instrumental in encouraging my return to live musical performance after I had taken a break from it to serve as a rabbi. Our friendship deepened while we shared our love of jazz (particularly David Murray and Miles Davis), the plastic arts, politics, the outdoors, and intellectual pursuits, as well as our parallel lives within academia. (He was the founding director of an art gallery at a nearby college.) Jim was one of the best friends I have ever had, as well as a discerning reader of both my manuscripts.

Jim spent his final two and a half years heroically battling cancer until his death in July 2014. That period was one of much personal sadness: my father, Stanley Gluck, had passed away the previous October. I miss both men deeply, but their memory, along with the ever-present support of my spouse, Pamela Faith Lerman, has spurred the creative thinking that enabled my completion of this book.

I dedicate these pages to Jim Richard Wilson and to Don Funes, two people whose friendship and steady support helped make my creative endeavors possible. I dedicated my recording of music for saxophone, piano, and electronics, *Tropelets* (Ictus Records, 2014), to my father's memory.

Faced as I was with competing possible narratives on which to focus *The Miles Davis Lost Quintet*, I owe many thanks to my editor, Elizabeth Branch Dyson, for helping guide my choice. Indeed, the Lost Quintet could be my major focus here while including two other elements from early drafts: Circle and the downtown loft scene in New York City. Both Circle and the Revolutionary Ensemble were personal discoveries made while I was at Potsdam. While I never saw Circle perform, I had the pleasure of hearing the Revolutionary Ensemble on two occasions, along with a solo performance by percussionist Jerome Cooper on a third. A conversation with Leroy Jenkins at that time (continued thirty years later) particularly sparked my interest. These were among many wonderful experiences I had while attending shows in venues like Studio Rivbea, Tin Palace, and the Public Theater. As I strove to identify a theme for this book, I came to recognize similarities between the music of Miles Davis's Lost Quintet, Circle, and the Revolutionary Ensemble. While writing, I increasingly appreciated their shared musical values and began to place all three on a single artistic continuum. Articulating the nature of that connective tissue, as well as the important differences, became an easy task.

Thank you, Elizabeth, and the entire staff at the University of Chicago Press, including Editorial Associate Nora Devlin, copy editor Sandra Hazel, and Promotions Manager Ryo Yamaguchi; I've had the pleasure of working with Elizabeth and Ryo on my earlier book as well. I am also grateful to the many discerning and encouraging readers of this manuscript, among them Pheeroan akLaff, Dawoud Bey, Andre Cholmondeley, Guy de Bievre, Douglas Ewart, Patrick Gleeson, Michael Heffley, David Katz, James Keepnews, Pamela Faith Lerman, Ras Moshe, Nashira Priester, and Jim Richard Wilson. They have made this a far better book than it would have been otherwise. For helpful contributions to my thinking and research, I extend my appreciation to Dawoud Bey, Stanley Cowell, Brent Edwards, Herbie Hancock, Jabali Billy Hart, Michael Heller, Dave Holland, George Lewis, Neil Rolnick, and Michael Veal. Thanks also to Shira Gluck for her work on interview transcriptions and editorial matters.

Many thanks to the many musicians who gave of their time to converse with me in formal interviews about that wonderful creative period of more than four decades ago: Barry Altschul, Karl Berger, Jerome Cooper, Chick Corea, Alvin Curran, Andrew Cyrille, Dave Liebman, John Mars, Michael Moss, Alphonse Mouzon, Wallace Roney, Warren Smith, and Richard Teitelbaum.

My writing is always informed by what I know and experience as a musician. One of the ways I learn more about music is by performing it. I began to explore the tune "Bitches Brew" as a performance vehicle—a collection of motifs to be variously structured and used as grist for improvisation—in 2005, initially playing solo piano with interactive computer software of my own design, and subsequently performing in trio and quartet settings. I am grateful to the various musicians who have contributed to this effort. Among them have been Michael Bisio, Don Byron, Benjamin Chadabe, David Katz, Jay Rosen, Dean Sharp, and

Christopher Dean Sullivan. Thank you to the staff at Cycling 74 (programming environment Max/MSP), Moog Music (PianoBar), and Yamaha (Disklavier).

One rarely anticipates what may prove to be a profound source of learning. My writing about music took a distinct turn in the past five years as I became aware of the strong acuity of Max, our family's finicky little shih tzu–poodle, to meter, spatial awareness, synchronicity, and levels of energy. While walking this remarkable dog, who very nearly reached the ripe age of sixteen, I began to think in terms of relational metaphors regarding improvisatory band interactions. I suspect that I am just beginning to assimilate all that I learned from Max.

Earlier drafts of this book included several topics that ultimately were not retained in the narrative and were instead spun off as articles. I extend much appreciation to the journals that provided a home for these: "Interview with David Rosenboom on His Early Career: Late 1960s–Early 1970s," *Journal SEAMUS* 22, nos. 1–2 (Spring–Fall 2011): 20–28; "Electric Circus, Electric Ear and the Intermedia Center in Late-1960s New York," *Leonardo* 45, no. 1 (2012): 50–56; "Nurturing Young Composers: Morton Subotnick's Late-1960s Studio in New York City," *Computer Music Journal* 36, no. 1 (2012): 65–80; "Morton Subotnick's *Sidewinder*," *New Music Box*, October 16, 2013, http://www .newmusicbox.org/articles/morton-subotnicks-sidewinder/; and "Paul Bley and Live Synthesizer Performance," *Jazz Perspectives* 8, no. 1 (2014): 303–22.

My family continues to be a source of joy and support, particularly during this year of mourning following the death of my father: my spouse, Pamela Faith Lerman, who deserves a second mention; my daughter, Allison Lerman-Gluck; my mother (and editor throughout my childhood), Aileen Gluck; my brother and sister-in-law, Arnie and Sarah Gluck; my aunt Myra Schubin; my nieces Ellie and Shira; and my cousins Wendy Haber and Peter Schubin, their spouses, and their wonderful children. Many other family members, too many to mention by name, have also been wonderful to me during this period. And I am grateful for my life, for my friends, and for the many musical colleagues who grace my existence.

I complete this book only weeks after the passing of Jerome Cooper and Ornette Coleman. No words can capture the depth of my gratitude to each of them.

One of the most serious problems confronted by jazz historians is that, while recordings offer the only tangible evidence we have of the music's development, some of the most important stages in that development were insufficiently recorded. Miles Davis's transitional protofusion period is a case in point. Miles spent a lot of time in the studio in 1969, and he came up with *In a Silent Way* and *Bitches Brew*, the two albums that are widely credited—or blamed—with ushering in the age of jazz-rock fusion. But Miles also spent a lot of time on the road that year, and the music he made with his working band was even more extraordinary than the music on those two remarkable albums.

PETER KEEPNEWS, "THE LOST QUINTET"[1]

Introduction

So exactly what *did* musically unfold during the period surrounding the recording of *Bitches Brew*? Until recently, only those who witnessed concerts by Miles Davis's "Lost" Quintet (1968–70; "lost" in the sense that it never completed a studio recording) or accessed bootleg recordings by the group really knew. The only "official" contemporaneous release—*Miles Davis at Fillmore: Live at the Fillmore East*[2]—represented a recording so dramatically edited as to obscure its essence.

So it is that *Bitches Brew* became the lens through which Miles Davis's work of that period became known. The music certainly confused some musicians and critics. *DownBeat*'s Jim Szantor wrote: "Listening to this double album is, to say the least, an intriguing experience. Trying to describe the music is something else again—mainly an exercise in futility. Though electronic effects are prominent, art, not gimmickry, prevails and the music protrudes mightily. Music—most of all music like this—cannot be adequately described."[3]

Some critics referenced *Bitches Brew* as the signal event initiating a fusion of rock and jazz, a perspective that added more heat than light. Stanley Crouch spoke of "static beats and clutter,"[4] while John Litweiler emphasized a "gravitational pull of the modern rock beat."[5] Yet the multiplicity of rhythmic layers and the intersections of cross rhythms within *Bitches Brew* and *Miles Davis at Fillmore* display few conventions of rock music. The slowly unfolding solos and unconventional mode of accompaniment suggest a different picture, as Langdon Winner wrote in *Rolling Stone*: "Dave Holland's bass and Jack DeJohnette's drums lay down the amorphous rhythmic patterns for Miles' electrified sound. To put it briefly, these chaps have discovered a new way to cook, a way that seems just as natural and just as swinging as anything jazz has ever known."[6]

A goal of this book is to explore how Davis's recorded performances from 1968 through 1970 illuminate the unfolding of his musical thinking during a period of personal transition. I will suggest the following: a careful listening reveals music that privileged an uneasy dynamic tension between sonic and structural openness, surprise, and experimentation and the rhythmic groove (which includes but doesn't overly favor beat-driven rock and funk elements). When viewed in this way, new webs of musical interconnection emerge. I am not suggesting a lack of continuity between the Lost Quintet and Miles Davis's subsequent funk-inflected bands. Yet by observing the more abstract, open aspects of the work of Miles Davis during this period, the listener can place the Lost Quintet within the context of highly exploratory bands, including Circle (cofounded by two members of the Lost Quintet) and the Revolutionary Ensemble.

Exploring these little-documented sister bands is my second goal. Certainly, they deserve a broader listening public, something I hope this book can help encourage. Thus, I narrate at some length their evolution, and describe and interpret their music with concrete examples. Yet if my purpose were simply to discuss Circle and the Revolutionary Ensemble, I would do so in a separate book. My reasoning here is to offer sufficient musical background and context about them to better understand a context that sheds new light on Miles Davis's own work, with the Lost Quintet.

A proper introduction requires more extensive narration, found in chapter 3, where we meet reed player Anthony Braxton and trace his journey with fellow members of the Association for the Advancement of Creative Musicians—particularly jazz violinist and violist Leroy Jenkins—from Chicago to Paris to New York; Braxton's encounter and tour with Musica Elettronica Viva; and then his meeting the Chick Corea, Dave Holland, Barry Altschul trio that invited him to join, forming Circle. Jenkins, now in New York, cofounded the Revolutionary Ensemble.

The musical world these musicians inhabited was intimately, interpersonally interconnected. From his Chicago days, Braxton was friends with Miles Davis's Lost Quintet drummer Jack DeJohnette. Both men were AACM members, as was Jenkins. When Braxton joined the musical collective band Circle, he partnered with the two other members of the Davis rhythm section. Within the same building where this pair lived was an existing collective organization that included members of future Davis bands. Few steps of separation lay between Braxton, Jenkins, Davis, and some of the others. Translating these connections from mere anecdote to significance requires articulating musical and social meaning.

Core musical values shared by Circle and the Revolutionary Ensemble drew from the pioneering work of the AACM, Cecil Taylor, Sun Ra, and most significantly Ornette Coleman and John Coltrane. Miles Davis paid close attention to Coltrane's every move, but as we will see in chapter 1, as soon as Coleman arrived in New York City in 1959, Davis was profoundly influenced by his ideas as well. We palpably hear the results in the 1960s Davis Quintet's increasingly collective improvisations[7] beginning in 1965. In this vein, Davis biographer Eric Nisenson observes of *Bitches Brew*: "The climax of 'Pharoah's Dance,' while Miles states and re-states the primary theme, the rest of the band reaches a cacophonous frenzy that is obviously an echo of [Coleman's] 'Free Jazz' or [Coltrane's collective improvisation] 'Ascension' at their most mind-bendingly intense."[8] Nisenson also suggests affinities between Davis's approach to modality in "Bitches Brew" the tune and that of Coltrane's later work such as "'Kulu Se Mama,' and in the improvising over pedal point and the use of two bassists, one serving as the anchor, the other playing far more freely, the classic 'India' or later Coltrane's version of 'Nature Boy.'"[9] It is in this light that critic Leonard Feather observed of Davis: "He is creating a new and more complex form, drawing from the avant-garde, atonalism, modality, rock, jazz and the universe. It has no name, but some listeners have called it 'Space Music.'"[10]

Yet these are musical details, and music is more than that. As a form of human expression, music is as much about the society that people create and inhabit as it is about pure sound. Each of these three bands existed within a distinct social and economic context, and these settings suggest differentiation as much as the bands' aesthetics point to resonances. Chapter 8 will summarize my third goal in writing this book, presented throughout the text, by identifying the profound distance that lay between Miles Davis and the Revolutionary Ensemble in their placement within the musical economy. This includes access to financial resources, recording contracts, and bookings, and the ability to reach an interested public. No matter how abstract Davis's chosen music might be, it would never have to inhabit small loft spaces rather than substantial concert halls, or suffer a lack in recordings rather than have steady studio access with guaranteed record releases. The gap between these musical worlds is vast. Circle was able to straddle a free-form aesthetic while performing on the jazz circuit, largely due to the association of half its band members with Miles Davis. This access, however, exposed Anthony Braxton, who did not identify himself as a jazz player (although he was then appearing on the jazz circuit), to the hostility of critics. The economic relationships and realities are important. Yet they should not detract from my thesis that from an aesthetic perspective the differences collapse.

In his original liner notes to Miles Davis's *Bitches Brew*, critic Ralph Gleason wrote:

> and sometimes i think maybe what we need is to tell people that this is here because somehow in this plasticized world they have the automatic reflex that if something is labeled one way then that is all there is in it and we are always finding out to our surprise that there is more to blake or more to ginsberg or more to trane or more to stravinsky than whatever it was we thought was there in the first place.
>
> so be it with the music we have called jazz and which i never knew what it was because it was so many different things to so many different people each apparently contradicting the other and one day i flashed that it was music.
>
> that's all, and when it was great music it was great art and it didn't have anything at all to do with labels and who says mozart is by definition better than sonny rollins and to whom.
>
> so lenny bruce said there is only what is and that's a pretty good basis for a start. this music is. this music is new. this music is new music and it hits me like an electric shock and the word "electric" is interesting because the music is to some degree electric music either by virtue of what you can do with tapes and by the process by which it is preserved on tape or by the use of electricity in the actual making of the sounds themselves.[11]

Gleason's conception of music beyond labels unites Miles Davis's work from 1968 through 1970 with kindred spirits—among them Circle and the Revolutionary Ensemble. Indeed, all "this music is new music," music that draws its expressive power from the legacy of Ornette Coleman, among others. While previous writers have generally treated Davis's electric ensembles from the perspective of biographical narrative,[12] it is my hope to offer a close, comparative look at the music itself and the musical relationships between players. In this way, the attentive listener can discover oft-obscured deep interconnections that uncover the profound originality of this important body of work.

1

Miles Goes Electric

For musicians within the world designated "jazz" who sought to expand their horizons, 1969 was ripe with possibilities. An arresting sense of urgency marked both Ornette Coleman's *Crisis*, symbolized by its album cover image of the Bill of Rights in flames, and Tony Williams Lifetime's searing *Emergency*, showcasing his new high-volume, high-energy drums, electric guitar, and organ trio. This was but one year after the assassination of Dr. Martin Luther King Jr. The night after King's death, at a televised concert in Boston, James Brown soothed an audience that was hurting and angry, and cities burned. Meanwhile, a black cultural renaissance was burgeoning. People were proudly assuming Swahili names and wearing dashikis. Politically, the Black Panther Party was at its height.

Nineteen sixty-nine was also the year of the first moon landing, a growing antiwar movement, and Woodstock Nation. Musicians mirrored and generated the high level of imaginative possibilities percolating throughout American culture. While this was the era of the concept album, the best examples display a startling depth

and breadth of emotional expressivity and sonic variety across a single recording. Among these are the Art Ensemble of Chicago's *People in Sorrow,* Herbie
Hancock's *The Prisoner,* and Frank Zappa's *Uncle Meat,* a mash-up of rock and
roll, 1950s doo-wop, exploratory improvisation, Stravinskian angularity, and
musique concrète.

Festival programming offered dramatic genre-crossing juxtapositions:
in Monterey, the Modern Jazz Quartet and Miles Davis performed alongside
Sly and the Family Stone; at Newport, Bill Evans and Freddie Hubbard were
paired with James Brown and Led Zeppelin. Even more extreme was the as-
semblage at Festival Actuel in Amougie, Belgium: an eclectic montage of the
Art Ensemble of Chicago, Sunny Murray, Don Cherry, and Archie Shepp; Pink
Floyd, Frank Zappa, keyboard whiz Keith Emerson and the Nice; and Musica
Elettronica Viva.

The permeability of musical boundaries was being tested and stretched. It
is not by chance that 1969 was the year when Miles Davis recorded two albums
that meditated on the wealth of musical influences that defined the 1960s. Each
took the vantage point of a jazz recording to look outward and inward. On one
hand, the albums balanced rock and funk's rhythmic dynamism with a relatively
static aesthetic sensibility. On the other, they sought grounding in Davis's lyrical
sensibilities while casting off familiar conventions of musical structure.

Along with Cecil Taylor, Charles Mingus, and Sun Ra (each of whom had released pivotal albums in 1956), Ornette Coleman had opened a new musical
passageway with the 1959 release of *The Shape of Jazz to Come* and premiere
performances of the material at the Five Spot in New York City. A growing
number of younger musicians were exploring the possibilities his music suggested. Coleman provided a way out of what some, including John Coltrane
and Miles Davis, had felt to be the growing tyranny of cyclical chord progressions. In an interview with Martin Williams, Coleman famously remarked: "If
I'm going to follow a preset chord sequence, I may as well write out my solo."[1]
What he meant was that the repeated cycle of harmonic movement shaped expectations of note choices based on what is suggested by functional harmony.
Within bebop, harmony had expanded to accommodate broader note choices.[2]
But Coltrane demonstrated the limitations of this approach. His recording of
"Giant Steps" (1959) traversed rapid-fire, cascading chord changes as if to say:
"You want chords? I'll give you chords!" An overabundance of chords pointed
to the need for new structural principles and the desire to balance freedom of
the individual with membership in a collective.

Saxophonist Sam Rivers described the new music of the period as "freeform," a "revitalizing force" in jazz. In place of the detailed intricacies of bebop, the goal was to play with "no pre-conceived plan," to "make every performance different, to let your emotions and musical ideas direct the course of the music, to let the sound of the music set up its own impetus, to remember what has been stated so that repetition is intentional, to be responsive to myriads of color, polyrhythms, rise and fall, ebb and flow, thematic variations, etc., etc."[3]

Although Davis publicly expressed scorn and, frankly, jealousy toward what he believed to be unwarranted attention given to Coleman, he was clearly listening.

Davis writes: "I used to go and check them out when I was in town, even sat in with them a couple of times." His reading of what happened could be viewed as reportage or as braggadocio: "I could play with anybody, in any style. . . . But Ornette could play only one way back then. I knew that after listening to them a few times, so I just sat in and played what they played."[4] He caustically adds: "He just came and fucked up everybody. Before long you couldn't buy a seat in the Five Spot. . . . They were playing music in a way everyone was calling 'free jazz' or 'avant-garde' or 'the new thing' or whatever."[5]

Critic Larry Kart reports Coleman's memories of the encounter, confirming Davis's presence at the Five Spot but adding an ulterior motive:

> Years later Ornette said, "I'm not mentioning names, but I remember one trumpet player who came up to me and said, 'I don't know what you're doing, but I want to let the people see me playing with you. Why don't you play some blues and let me come up and play.' So I said, 'Ok,' and we did some song that he had played with Charlie Parker. Then when they asked him what he thought of my music, he said, 'Oh, the guy's all messed up—you can tell that just by listening to him.' And it wasn't true."[6]

Davis commented that he liked Coleman and trumpeter Don Cherry as people but saw them as neither talented nor original and revolutionary. He reserved particular scorn for Cherry: "I didn't like what they were playing, especially Don Cherry on that little horn he had. It just looked to me like he was playing a lot of notes and looking real serious." Davis challenged not only Coleman's choice of this fellow trumpeter but Coleman's own performance on trumpet and violin, for which he lacked formal training: "[He was disrespecting] all those people who play them well."[7] But this wasn't the first time Davis had disparaged a musician. Robin D. G. Kelley reports a screaming match Davis had with Thelonious Monk at Monk's house in the early 1950s; while playing one of the pianist's compositions, Davis reportedly told him that he wasn't playing the music correctly. Monk's father asked Davis to leave.[8]

Davis's rivalry with Coleman seems at least in part generational, as both men were close in age. Coleman's dramatic appearance on a scene where Davis had staked a claim as a central innovator could not have been easy for him. Even with fifteen years of history in New York, he was already contending with the rising star of another contemporary, former sideman John Coltrane. In his autobiography, Davis expresses appreciation for Coltrane's late work, both musically and in terms of its sociopolitical meaning for young black people. But it was Coleman who commanded the attention that had previously been directed Davis's way; rattled by this, he sought to reassert his dominance.[9] Davis's tensions with Coleman can also be viewed with respect to the comparative ease and esteem with which a younger generation of musicians related to Coleman. Anthony Braxton, Leroy Jenkins, and drummer Jerome Cooper, all of whom we will meet in this book, were among the many who saw Ornette Coleman as a mentor and generous supporter.[10]

Despite his complicated feelings toward Coleman, Davis learned from him. Although years later he continued to diminish the import of Coleman's method and execution, he acknowledged the significance of his methodology: "[The group was] just being *spontaneous in their playing, playing 'free form,' bouncing off what each other was doing* . . . it had been done before, only they were doing it with no kind of form or structure . . . *that's the thing that was important about what they did*, not their playing." And Davis added a respectful postscript: "Now, what Ornette did a few years later was hip, and I told him so."[11]

The influence of Coleman's approach, his use of intuition to govern improvisation and his application of a democratic principle to guide collectivity,[12] can be heard in Davis's quintet of the 1960s as the band turned toward open forms. By 1965, it was deeply engaged in what Chick Corea calls "that thing of vaporizing themes and just going places."[13] "Going places" was the result of a collective musical mind at work. Davis's new electric quintet of 1969 was primed to take these principles further.[14]

The musically democratic principle had gained influence across North America and Europe. In 1964 in New York, a cluster of creative musicians participated in a four-day festival named the October Revolution in Jazz; some of these players later formed the Jazz Composers Guild.[15] The next year in Chicago, black musicians gathered under the banner of the Association for the Advancement of Creative Musicians (AACM), with sister groups springing up in other parts of the United States.[16] London had its own "free jazz" scene; among its participants were guitarist John McLaughlin and bassist Dave Holland, future musical associates of Miles Davis.

From where else did Davis draw inspiration during this time? Drummer Tony Williams was an important source of new ideas within Davis's 1960s quintet.[17] His own first two recordings, *Lifetime* and *Spring!*, anticipate the developing musical abstraction[18] soon to be found within that band. By the late 1950s, when Williams was thirteen years old, he had played with saxophonist Sam Rivers's band and participated with those musicians in the Boston Improvisational Ensemble.

Rivers described the group in this way: "We'd go to museums and we'd play the lines on the paintings, he [an art historian and musician who led the group] would explain the painting, and then we'd play the music like this. . . . The usual Dada kind of stuff. We'd throw ink splats on the paper, and do the rise-and-fall of this."[19] He refers here to the way some musicians interpreted graphic scores, translating visual information into sound.[20]

Three years later, in 1963, following dates with icons of the avant-garde, pianist Cecil Taylor[21] and saxophonist Eric Dolphy, Williams joined saxophonist Jackie McLean's band. He gained Miles Davis's ear, netting an invitation to join his quintet; in 1965, he subbed for Elvin Jones with the John Coltrane Quartet.[22]

Coltrane's work during this period was of great interest to Davis, Trane's former employer, and to his band. Coltrane's quartet took an expansive approach to the concept of soloist-with-accompaniment, offering the kind of distinct flexibility and adaptability that saxophonist Wayne Shorter could build on with Davis.

Regarding Davis's influence, trumpeter Wallace Roney, a protégé of his, observes:

> This band had participated and assimilated the innovations of The John Coltrane Quartet, Ornette Coleman Quartet, and Miles Second Great Quintet and utilized them freely with the new Pop avant-garde. They were on the front line of these innovations along with individual members of the Second Quintet, and Miles himself! The difference between the Second Quintet and the Lost Quintet was the second Quintet innovations were conceived adjacent to the John Coltrane Quartet and although inspired by the happenings of that Quartet, and by Ornette and Mingus, they were developing their ideas, whereas the lost Quintet was free to use both concepts at any given time. In other words the lost Quintet might play things pioneered by the

Second Quintet behind Miles, play something pioneered by the John Coltrane Quartet behind Wayne or vice versa or a hybrid behind either one, or play totally abstract.[23]

As the Miles Davis Quintet evolved during its most exploratory period, 1965–68, Davis sought something akin to what in politics is sometimes called a "third way."[24] He kept one foot planted in inherited forms and the other in the new order. While seeking musical cohesion in the qualities of sound, he was not yet prepared to depart from song forms. His own playing remained committed to melody[25] and a rootedness in the blues.[26] But his band was also beginning to embrace spontaneous collective invention. By the late 1960s, the idea of weaving sonic fabric from melodic or rhythmic germs—concepts developed by Coleman, Coltrane, and Taylor—had worked its way into Davis's creative imagination.

My favorite example is from the quintet's appearance at the Paris Jazz Festival, held at Salle Pleyel on November 6, 1967. Wayne Shorter's "Masqualero," a constant on the November 1967 European tour, receives a striking treatment, beginning with a dramatic and forceful statement of the theme. This opening is followed by a quiet, spare solo by Davis, punctuated by short spikes by Herbie Hancock, a steady pulse by Tony Williams, and a stream of repeated notes by bassist Ron Carter.[27] Suddenly, Hancock initiates a change in course by playing a downward, stepwise series of chords, which Davis imitates in his solo line, echoed by Hancock. As Davis's solo unleashes an outpouring of faster notes, the rhythm section builds energy and tension, reaching a peak, and then shifting to a pastoral mood. It is difficult to tell whether one musician has initiated this shift or it is simply a collective action. Either way, the entire band is instantaneously together. When Davis plays a more upbeat phrase, the band again responds, shape-shifting as a unit.

This reconfiguration of mood, texture, and intensity occurs again and again throughout the performance. It happens next at the start of a Shorter solo that begins with a beautiful yet simple figure, juxtaposed to an equally lovely Hancock accompaniment. Again, it is difficult to tell who has initiated the change. Thirty seconds into his solo, Shorter reaches into a higher register to play a variant of his starting motif, then descends slowly. Before we know it, another moment of musical grace unfolds, beginning with a spontaneous, new Shorter melody, maybe a recasting of the previous one, joined by Hancock. Williams and Carter are immediately present to capture the subtle shift in mood. For most of the solo, Williams has played a repeated-stroke snare figure, akin to a very gentle military cadence. With only a slight shift in volume and intensity, the same material has been transformed into a perfect complement for the new emotional tone.

While Miles Davis was exploring—and, in a sense, mainstreaming—abstraction and spontaneous invention, other musical worlds beckoned to him from beyond the jazz realm: rock, rhythm and blues, and funk. His eyes and ears were trained simultaneously on both abstract and populist principles.[28] Chick Corea remarks: "In retrospect if I look at it now, it's pretty obvious where Miles was going. He wanted to reconnect with audiences. And to do that, he put a groove and rhythm back into his music. He more and more put flavors of the youth of the times into his presentation, the way he dressed, the musicians he hired, the way they played, the electric guitar."[29] Davis's repertoire began to draw from vamps and grooves, the steady, repetitive rhythmic pulses and bass lines of rhythm and blues, and rock and roll.[30]

His path would lead from the blues-gospel bass line of "It's About That Time" (from *In a Silent Way*, 1969) through the funk riffs of James Brown and Sly and the Family Stone that ground his 1970 recording *A Tribute to Jack Johnson*, and ultimately to his vigorously percolating, multilayered, polyrhythmic guitar and electric organ bands that produced *Dark Magus* (1974), *Agharta* (1975), and *Pangaea* (1975).

While a youthful, more contemporary black aesthetic was guiding Davis toward a more pronounced, regular metric pulse, his music continued to tap into a deep well of experimental influences. As Corea notes: "Experimentation and the search for new combinations was definitely 'in the air.' . . . The excitement over search for new forms was at a peak, and as improvisers, the best place to start seemed to be with free-form improvisation, where the rules were made up as you go."[31] Aspects of this sensibility continued to shape his even more funk-oriented music until his first retirement in 1975.

What drove Corea's and Dave Holland's passions while playing with Davis wasn't the beat but, as Corea continues, "the free music aspect of the band; that's what interested us. . . . Miles was 'in kind of a search.'" Although "as the concerts developed, Miles kept going more and more to a groove rhythm. He'd start a groove rhythm and the band would go in all kinds of different directions, with Wayne's solo and mine and what Dave and Jack were doing."[32] The "free music aspect" of this Miles Davis Quintet was equal in importance to the grooves, and the flexibility and open instincts of Jack DeJohnette rendered his drummer as deeply implicated in these directions as Corea and Holland.

What is notable is Davis's ability to maintain his balance while remaining on a leading edge. Greg Tate speaks of his deep rootedness in his sense of himself as a black man, culturally confident. Tate adds: "Miles' music makes you think of Nat Turner, proud without being loud because it was about plotting insurrection. In this sense Miles never changed. His agenda remained the same from day one: stay ahead."[33] Despite his ambivalence about what has been termed the "freedom principle"[34] linking open improvisation, black identity, and political freedom, Davis at various points embraced elements of all three concepts. As in most things, he did so in his own way and in his own time.

He was at the time a nondirective bandleader. Members of his quintet were given wide latitude to play what they wished. The "just going places" ethic noted by Corea was pregnant with possibilities, opening tremendous space for unanticipated musical creativity. Corea observes that Davis's method was focused on the *choice* of musicians:

Miles . . . was a chemist—a spiritual chemist—as far as putting musicians together, because he himself didn't really compose tunes that much, although he developed styles and arrangements but he chose musicians that went together a way that he heard and that he liked. And he went from this piano player to that piano player or from this drummer to that drummer—he chose these guys so that it went together in a way that he heard it. And I guess that's leadership, you know, it's like the choosing of the way and the treatment of the group.[35]

In a 1969 *DownBeat* interview with Larry Kart, Corea relates that in their first conversation, Davis told him about how to interpret Shorter's compositions: "I don't know what else to tell you except that we'll go and play, but whatever *you* think it is, that's what it is."[36]

Hancock remembers Davis's leadership of the previous quintet in a similar way. He explains in a 1971 *DownBeat* interview:

With Miles' band we were all allowed to play what we wanted to play and shaped the music according to the group effort and not to the dictates of Miles, because he really never dictated what he wanted. I try to do the same thing with my group. I think it serves this function that I just mentioned—that everybody feels that they're part of the product, you know, and not just contributing something to somebody else's music. They may be my tunes, but the music belongs to the guys in the band. They make the music—it's not just my thing.[37]

Wayne Shorter

Shorter's first decade on the national stage began in 1959 with sessions with John Coltrane and fellow members of Davis's first quintet (Wynton Kelly, Paul Chambers, Philly Joe Jones), a recording under his own name, *Introducing Wayne Shorter*, and the beginning of a five-year stint with Art Blakey and the Jazz Messengers. Blakey's group was the preeminent hard bop ensemble of its time and a training ground for young musicians. With Blakey, Shorter joined a front line with trumpeter Lee Morgan (later replaced by Freddie Hubbard); all three horn players recorded on one another's Blue Note Records sessions. Shorter became the Blakey band's chief composer, a role he continued when he joined the Miles Davis Quintet in 1964.[38]

Shorter was always an arts man, majoring in visual art in high school and graduating with a degree in music education from New York University. The university's Greenwich Village location afforded him the opportunity to hear Duke Ellington, Dizzy Gillespie, Charlie Parker, and other prominent musicians at a neighborhood theater, and at Birdland and the Open Door farther uptown. The timing of his graduation proved prescient: "One week I was hanging out at the Café Bohemia [in the Village]. Everybody was in the joint—Kenny Clark, Donald Byrd, Max Roach, Jimmy Smith had just come to town, and Cannonball [Adderley] had come from Florida—all in that same week. I was standing at the bar, and Donald Byrd said, 'Hey, Wayne, come on up.'"[39] After serving in the army, he returned to New York. Shorter built a close association with Coltrane—he recalls Trane inviting him over to play: "Hey, you're playing that funny stuff, like me. Come on over to my house." There, he heard Coltrane experimenting with what would become the chord patterns of "Giant Steps." He realized that "if there is anything new that I am going to do, I'm going to have to do it all by myself."[40]

One year into Shorter's tenure with Davis—around the time of the famous concerts at Chicago's Plugged Nickel—the band members began to actively ground their musical structures in intuition. This shift is documented on the recordings *ESP* (1965), *Live at the Plugged Nickel* (1982/1995, recorded in 1965), *Miles Smiles* (1966), *Nefertiti* (1967), and *Sorcerer* (1967). The new approach also served as the engine that would guide the Lost Quintet.[41] It was one that suited Shorter well, provided there was attentive and flexible support from his bandmates. His improvisational approach is described by Kart as one "in which emotion is simultaneously expressed and 'discussed' (i.e. spontaneously found motifs are worked out to their farthest implications with an eyes-open conscious control)." These "workings out" are anything but clinical, as Kart adds: "His playing has more overt emotional qualities of tenderness or passion which can give pleasure to the listener."[42] Indeed, what Shorter brought to both Davis bands was great imagination, intensity, and emotion. Four years with the 1960s Davis Quintet gave him a deep knowledge of the give-and-take chemistry Davis sought within his new ensemble.

Transitions

At first, Miles Davis's Lost Quintet seemed less oriented toward free exploration than the previous band, composed of Wayne Shorter, Herbie Hancock, Ron Carter, and Tony Williams. That situation changed as the band shifted in personnel, allowing a new chemistry to develop. First, in August 1968, twenty-one-year-old British bassist Dave Holland replaced Carter. In July, Miroslav Vitous had filled the gap left from Carter's departure. Davis, vacationing in London, came to Ronnie Scott's club one night to hear pianist Bill Evans, but unexpectedly discovered Holland, who was playing that night with a group opposite Evans.[43] Jack DeJohnette was Evans's drummer but was also playing melodica in the group with Holland.[44] Holland relates: "Miles dropped in, and between two sets his former drummer Philly Joe Jones passed on the message to me. But when I got off, he had left, and I missed him the next morning at his hotel, as he had checked out and was on his way back to New York. Three weeks later, his agent called, informing me I had to be there in three days. That's when I met him for the first time, in the studio."[45]

Holland played both electric and acoustic bass—Carter had not wanted to play electric—and once Davis heard him, the bandleader immediately surmised that he just might be the right person for his band.[46] The choice proved prescient, because Holland could play not only what Davis was seeking but much more, since his musical interests had been shaped in part within London's open-improvisation world.

In September 1968, Chick Corea replaced Herbie Hancock, at Tony Williams's recommendation.[47] Hancock told John S. Wilson of the *New York Times* on the eve of the premiere of Hancock's new sextet: "Miles had heard Chick Corea and felt he would be the best new piano player for him. While Chick was with Stan Getz, he had six weeks off so Miles decided to use him for that period."[48] Holland and Corea's first studio session with Davis was on September 24, 1968, recording two tunes that would appear on *Filles de Kilimanjaro*.[49] The pair recorded in the studio with Davis throughout November and into early December. These sessions often involved multiple keyboardists, including Hancock and Josef Zawinul. Guitarist John McLaughlin was another regular participant.[50]

A New Bassist: Dave Holland

Dave Holland was born in Wolverhampton, a town in the West Midlands of England. During the nineteenth and twentieth centuries, the region became home to automobile, glass, and other manufacturing industries.[51] According to Holland, "There were no musicians in my family, but my uncle brought a ukelele home and started strumming some chords. I wanted him to show me, so that's how I picked up my first things, and I was just five years old then. There was a piano, too; my mother and grandmother sang songs from sheet music, so I began to pick out tunes with it."[52]

The young Holland took up rock guitar but switched to bass as a teenager, playing in local "beat . . . C&W-style [country and western] pop" groups[53] and "studying Ray Brown's work on Oscar Peterson's albums *Night Train* and *Affinity*, plus two Leroy Vinnegar records, *Leroy Walks* and *Leroy Walks Again*."[54] When he was eighteen, he left Wolverhampton for the musically more cosmopolitan London scene. "For kids like myself, music was like a ticket to ride, a way out of that dreadful working environment and rigid class system."[55]

In London, Holland played clubs and restaurants; his diverse repertoire included Dixieland, which was sweeping England at the time.[56] He also joined visiting American saxophonists Coleman Hawkins, Ben Webster, and Joe Henderson and British sax player Ronnie Scott at the eponymously titled premier London jazz club, Ronnie Scott's.[57] Holland recalled in 1968: "When I came to London four years ago, I couldn't read music and had to take all kinds of jobs — even worked in a Greek restaurant playing bouzouki."[58] During this period, he was studying bass with James Merrett at the Guildhall School of Music and became involved with the growing British open-improvisation world, which included a trio he joined in 1967 with guitarist John McLaughlin and drummer Tony Oxley.[59]

Among Holland's musical associates was saxophonist John Surman, and he played with John Stevens's Spontaneous Music Ensemble, recording *Karyobin Are the Imaginary Birds Said to Live in Paradise* in early 1968.[60] The recording included musical pioneers Derek Bailey, Evan Parker, and Kenny Wheeler. This collective improvisation was organized as a series of short spurts of activity, each one a phrase played in parallel (not unison), each separated by a brief pause. In this form of improvisation, embedded within each cluster of activity, individual musicians listen closely and respond to one another, completing and commenting on the other's gestures. At times, one or more of the players are akin to a relay race, where one person hands a baton off to the next. Holland's rapid, mellifluous phrases, first pizzicato and later arco, reflect the kind of individual-within-the-collective thinking that would serve him well with Miles Davis and later with Circle, Anthony Braxton, and Sam Rivers. He is rarely in the foreground, yet is an integral element in the group chemistry, an ever-active, highly engaged presence, crafting well-shaped phrases and thinking on his feet.

Holland came to the States to join Miles Davis's band after completing his final semester at the Guildhall School of Music. "I had only four days to prepare. Luckily I knew most of his music from the records. Right after I got to New York, we opened for 10 days at Count Basie's Club in Harlem."[61] *Melody Maker* critic Jeff Atterton gave the band a rave review, noting "the strong bass playing of Dave Holland who seemed very much at home with the group and more than able to hold his own in this fast company."[62]

The move to the States represented a big change for Holland, but he quickly learned to navigate the New York scene. "I had been out of the country [England] only once before that and being there at that time was a real eye-opener. There was a cultural revolution going on then: you had the Vietnam War and the Civil Rights Movement coming to a head, then the political assassinations, so it was such an incredibly intense period. Sure, the language was the same, but I was learning a new culture as well as finding my way around and making contacts."[63] An informal recording from October 28, 1968, has Holland playing with John McLaughlin, Jack DeJohnette, and an unidentified pianist in a relatively open improvisational setting.

A New Pianist: Chick Corea

Chick Corea was raised in a musical household; his father was Armando Corea, a trumpeter and bassist who played the jazz clubs around their hometown, Boston, and nearby Cape Cod. Corea notes that his dad was "a musician all his life and he gave me my first instruction. He was really kind and gentle. He got me off to a real safe start. My parents were both always very encouraging and allowed me total freedom to pursue music."[64] Armando was active from the 1930s through Corea's adolescence in the 1950s. When he was around four years old, Corea "first heard Bud [Powell] play, on my dad's seventy-eight RPM vinyl . . .

[and] I do remember the spirit of his playing, and the 'bubble-iness' of his piano playing attracting me and I just liked it. I kept listening to him."[65]

Chick Corea's formal musical education was limited to "a six-year stint that I spent with a great classical pianist who lives in Boston whose name is Salvatore Sullo. . . . I began to study with him when I was about eleven, twelve years old and stayed with him until I was about sixteen or seventeen years old. Bach, Beethoven, and Chopin were prevalent in my classical music studies on the piano, along with a little bit of Mozart and Scarlatti."[66] Corea also developed skills as a trumpeter and drummer.[67]

When he was a teen, it was Bud Powell's musical approach and feel that he was the most strongly drawn to. He became interested in Powell's compositions and "transcribe[d] some of Bud's piano playing note-for-note and I would try to play the notes." Literal transcription was but the first step in learning to emulate Powell. "I would play the notes, but it still wouldn't sound like Bud. I knew something was missing from the phrasing or the rhythm or whatever." Corea began to play along with the recordings, "trying to get it so that my playing would just kind of exactly duplicate what was coming off the record. Bud's playing was just completely innovative and interesting to me—everything he did was so spirited . . . and so creative."[68]

It was not unusual for a young jazz pianist to view Bud Powell as a model. After all, Powell had played a substantial role in establishing core traditions of bebop, crafting a harmonic grounding of its highly chromatic musical language—with left-hand voicing of ninth and thirteenth chords—while backing Charlie Parker and Dizzy Gillespie. Powell translated the angularity of Parker's horn lines for his right hand. But equally important to Corea was his simplicity, symmetry, and directness.[69] Over time, like Powell, he developed a style that is simultaneously rhythmically energetic and in equal measures virtuosic and to the point. Corea's solos came to present well-developed ideas, often symmetrical in phrasing.[70]

During his teen years, the pianist started playing on his father's gigs. In high school, Corea's interests expanded to hard bop trumpeter Blue Mitchell and pianist Horace Silver, whose solos he also transcribed and played in a trio. "Horace's music and his piano playing was a little bit more accessible to me because it wasn't so technically demanding as Bud's." In the late 1950s, Corea continued to follow many of the leading jazz pianists of that decade: "I listened to John Lewis. I listened to early Thelonious Monk on Miles' records. . . . Hank Jones played some with Miles, and then finally into the . . . mid-fifties somewhere is where Red Garland showed up. And Red's style just, you know, captured me—I loved. It. Then, even after that, Wynton Kelly was a real favorite of mine and after that came Bill Evans—this is all Miles's career. Then after Bill Evans came Herbie Hancock. So all of these guys were tremendous inspirations to me, piano-wise."[71] And all these pianists had played with Miles Davis.

After following his father to the senior Corea's gigs, his first hit on his own, "outside of my father's circle," was as "a junior in high school—I guess I was 15 or 16 years old—I was called to do a gig with Cab [Calloway]'s band for a week at Boston's Mayfair Hotel. That was my first real stepping-out. I was stunned. All of a sudden I had to wear a tuxedo and it was like a big show with lights on the stage. It was kind of scary, you know? He had a dance line of ladies who were only dressed a little bit. They seemed huge to me. They were daunting. After a little while I got into the swing of it and started really loving being out on my own like that. As for the entertainment value of it all, I was just thrilled to be there."[72]

Corea moved to New York City in 1959 after his high school graduation, and his recording career began in 1962 in the Latin jazz bands of Willie Bobo and Mongo Santamaria. Joining Montego Joe's band in 1964 continued Corea's experience playing Latin. He first recorded with Blue Mitchell that year and joined his band in 1965. Also in 1965, Corea recorded with flutist Herbie Mann (*Roar of the Greasepaint*). The following year, he played with Latin vibraphonist Cal Tjader. He also recorded his first album as a leader, *Tones for Joan's Bones*, "a breakout hard-bop date with a modal feel."[73]

Corea's jazz interests continued to be augmented by an appreciation of contemporary European art music: "My favorite contemporary composers are Bartok and Stravinsky. Also, I admire Eric Satie's music an awful lot."[74] We find throughout Corea's mature playing—particularly as a member of Miles Davis's Lost Quintet and Circle[75]—rapid runs and other figures built on tone clusters (collections of adjacent notes that are played simultaneously).[76] Many examples can be found throughout this book. These are devices well represented within Bartok's piano repertoire, for example in *Microcosmos*, volume 5.[77] An overlapping influence in this regard may have been Thelonious Monk, who also made use of tone clusters throughout his work.[78]

A 1966 stint with Stan Getz[79] was followed by a tour with Sarah Vaughan in 1967, and then his tenure with Miles Davis. Corea's trio recording *Now He Sings, Now He Sobs*, with Miroslav Vitous and drummer Roy Haynes, followed in 1968.[80] Accepting an invitation from Miles Davis was of course an excellent move for an aspiring jazz musician.

A Rhythm Section Two-Thirds Rebuilt: The Band's Final Shows with Tony Williams

On October 5, 1968, Davis's band, now with Dave Holland, Chick Corea, Wayne Shorter, and Tony Williams, played a show at UCLA that *Los Angeles Times* critic Leonard Feather hailed as "not likely to be surpassed this season by any other group that works at this high level of abstraction. . . . The sensitivity that bound the five men in a jagged unity often seemed to attain extra-sensory peaks of invention." Feather also lauded the new band members: "In this new and more challenging context, [Corea] drew on inner reserves of creative strength that were rarely apparent in the relatively conservative groups with which he had previously been heard [Herbie Mann, Stan Getz]. Holland displayed great sensitivity and a rich, big sound. Although meters, accents, volume and moods shifted around with the liquidity of a light show, nothing seemed to phase him." He referred to Davis as "a spellbinder" and described Williams's drumming as "frenzied." The repertoire drew largely from the 1965–67 Davis Quintet's song-book, largely composed by Shorter: "Agitation," "Footprints," "Paraphernalia," "Pinocchio," and "Nefertiti," plus "'Round Midnight" and "an oblique, restless up tempo blues excursion based on one of his early records, 'Walkin'.'" All in all, a propitious public start for a band that by this time had replaced bassist Ron Carter and pianist Herbie Hancock.[81]

The same outfit, continuing with Williams, appeared at the Jazz Workshop in Boston for a four-day stand on December 5–8. This was four months after Holland's first performances with the band at Count Basie's club in Harlem.[82] Shows from this period represent Davis's first experiments using two electric pianists in concert settings. One track of an audience recording from Boston pairs Corea with Wynton Kelly on "Round Midnight." Kelly is likely playing a Wurlitzer, but is barely audible until he takes the first piano solo. Around this time, Davis also paired Corea with Stanley Cowell, in Montreal and probably Boston. Cowell views the combination to have been unsuccessful.[83]

The Miles Davis Quintet was not an easy band for newcomers to join. By 1968, five years of chemistry among the players had been amassed with a distinct experimental trajectory, particularly since 1965. Holland remembers that it took him nearly a year to gain enough confidence in this new setting.[84] Corea, stepping into Hancock's seat, remembers:

> The main challenge [upon joining Miles's band] was to step into a hot-seat that had developed over six or seven years with Tony Williams, Ron Carter, Herbie

Hancock and Wayne Shorter, as one of the great, great groups of jazz in live performance. . . . It was a pretty big challenge to step in there and try and make some sense. Tony was still playing with Miles, he was in his last six months of his tenure and was full-blown in the freedom with which he was approaching the music, and it was a challenge to try and fit in. But, Miles was really encouraging and told me to just play right here, and I did. It was very rewarding.[85]

Four months after Corea joined the band, on February 18, 1969, Davis returned to the studio to record the groundbreaking *In a Silent Way*, using three electric pianists in tandem: Corea, Hancock, and Joe Zawinul, with Williams on drums.[86] By this point, the only members of the previous quintet remaining with the touring band were Wayne Shorter and Miles Davis; Williams had already left to form Tony Williams Lifetime. As we shall see, the emerging new quintet remained musically in transition until Jack DeJohnette, who had been periodically subbing for Williams,[87] joined in time for a March date in Rochester, New York.

The New Drummer: Jack DeJohnette

Chicago-born Jack DeJohnette was first a pianist, and only later a drummer. He began piano lessons at age four and took up the drums at thirteen. His musical interests were cultivated by his uncle, Roy I. Wood Sr., a disc jockey. DeJohnette's professional background became as eclectic as the music of the city's South Side, where he grew up. He played rhythm and blues; hard bop, the newly dominant form of jazz in black communities; and open improvisation. His first experience touring was with saxophonist Eddie Harris, who encouraged DeJohnette to focus on the drums: "He thought I was a natural drummer, and he thought I'd be more successful at it and as it turned out, he was right. When I came to New York in '64 or '65, I went up to Minton's, and Freddie Hubbard was there, and I sat in with him. John Patton was there, he heard me play, and he said, 'Hey, man, you got a set of drums?' I said, 'Yeah.' 'Well, you got a gig.' That's when I decided, 'Ok, I'm going to make drums be my main instrument.'"[88]

A highlight of DeJohnette's time in Chicago, around 1958, was playing with visionary big-band leader Sun Ra. "When I had the time I'd always make his rehearsals. I was trying to develop myself as a drummer, and it was a great experience to play with him." He played a set with the John Coltrane Quartet, sitting in for Elvin Jones in 1962, and joined Coltrane's band again four years later as a second drummer to Rashied Ali.[89]

DeJohnette was present at the founding of the Association for the Advancement of Creative Musicians (AACM) in 1965, and he developed a close connection with early members. He attended Wilson Junior College with saxophonists Anthony Braxton, James Willis, and Roscoe Mitchell, who introduced him to reedist Joseph Jarman. DeJohnette recalls playing with these musicians and introducing Mitchell and bassist Malachi Favors to Muhal Richard Abrams, who cofounded the organization.[90] Also among DeJohnette's AACM friends was Steve McCall, the drummer in one of his early trios as a pianist and later a Braxton collaborator.

DeJohnette:

> It was a time of exploration and changes. There was no outlet for an alternative music. Roscoe and Joseph and I would get together to play our music and our concepts of improvisation. Muhal realized that we needed to have a space and an organization, we needed a structured outlet to get that creative energy out and so he got together a charter and a performance space and formed the AACM, with an orchestra that then spun off smaller groups. Muhal was one of my mentors. He helped me a lot with my music and with life problems, and he was the one who encouraged me to come to New York.[91]

Drummer Billy Hart keenly recalls this circle of musical connections: "I had met Jack DeJohnette and Muhal Richard Abrams in Chicago when I traveled there with Shirley [Horn]. Anthony [Braxton] and I were very close friends for a while [in the mid-1960s], to the point where when I'd go to Chicago, I would actually stay with him. We used to listen to John Cage, David Tudor, and Stockhausen."[92]

The AACM can be approached from overlapping perspectives—aesthetic, cultural, political, organizational, and business. Among its founding principles were black financial and organizational autonomy guided by collective action, and as scholar and AACM member George Lewis observes, "collective working-class self-help and self-determination; encouragement of difference in viewpoint, aesthetics, ideology, spirituality, and methodologies."[93] Aesthetically, the group championed a broad musical eclecticism, an interest in open musical forms, a balance between composition and new models to relate composition and improvisation, and, in Lewis's words, "new ideas about sound, timbre, collectivity, extended technique and instrumentation, performance practice."[94]

The same year that the AACM was founded, DeJohnette moved to New York, choosing the Lower East Side neighborhood where many jazz musicians were living. During this period, he played with Sun Ra (who had moved from

Chicago to Montreal and then to New York), Betty Carter, Charles Tolliver, Henry Grimes, Herbie Lewis, and Jackie McLean, with whom he recorded.[95] DeJohnette was playing with McLean at the neighborhood jazz club Slugs when Miles Davis first heard the drummer play. "Miles and Jackie McLean had similar taste in drummers. Jackie always said to me, 'Miles is going to hire you, because Tony [Williams] was with me before Miles hired him, and we have the same taste in drummers.' Sure enough, one night I was in Slugs, and Miles came in to hear me. He'd heard about me, so he came."[96]

DeJohnette caught the attention of a broader group of musicians, listeners, and critics while touring internationally with saxophonist Charles Lloyd. Lloyd had been part of the West Coast jazz scene, where he encountered Ornette Coleman's circle of musicians. His quartet was formed in 1965 with DeJohnette plus pianist Keith Jarrett and bassist Cecil McBee, both invited at DeJohnette's suggestion. The band's musical eclecticism, bridging elements of Coltrane's music, straight-ahead jazz, rock beats, Indian musical influences, and open improvisation, was a tremendous commercial success, particularly among young white audiences. The quartet toured rock halls as well as jazz festivals.

After a stint with Stan Getz in 1968,[97] DeJohnette joined Bill Evans's trio with bassist Eddie Gomez. Their work is documented on *Bill Evans at the Montreux Jazz Festival*.[98] It was of course on an evening with Evans that Davis first heard both DeJohnette and Holland play in London. During this period, DeJohnette began subbing for Tony Williams in Miles Davis's Quintet.

When Davis was seeking a new drummer, it was DeJohnette's synthesis of many musical influences and sensibilities that captured the bandleader's imagination. "I adjusted what I played to what the musical situation was. I had influences. I had Elvin, or I had Tony, Roy, Max, and all those, but I also knew very consciously that I had to develop my own voice. So I took what I liked from the other drummers, and tried to turn it around into Jack DeJohnette, and basically had the good fortune to be in situations . . . where musicians are taking risks and trying different things. I had a chance to experiment." Key to working with the Miles Davis Quintet was his "concept around utilizing drums as an integral part of the ensemble, as well as solos."[99] DeJohnette shared that adaptive quality and skill at balancing individuality and collectivity with Tony Williams, his predecessor in the band. Williams had developed a way to engage with and interconnect his fellow band members,[100] as would DeJohnette.

DeJohnette brought tremendous drive and intensity to his playing. His beat could be simultaneously direct and flexible, in part thanks to his foot dexterity. He listened carefully to his bandmates and brought constant variety and a deep level of complexity to what he played.[101] In Davis's Lost Quintet, Chick Corea's use of the electric piano (and eventually Dave Holland's electric bass) raised the volume level of the rest of the rhythm section, allowing DeJohnette to draw from the full dynamic range of his instrument. The interplay between him and Corea could become one of the first strikingly creative developments to unfold within the new band. Dave Holland told trumpeter and Davis biographer Ian Carr: "When Jack came in the band, a whole new feeling happened for me because I had played with Jack before and I'd felt this affinity with him; so when he came into the band, the whole feeling of the music changed for me." He noted that he "hadn't been able to make the kind of musical contact" he needed when playing with Williams, whom he felt "was a sort of immovable object to me: he had his place where he played and I was either to play with him, or on my own. But . . . I never felt that he came over to my space too much."[102]

DeJohnette found it a joy to play with Davis:

It was great to play with Miles, because Miles loved the drum. Everything came from the drums. He liked boxing, he was a big boxing fan, and he saw drums in jazz as having similar aspects. The drums and the horn player have to set each other up. He would talk about that, "Ok, now you've got to set this way. . . ." If you play a phrase, you have to know how to set a guy up. The same thing with boxing. You set a guy up, you feint with a left hook and then catch him with an overhand or uppercut right. It's in the rhythm.[103]

All the Pieces in Place: The Davis Band Develops a New Chemistry

Jack DeJohnette's presence in the drummer's seat during the band's stand at Duffy's Backstage in Rochester, New York, in March 1969,[104] marks the real beginning of Miles Davis's Lost Quintet. DeJohnette ably continued the tradition of Tony Williams's percussive dynamism, but when he joined, something changed in the chemistry of the group. We immediately sense that the newly formed rhythm section gels in its own way, unique yet parallel to the power of the previous Herbie Hancock–Ron Carter–Tony Williams rhythm section. Both men provided the band's connective tissue and were key to its ability to continuously reconfigure the ever-changing textures at the core of its music.

The new quintet's rhythm section was more extroverted than its predecessor's. The increased volume level meant not only a louder sound but also different relationships between instruments. The electric piano's more percussive attack, the sound swelling into a longer, richer sustain,[105] the ability to play as loudly as the drums, and the possibility of electronically altering the resulting timbre rendered the instrument a sonic change agent. Corea's newfound timbral variety allowed him to inject his presence within the textural environment of horn soloists. The potential to foreground rhythmic interplay between Corea and DeJohnette increased, and space had to be consciously made for Holland to be heard and for Corea and Holland to interact.

Finding an ideal balance and synergy between instruments was not going to be a simple matter. Davis's aesthetic was evolving, leaning in two seemingly contradictory directions: improvisationally open yet with a strong beat. De-Johnette's experiences attuned him to both of Davis's new musical inclinations, having played rhythm and blues, backed open improvisations by members of the AACM, and engaged in more straight-ahead playing. Although Davis first heard Holland in a relatively conventional musical setting, the bassist was an active participant in London's avant-garde. Corea built a reputation in hard bop and Latin jazz, but he was also a drummer. With Davis he was asked to play a new instrument—electric piano—in a setting unlike what he had experienced. Miles Davis was asking a lot from his new bandmates, tossing them into a setting whose trajectory even he couldn't predict. Yet in its earliest stage, on that March gig, we sense the rhythm section cohering and functioning as an integral, organic unit, making compelling music as a team.

It is difficult to draw firm conclusions about the rhythm section before De-Johnette's arrival simply from the one extant audience recording. What is clear is that drummer Tony Williams was a dominant presence in the Boston Jazz Workshop shows.[106] That four-day stand came amid Miles's first multi-keyboard recording sessions leading toward *In a Silent Way*, a recording (reuniting Hancock, Williams, and Davis) on which the delicate balance of the previous quintet remains much in evidence. But the Jazz Workshop recording with the new lineup seems quite different. Williams's thundering drumming surges into Wayne Shorter's solo in "'Round Midnight," ebbing and flowing while rarely ceasing to drive hard. It is when Williams lays out after one final drumroll that we hear glimpses of the new quintet: Holland's walking bass line takes over as Shorter's sole partner, eventually leading to Corea's electric piano solo.[107]

While the inferior recording quality contributes to the perception that Williams dominates the proceedings, there is little doubt that his role that evening was central.[108] There are hints of both past and future quintets, such as Corea's intuitive approach to comping[109] for Shorter. Here, the pianist responds to the nuance, phrasing, and sound of the saxophonist's lines, providing only hints of the chord changes. Otherwise, the band on this night offers a linear, soloist-centered model closely adhering to the forms of the tunes. It is as if Williams were seeking to provide the glue that holds together what otherwise might be a band lacking the time and opportunity to have developed its own chemistry. His driving drumming on Joe Zawinul's new tune "Directions," soon to become a core part of the band's repertoire, offers a fascinating snapshot of where his musical instincts were taking him as Tony Williams Lifetime was taking shape. The give-and-take between Williams and Corea, whose sharply attacked chords punctuate the rhythm, is exciting. As Wallace Roney observes: "Tony's Lifetime was the instigator of the electric direction Miles would take."[110]

In April 1969, Corea reflected on how challenging it was to figure out what to play in this new band:

> When Tony had called me for the gig, he said that he thought Miles was more interested in an accompanist than a soloist, but the first few weeks I hardly comped at all. I didn't know what to comp. Previously, I had started to play in a very unharmonic atmosphere, using harmonies as sounds and textures rather than as voice leaders in song-like fashion. But when I got in the band the things that Miles and Wayne were playing were so harmonically oriented (single notes they would hang onto would imply so much harmonically) that I was at a loss for what to do . . . so I didn't play at all until Miles told me, "Whatever you have, just drop it in." So I began doing that. Whenever I would have something, rather than hesitating because it might conflict, I would play it, and what started to happen (maybe just to my own ears) was that Miles and Wayne began to play all inside what I would put down. It would seem to be so apropos all the time that there was nothing that could be played which was "wrong." Whatever is presented always seems to fit. That really makes it very relaxed.[111]

Heading in a New Musical Direction

In contrast, the new rhythm section playing together in March 1969 at Duffy's Backstage provides glimpses of a collective cohesiveness that would flower over time. We hear that like his predecessor, Jack DeJohnette's drumming is dramatic and virtuosic. He is well supported by Dave Holland's solid and steady walking bass.[112] DeJohnette plays as if he were a partner in an organic whole, rising and falling in levels of energy, punctuating each soloist's ideas, periodically sparking a rise in intensity. He raises the temperature of the ensemble by subdividing beats, creating variations on a tune's rhythms, tossing in surprising rhythmic accents.[113] He crafts polyrhythms by intently inserting a series of strongly played beats across the bar lines. He attentively follows each soloist, particularly Chick Corea. Listening to the drumming, we immediately sense a high level of interdependence and a growing trust.

When we listen to the other two members of the rhythm section on this date, we can hear how all three members' contributions cohere. There are moments when one player changes mood, speed, or direction, and the other band members quickly reconfigure in a tightly interwoven manner. Sometimes each musician finds his own way to respond. Two minutes into Shorter's solo on "So What," there is a stutter in Holland's bass line, followed by a rapidly repeated three-note phrase, which forms an ostinato. Corea incorporates this particular figure within his chordal accompaniment, which DeJohnette completes with a drum flourish. When Corea contributes a series of two-handed rising and falling melodic lines in contrary motion, the level of complexity increases within the band, interrupting the linear flow of Shorter's solo. After Corea plays a series of brief ostinato figures and one upward glissando after the next, his bandmates build on his musical ideas. Although this is Shorter's solo, it is Shorter who imitates Corea's gesture and DeJohnette who extends it.

Early in Corea's own rapid and fluid solo, he listens closely to Holland, who is multiply repeating a note, creating a holding pattern. Corea develops the figure further and then also uses the principle of constructing phrases from repeated notes. A dance emerges between piano and bass, while DeJohnette's drums continue steadily behind. At various points, Holland and DeJohnette show remarkable rhythmic elasticity as they change speeds, building and releasing tension. The three members of the rhythm section are engaged in a delicate interplay.

On this March 1969 recording, we can discern Corea's emerging approach to the electric piano: his solos and comping offer textural variety, rhythmic creativity, and moments of surprise and invention. Ostinati—built from repetitive rhythmic, harmonic, and textural patterns—are peppered throughout. At this point, Corea's solos remain generally linear, hinting at the greater chromaticism and complexity to come. His serpentine lines give way to rhythmic figures and whimsical variations of motifs spun from just a handful of notes. In the up-tempo "Paraphernalia" (second set), Corea begins with small amounts of material to construct grand textural events built on trills or tremolos, or slowing rising chordal structures. In his solo during "No Blues" (second set), he makes use of the tremolo feature on the Rhodes to create a changing delay-like effect that turns sustained chords and then single notes into throbbing, vibrating sonorities. DeJohnette joins Corea with rising and falling levels of drum and cymbal rolls. We can hear Corea's satisfaction confirmed by the increased volume of the Fender Rhodes electric piano, which "really makes me feel like part of the band."[114] His playing reflects his own vitality and creativity and a keen awareness of his fellow players, a sign of the coming interdependence in the Miles Davis Quintet as it matured.

The Village Gate as Incubator

Later that spring,[115] Davis rented the Village Gate, a club on Bleecker Street in Greenwich Village,[116] for several appearances. It was a hip place to fine-tune his new band before taking it on the road. The finger-popping "Miles Runs the Voo-doo Down" was introduced during these shows, supplementing repertoire from the previous 1960s quintet. This was the first tune developed that would appear on the recording *Bitches Brew*.

Led by the fashion-conscious Davis, the band dressed in the latest "mod" clothing, an analogue to its increasingly electric and exploratory music and the Village setting. Critic Richard Williams reported: "These days Miles wears fringed buckskin waistcoats and flowering Indian-print scarves, and the import-ant thing is that he does it with a natural elegance worlds away from the jowly executive who goes out frugging in order to learn to relate to what the young and the free-spending are digging."[117] Wayne Shorter remembers one night in partic-ular: "I was wearing a Spanish leather vest, and chopper boots with a heel, in two different colors, brown and black, Spanish conquistador riding-the-horse boots. People in the audience were looking up there at me and Miles, and after the set they were asking, 'which one is Miles.'"[118] Chick Corea wore a "purple headband and the blue corduroy pants, a stick of incense burning on his keyboards; Dave Holland with his curly long hair and velvet fringed shirt."[119]

A Musical Affinity Develops between Corea and DeJohnette

One of the most striking elements in the quintet's evolution was the close musi-cal connection developing between its electric pianist and its drummer. In part this may have been because Corea and DeJohnette had a background in both instruments, which in turn explains the highly percussive nature of their pairing within the band.

Musical Example I: Live at the Village Gate

The extant recording from the Village Gate, possibly from May 1969, opens with the title track of Chick Corea's recording *Is*.[120] Originally an extended abstract work, the composition is used here as a vehicle for driving solos given shape by Corea's chordal ostinati. At times these are played in sync with De-Johnette's drum hits. We hear this synchronicity between pianist and drummer again on "Footprints," where coordinated ostinati and drum accents heighten the drama and tension during Davis's and Shorter's solos. DeJohnette's repeated hits, something like a minor volcanic eruption, repeatedly create a pattern of disruption. Later in Shorter's solo, DeJohnette builds waves of energy, calming and slowly building, peaking with multiple bass-drum-pedal hits in a drummer's tour de force. Corea's drummer-like ability to vary his chord articulations— from highly staccato to sustained—adds contour to the band's collective texture. Davis's beautiful, elegiac closing solo backed by the band's textural playing is a high point of the show.

Davis's "Miles Runs the Voodoo Down" lightens the mood from the heightened intensity of the set opener. Holland provides an anchor on the tune's bass vamp, accompanied by Corea and DeJohnette. DeJohnette alternately follows and elaborates on Holland's figures, offering a boogaloo rhythm played with much flourish and virtuoso fills, sixteenth-note hits, and rolls that connect segments. Corea's Rhodes adds a funky flavor. The three work as a team. Shorter's and Corea's solos each develop from small gestures; DeJohnette fills in the spaces between Corea's figures, heavily accenting each beat. Corea's lines soon become lengthy and angular, eventually tossing in contrasting phrases filled with repeated notes. A standout feature of this performance is in fact the close connection between drummer and keyboardist. DeJohnette alternately follows and interlocks with Corea and presides with great energy and invention, varying his choice of accented beats to shift the rhythmic feel.

A better-recorded show from the Blue Coronet,[121] a club in Brooklyn, demonstrates Corea's highly rhythmic approach and the growth of his partnership with DeJohnette. This is most in evidence when he is backing Wayne Shorter's solos. Larry Kart, in his review of the band's early June stand at the Plugged Nickel in Chicago, observes that Corea had assumed the role of "pattern maker in the rhythm section," partly due to the electric piano's "ability to sustain notes and produce a wide range of sonorit[i]es."[122] Yet Corea was also in many ways thinking like a drummer, which freed Holland and DeJohnette to flexibly vary their roles in the ensemble. We hear evidence of Corea functioning like a second drummer, albeit at the keyboard, even back in Rochester. On the opener to the second set, Jimmy Heath's "Gingerbread Boy," he peppers the rhythmic flow with percussive staccato chords. This provides a preview of a later point in the life of the quintet, when Corea sometimes actually played a second set of drums. But whether he was at the keyboard or the drums, the sympatico rhythmic relationship between DeJohnette and Corea was an early source of the band's dynamism.

On Tour

After the opportunities for its members to bond afforded by a brief but steady residence in New York, the Miles Davis Quintet began to tour steadily. It traveled from New York and Washington, DC, to Chicago, crossing the ocean for a show at the Juan-les-Pins Festival at Antibes, France. By July, Davis's tune "It's About That Time" from *In a Silent Way* (the recording wouldn't be released until late that month) and Wayne Shorter's "Sanctuary" (soon to be recorded on *Bitches Brew*) were added to the set lists. The band played a short quartet set (without Shorter) during its July 5 appearance at the Newport Jazz Festival in Rhode Island. It was on this date that Davis was reportedly taking notice of the audience response and size. He seemed transfixed by singer James Brown's ability to engage the audience through his personal magnetism and the infectiously funky beat of his music.[123]

By the July 7 show in New York's Central Park, "Directions" had become the opener and increasingly the vehicle for the band's more exploratory side.[124] Then Davis's clarion calls, driven by DeJohnette's drumming, would usher in "Miles Runs the Voodoo Down." By this point, the tune had lost its simplicity of prior shows. Corea made increasing use of ostinati in his often highly chromatic chordal accompaniment, inserted when a space opened or wherever he could offer commentary on the proceedings.[125] Holland played repeated fragments and variants of the vamp, creating a steady rhythmic fabric that allowed ample room for DeJohnette's dramatic displays. The lively tempo and high energy continued unabated through "Masqualero" and into "Spanish Key" (also later to be recorded on *Bitches Brew*). The developing pattern—of Corea comping in a more complex manner behind Shorter than behind Davis—was clearly in play, while rhythmically he remained equally alive and constantly responsive to each soloist. Holland contributed a steady, infectious rhythmic pulse beneath DeJohnette and Corea.

A Growing Corea-Holland Connection

While the focus up to this point has been the connection between Jack DeJohnette and Chick Corea, the budding musical symbiosis between Dave Holland and Corea was also developing.

Musical Example 2: Live in Central Park

In a July 7, 1969, rendition of "Miles Runs the Voodoo Down" (first show), Holland and Corea create rhythmic ostinato after 4:30; Corea leads by playing tone clusters in groupings of three and later four, and Holland responds in kind. A moment later, Holland plays a series of figures built from rapidly repeated notes; this will become a characteristic feature of his playing during the 1970s. During Corea's solo, Holland closely locks within Corea's repetitive patterns, at one point crafting a several-note phrase that speeds and slows like a roller coaster, spinning with myriad variation. Eventually, the two players become so enmeshed that it is difficult to tell who the soloist is.

The empathetic, closely interlocking nature of Corea and Holland's musical embrace is on display during "Milestones." Holland picks up on the smallest nuances and patterns that Corea uncovers, then just as quickly shifts into a walk when the pianist plays more bop-like lines. This requires exquisite attentiveness on Holland's part, even within the head of the tune, where Corea tosses off-pulse notes, chords, and clusters. When Corea plays behind Shorter, drawing from pointillism, pantonality, highly angular gestures, and asymmetrical groups of rapidly played notes,[126] Holland has to listen even more closely as he continues to change up the pace of his note-pattern groupings, which are interspersed with rapidly repeated single notes.

The interplay between pianist and bassist is particularly in evidence during the second show, in Corea's solo on "Masqualero." There, Holland and Corea play nearly in tandem, joined by DeJohnette's cymbals, which provide the source of energy expansion and contraction. Corea builds intensity by repeating short phrases and chordal fragments, pulling from them new phrases.

Even when the band makes only subtle shifts away from a straight-ahead approach, its members are beginning to display fascinating sleights of hand. After a smart groove has been laid down by Holland and DeJohnette during "Miles Runs the Voodoo Down" (second show), the rhythm section plays double time during Davis's solo, creating the perception that the pulse has sped up. Indeed, Davis's lightning-fast lines during the early portion of his solo support this notion. Corea's solo begins in a highly atonal manner, with Holland on arco bass, heavily scraping the strings. A pointillistic dialogue emerges between Corea and Holland, joined soon by DeJohnette. But again, the real action is between the bassist and the pianist before they return to the original groove.

During the band's fall 1969 European tour, these dynamics show expansive growth. At a November 7 show in Berlin (second set) during "It's About That

Time," Holland responds to Corea's brief, frolicking groupings of notes with sparse figures sometimes imitative of Corea. When Corea crafts a repetitive spinning, textural display, the rhythmic work of a drummer at the keyboard, Holland lays out and DeJohnette takes over, very sparingly, building in response to Corea's more elaborate and intense playing. Holland joins with rapidly played arco figures. "Masqualero" displays the delicate interchange between Corea and Holland, their duet held together by a thread. They both play breath-long phrases. Holland's bass is barely one step behind Corea, responding to the direction, speed, and density of the pianist's playing. This is a refined form of counterpoint invented on the spot. The level of sensitivity and empathy between the players is substantial.

A Unique Team

The Corea-Holland-DeJohnette rhythm section had grown remarkably in its own right during this first year of the band. Corea developed an empathetic symbiosis with each of his rhythm partners that would continue to thrive. Together, the three musicians provided lithe and creative support for the horn soloists. But they were also growing as a subunit that functioned according to its own internal logic. Ultimately, this would lead to the band's split, with two of its three members departing to explore further the new directions they had uncovered and Davis reconfiguring the ensemble.

With that band we were playing our butts off, everybody was raising hell.

JACK DEJOHNETTE[1]

2

"Bitches Brew," in the Studio and on the Road

Back home in New York after a spring European tour, Miles Davis brought an expanded band into the studio to record *Bitches Brew* on August 19–21, 1969. The sessions included tunes that had been honed on the road—"Miles Runs the Voodoo Down," "Spanish Key," and "Sanctuary," plus two new compositions: the opening track, "Pharaoh's Dance," and the title tune, "Bitches Brew."[2]

The band in the studio included three electric keyboardists (Chick Corea, Joe Zawinul, Larry Young[3]); four drummer-percussionists and two bassists (one electric, one acoustic), of which Jack DeJohnette and Dave Holland were core members; and two reed players (Wayne Shorter, plus Bennie Maupin on bass clarinet). A guitarist, John McLaughlin, took a highly rhythmic approach, adding a solo voice and also another percussionist. (He and Young were two-thirds of the Tony Williams Lifetime.) What this expanded band created is the "brew," shaped by the rich, ever-changing, swirling mix of keyboards and multiple percussion.

35

Davis describes the process of conception through recording in his auto-biography:

I had been experimenting with writing a few simple chord changes for three pianos. Simple shit, and it was funny because I used to think when I was doing them how Stravinsky went back to simple forms.[4] So I had been writing these things down, like one beat chord and a bass line, and I found out that the more we played it, it was always different. I would write a chord, a rest, maybe another chord, and it turned out that the more it was played, the more it just kept getting different. This started happening in 1968 when I had Chick, Joe, and Herbie [Hancock] for those studio dates. It went on into the sessions we had for *In a Silent Way*. Then I started thinking about something larger, a skeleton of a piece. I would write a chord on two beats and they'd have two beats out. So they would do one, two, three, da-dum, right? Then I put the accent on the fourth beat. Maybe I had three chords on the first bar. Anyway, I told the musicians that they could do anything they wanted, play anything they heard but that I had to have this, what they did, as a chord. Then they knew what they could do, so that's what they did. Played off that chord, and it made it sound like a whole lot of stuff.

I told them that at rehearsals and then I brought in these musical sketches that nobody had seen, just like I did on *Kind of Blue* and *In a Silent Way*. . . . So I would direct, like a conductor, once we started to play, and I would either write down some music for somebody or I would tell him to play different things I was hearing, as the music was growing, coming together. It was loose and tight at the same time. It was casual but alert, everybody was alert to different possibilities that were coming up in the music. While the music was developing I would hear something that I thought could be extended or cut back. So that recording was a development of the creative process, a living composition. It was like a fugue, or motif, that we all bounced off of. After it had developed to a certain point, I would tell a certain musician to come in and play something else, like Benny Maupin on bass clarinet. . . . Sometimes, instead of just letting the tape run, I would tell Teo [Macero] to back it up so I could hear what we had done. If I wanted something else in a certain spot, I would just bring the musician in, and we would just do it. That was a great recording session, man, and we didn't have any problems as I can remember. It was just like one of them old-time jam sessions we used to have up at Minton's back in the old bebop days. Everybody was excited when we all left there each day.

What we did on *Bitches Brew* you couldn't ever write down for an orchestra to play. That's why I didn't write it all out, not because I didn't know what I wanted; I knew that what I wanted would come out of a process and not some prearranged shit. This session was about improvisation, and that's what makes jazz so fabulous. Any time the weather changes it's going to change your whole attitude about something, and so a musician will play differently, especially if everything is not put in front of him. A musician's attitude *is* the music he plays.[5]

Jack DeJohnette:

Miles had some sketches and bass patterns. He'd ask me, "play a groove, play this," and he'd count off a tempo and if that wasn't it he'd say, "No, that's not it!" and he'd say to try something else. I'd start something and if it was okay he wouldn't say anything and it would continue, then he'd cue each instrument in and get something going. When it would start percolating, then Miles would then play a solo over that and then let it roll, let it roll until he felt it had been exhausted. Then we would go on to something else.[6]

On another occasion, DeJohnette noted:

As the music was being played, as it was developing, Miles would get new ideas. This was the beautiful thing about it. He'd do a take, and stop, and then get an idea from what had just gone before, and elaborate on it, or say to the keyboards "play this sound." One thing fed the other. It was a process, a kind of spiral, a circular situation. The recording of *Bitches Brew* was a stream of creative musical energy. One thing was flowing into the next, and we were stopping and starting all the time, maybe to write a sketch out, and then go back to recording. The creative process was being documented on tape, with Miles directing the ensemble like a conductor an orchestra.[7]

Various participants in the sessions have pointed out that while the music spontaneously unfolded, there was more advance preparation than Davis acknowledged.[8] *DownBeat* writer Dan Ouellette quotes Joe Zawinul: "There was a lot of preparations for the sessions. I went to Miles' house several times. I had 10 tunes for him. He chose a few and then made sketches of them."[9] Paul Tingen quotes drummer Lenny White: "The night before the first studio session we rehearsed the first half of the track 'Bitches Brew.' I think we just rehearsed that one track. Jack DeJohnette, Dave Holland, Chick Corea and Wayne Shorter were all there. I had a snare drum, and Jack had a snare drum and a cymbal. I was a 19-year-old kid, and I was afraid of Miles. My head was in the clouds!"[10]

Bob Belden, producer of *The Complete Bitches Brew Sessions* boxed set released in 1998,[11] lays out the sequence of the three days of recording. On August 19, the order was "Bitches Brew," followed by the music later titled "John McLaughlin," "Sanctuary," the various segments of "Pharaoh's Dance," and then "Orange Lady." August 20 began with "Miles Runs the Voodoo Down," and on the twenty-first, "Spanish Key" and further work on "Pharaoh's Dance."[12] He also offers a "score" and narrative detailing the various edits involved in the assembly of "Pharaoh's Dance" and "Bitches Brew." Enrico Merlin's "Sessionography, 1967–1991"[13] offers a more detailed analysis of the construction of "Pharaoh's Dance," noting slight differences between the LP and CD versions.

The process that unfolded during the studio sessions is apparent within the original session tapes. These can be heard in compilation CDs that have been in unofficial circulation for years. They include fragments of various takes recorded during the sessions. Some fragments are as short as twenty seconds, and most are under two minutes. Some seem to be microphone checks. Particularly tantalizing are those that fade out after a minute or two. Together, they survey the two days of recording, presenting something like an X-ray of the events. Periodically among the in-studio banter, we hear the voice of record producer Teo Macero announcing a code number for the take—"this will be part 2 of CO103745 take 1," "part 2 take 2." A phone rings. Dave Holland asks questions. At one point, Miles Davis says, "Hey, Teo, come on!" At the end of his solo on one of the takes of "John McLaughlin," Davis declares: "Hey, Teo, I can't hear nothing. . . . I can't hear myself."

We hear the band members trying out various thematic elements, such as Chick Corea experimenting with possible ways to approach material around and about the "Bitches Brew" vamp, varying the degrees of chromaticism. The two bassists try out their parts on "John McLaughlin." There are two approximately seven-minute runs of the tune, complete with solos. "Spanish Key" receives a range of treatments, some with a lighter rhythmic feel than the one we know. That final version clearly works better than one that begins with a Corea solo, or another, echo drenched, that opens with a denser ensemble, the texture more akin to "Pharaoh's Dance." Here, the editing process involved more selecting between takes. Some material, such as rehearsals of Joe Zawinul's "Orange Lady," simply isn't included on the recording.

"Miles Runs the Voodoo Down" receives several rehearsal segments and eight actual takes, some between two to more than nine minutes long.[14] Davis and the rhythm section approach the material in a variety of ways. Several times, Davis opens with a slow, unaccompanied presentation of the theme; elsewhere, it is the rhythm section that begins the tune, similar to how it appears on the recording. Another take features a slow and breezy solo bass opening, and then abruptly ends. On three of the latter takes, Bennie Maupin's bass clarinet immediately joins with the rhythm section. Take 7 has from the start a more rhythmically interlocking funk feel, continuing through Wayne Shorter's solo. John McLaughlin continues in this vein during the first section of his solo.

By Davis's solo, the rhythm section has simplified its beat structure, and the electric piano is limited to long, sustained notes and chords. In Belden's essay, percussionist Don Alias recalls that after a few failed takes, he remembered a drum rhythm he had recently heard at Mardi Gras in New Orleans that he thought would work. Davis suggested that Alias sit at Lenny White's kit, and he ended up leading the rhythm section during the version that appears on the final recording.[15]

The most interesting takes from the perspective of this discussion are of "Pharaoh's Dance," in which the band rehearses various possibilities for segments of the tune, moving from section to section. The bassists and Corea try out variants of lines, sometimes in unison, that do not appear on the final recording. There is a five-note unison passage, really a cadence, rehearsed several times, that remains on the editing room floor. Another option is tried a few times, and then a third. Portions of composer Joe Zawinul's original conception, rehearsed and recorded in the studio, don't make it into the final mix.

Tiny phrases are rehearsed in multiple ways. In one instance, after several takes, Macero is heard saying without irony, "Want to do that again?" And that is exactly what happens. Corea's double-time passages near the end of "Pharaoh's Dance" are rehearsed several times. After a particularly successful attempt, Holland can be overheard saying, "Yeah!" Listening with 20/20 hindsight, we can hear some elements, but not others, that will ultimately be stitched together to form the fabric of *Bitches Brew*. Clearly, Davis rehearsed and rehearsed segments of material, and then moved on to others. The musicians could have no clear sense of what form the music would ultimately take, but they knew what some of its ingredients would be.[16]

The basic material that ultimately comprises "Pharaoh's Dance" includes a lively melody that appears at the beginning of the recording; a repeated, single-note vamp to ground solos; one or more unison passages designed to conclude sections; and a second melodic theme that is performed by Davis toward the end of the recording. The crafting of the tune involved organizing a coherent structure from bits and pieces of studio takes, a vast assemblage of these thematic elements and ever-morphing textural material.[17]

Postproduction as a Compositional Process

"Pharaoh's Dance" and "Bitches Brew," the compositions that open *Bitches Brew*, are the album's most extended compositions. They are the most densely layered, the most heavily edited and postproduced. Since they lead off the recording, the listener's experience was going to be shaped by these first compositions. *Constructions* might be a better term than *compositions*, since in this context the word *composition* is freighted with the question of who the composer was. "Pharaoh's Dance" is credited to Zawinul (albeit substantially reworked by Davis), and "Bitches Brew" to Davis. Yet, as several writers have noted, Macero played a significant hand in the final versions that appear on the record. As Davis observes in his autobiography, Macero recorded every note played during the recording sessions, sometimes multiple takes of those tunes and oftentimes just fragments of varying lengths; consequently, the material was going to require structuring in postproduction. The new recording shifted the balance between Davis and the band's contributions and those of Macero, who treated the studio recordings as material in search of structure, if not quite operating in the tradition of sonic collage within electronic music.

One point of reference for this discussion is Karlheinz Stockhausen's early electronic composition *Gesang der Jünglinge* (Song of the Youths; 1956).[18] The work is crafted by a process of interweaving recorded fragments of sung texts with electronic sounds. Working in Cologne, Germany, Stockhausen drew from the emerging Parisian tradition of musique concrète pioneered by radio engineer Pierre Schaeffer.[19] Schaeffer had recorded, collected, and edited sounds (*objets sonores*, sonic objects) on tape, abstracting them from their original source and complex of meaning. He then composed by arranging the sounds according to purely aesthetic criteria unrelated to their original context; his aesthetic roots are in the collage forms of visual artists Pablo Picasso and Georges Braque.[20]

In *Gesang der Jünglinge* and later works, Stockhausen changes the terms of this process by taking into account the referential meaning of the text and sound material and by adding purely electronic sounds. His sound collage provided a model for early pop music producers—and Teo Macero—who edited studio-recorded material in postproduction. What began first as documentation of performance and then as error correction came to represent a compositional process. As Albin J. Zak III observes: "In their lack of any real world counter-part and their frank artifice, pop records of the early fifties rendered the goal of real life sonic depiction meaningless."[21] Tape splicing migrated to popular music most famously with the Beatles, as early as "Please Please Me" in 1962.[22] Segments of one take of a song could be edited together with segments of another to create a new track. Beatles' producer George Martin and Davis producer Teo Macero each crafted sound collages, new compositions that drew from what had been recorded in the studio.

Macero had already begun using editing techniques in his work with Davis in the late 1950s. In his autobiography, Davis recalls that Macero "had started to splice tape together on *Porgy and Bess* and then on *Sketches of Spain*, and he did it on this album, too [*Someday My Prince Will Come*, 1961]. We post-recorded solos on those albums, with Trane and me doing some extra horn work." When he adds, wryly, "It was an interesting process that was done frequently after that,"[23] he is referring to a more radical use of the technology.

In the 1960s, rock musicians and producers grew increasingly expansive in their use of their inheritance from Schaeffer, Stockhausen, and early pop studio engineers, most famously in 1967 recordings; notable among these are the Beatles' *Sgt. Pepper's Lonely Hearts Club Band*, Frank Zappa's *You're Only in It for the Money* and *Lumpy Gravy*, and the Beach Boys' *Pet Sounds*. Recordings of studio sessions plus, at times, unrelated sounds are sped up, slowed down, played backward—in sum, rock music merged with sound collage. It is that hybrid into which Teo Macero stepped while working on Miles Davis's recordings of the late 1960s.

The construction of final versions out of recorded fragments may have been the plan from the start, a simple necessity, or both. As mentioned above, Davis later recalled: "I didn't write it all out. . . . I knew that what I wanted would come out of a process. . . . This session was about improvisation, and that's what makes jazz so fabulous." Yet the need for deft tape splicing doesn't explain the use of Echoplex and brief, looped segments, all accomplished in postproduction. The triple repetition of the opening section of "Pharaoh's Dance," all copies of the same recorded take, before leading into an extended through-performed segment, points to a compositional scheme not evident in advance. Was it part of an advance plan that Davis's solo during the latter portion is really a pre-composed theme on which he comments during his opening solo? This is an inversion of the usual head-solo arrangement: here, variations and elaborations appear long before we hear the actual melody. The full compositional details surely emerged in Macero's editing room, where he sought to craft a coherent

extended work a half hour in duration. Yet questions remain regarding authorship of the overarching musical structure. The form of side 2 of Davis's previous
recording, *In a Silent Way*, sandwiching "It's About That Time" between two
exact copies of the title tune, seems to have provided a working mode that was
agreeable to Davis.

Macero testifies to the compositional hand he exerted during postproduction:

> I had carte blanche to work with the material. I could move anything around
> and what I would do is record everything, right from beginning to end, mix
> it all down and then take all those tapes back to the editing room and listen
> to them and say: "This is a good little piece here, this matches with that, put
> this here," etc. and then add in all the effects—the electronics, the delays and
> overlays.... [I would] be working it out in the studio and take it back and re-
> edit it—from front to back, back to front and the middle somewhere else and
> make it into a piece. I was a madman in the engineering room.[24]

Herbie Hancock's producer during the 1970s, David Rubinson, observes
that while true partnership between producers and musicians may have been
growing within rock music, this was "[less so in jazz, where] the musicians were
grist for the mill, and had little or no control or participation in the creative
process of post-production or mixing, as little as there was of that then.... [His-
torically] the structure of the record business is basically a plantation where the
white guys ran the record business and the studios."[25] Rubinson understands the
relationship between Davis and Macero as having been in this mode, as Macero
himself attests. In his autobiography, Davis alludes to his ambivalence about the
substantial control Macero assumed over the final versions of his work. He asserts: "[I] ... started putting 'Directions in Music by Miles Davis' on the front of
my album covers so that nobody could be mistaken about who was the creative
control behind the music."[26] This may reflect a reality that Davis ultimately had
limited choice in the production of his music.

Writer Victor Svorinich places Davis more firmly in the compositional driver
seat. He resolves conflicting claims of authorship by citing a contemporaneous
letter from Davis to Macero. In it, Davis explicitly directs how Macero should
order much of the recorded raw material for the title track "Bitches Brew."[27] Davis identifies which segments from two studio takes should begin and conclude
the piece, and he insists that continuity be maintained between the opening

figures and the entry of the bass clarinet. Improvisatory sections should "run together whether they are high in volume or low in volume." Svorinich finds support for the Davis letter in an interview with the album's mixing editor, Ray Moore. Moore recalls Davis unexpectedly sitting by his side in the postproduction studio in September during the final edits, going through the entire project with a fine-tooth comb.

Svorinich proposes that Macero's memories of postproduction—seasoned with complaints about not being adequately credited—may indeed reflect his frustrations about the amount of detailed legwork Davis had entrusted to the engineers. Further, Macero may have conflated memories of *Bitches Brew* with his exasperation with the trumpeter's diminished presence in later years. In Svorinich's view, Davis was truly the director, leaving Macero's team responsible for the realization of a wide range of details.[28] These numerous decisions did, however, represent compositional thinking on the part of both Davis and Macero.

Macero's consistent record-producing method can be seen in the distinct similarities found between *Bitches Brew* and the highly edited *Miles Davis Live at the Fillmore East* (1970).[29] The net result is that he structured the outcome of Davis's recording sessions in a way that was alien to the aesthetic of the live band. This outcome may have been acceptable to Davis, because the trumpeter personally privileged his live performances over the recordings, and because Macero produced commercial products out of exploratory, structurally amorphous material. Davis wished to release recordings but was most engaged in performing with his musicians, on the road and in the studio. Creatively, he was ever on the move, performing abstract music with the Lost Quintet one day and recording funk-oriented music in the studio the next, rarely if ever looking back.

"Bitches Brew": Structure

The basic elements of the tune "Bitches Brew" remain relatively constant, starting with the recorded version and continuing throughout the live band's performances. How Miles Davis and his band made use of these materials changed over time, from the initial "construction" of "Bitches Brew" in postproduction through the next year of performances. Opening the work is a series of motifs; the performers move from one to the next as if they were modules to be assembled. On the recording, the full set of modules is on display; later, the material was treated more flexibly.

On the recording, "Bitches Brew" is organized into five sections (time units here are approximate). During subsequent live shows, Chick Corea embroidered various forms of musical commentary and filigree around all the opening figures.

1. The opening motifs (2:50)
2. First series of solos over a vamp[30] (10:30)
3. Return of the opening (1:30)
4. Second series of solos over the vamp (4:00)
5. Coda: Exact repetition of the opening (2:50)

In live performances, a more malleable form of a coda, in which elements of the opening motifs are reiterated, replaced the repetition.

Opening Motifs

The opening section consists of a series of five interconnected motifs. On the recording, the sequence becomes fixed, because the repetitions are copies from the session tape. In live performances over time, the elements were treated more freely.[31]

1. "Pedal":[32] A pattern of repeated low Cs separated by silences
2. "Alarm": Rapid-fire pairs of high Cs played on trumpet, with an accent on the first
3. "Crashing chord": A sustained chord with a short attack, played by the rhythm section. Harmonically, it is ambiguous. The chord is a C-minor +7 in three simultaneous flavors: diminished, minor, and augmented. It can be thought of as much a tone cluster as it is a highly unstable chord.
4. "Staircase": Three pairs of descending minor thirds (sometimes harmonized as three pairs of major triads), each pair beginning a major second below the previous pair—as if descending a staircase. The upper notes of the chords are F D–E♭ C–D♭ B♭. On the recording and in some live performances, each chord is repeated twice before descending to the next.[33]
5. "Clarion call": A melodic phrase played on trumpet that concludes with descending notes of a C-minor chord; the penultimate note bending, following blues conventions, to suggest ambiguity about whether it is a minor or major third.

Vamp and Solos

In "Bitches Brew," the vamp is a simple, repeated bass line—G–C–pause–F♮–B–pause–G♮–E–pause–B—that underpins a lengthy section of solos.

The studio recording of "Bitches Brew" includes two sets of solos, played over the vamp. These solo sets are separated by a repetition of the opening section.

In the first series, Davis plays two solos, each two and half minutes long, that sandwich one of the same length by John McLaughlin. A curious aspect of McLaughlin's solo is an extended pause in the middle as the vamp continues. Wayne Shorter follows for one minute, Dave Holland for just several seconds, and then Chick Corea for nearly two minutes. Corea's first solo is introduced by ten seconds of a Jack DeJohnette solo.

A quotation generally said to reference "Spinning Wheel," a hit song by the jazz-rock group Blood, Sweat and Tears, appears during Davis's first solo, around six minutes in. The quotation seems to emerge logically from the melodic material he is playing, and it nicely offsets the vamp; McLaughlin hints at the motif, quickly responding to one of Miles's phrases while comping early in Davis's solo. Davis briefly referred to this recorded quotation during a concert at the Fillmore West in San Francisco, on April 10, 1970. Might he have also been thinking about "Lulu's Back in Town," a song featured in a movie and performed by both Fats Waller and Thelonious Monk, which opens with related thematic material?[34] Was Davis signifying on his relationship with the jazz-rock ensemble or on its musical world?[35]

In the second series of solos, Dave Holland opens, then Bennie Maupin takes over, followed by an additional Davis solo (the general length of solos is around two minutes) and then a quiet, extended collective improvisation in which there are segments when Maupin moves forward in the collective mix. There is an ebb and flow in the brief vamp segments between solos, which serves to connect them all into a more coherent whole. In between the two sets of solos played over the vamp and again afterward lies a coda, which consists of an exact repetition of the opening 2:50 of the work.

Maupin's contribution on bass clarinet is one of the most distinctive aspects of this recording. His playing lurks beneath the surface in a couple of places: during the opening, and in the opening seconds of the vamp (a recorded segment that is repeated several times). The addition is both textural and contrapuntal. Maupin also provides an added ingredient juxtaposed to Shorter's solo.

Holland's solo, which opens the second set of solos, is enhanced by Maupin's presence within the quiet comping that includes guitar, keyboards, and drums; Maupin gradually emerges more prominently partway into the solo, shifting the balance from accompanied solo to duet. He adds a layer beneath Davis's solo in section two, continuing underneath as counterpoint during the brief vamp that bridges Davis's solo and his duet with Corea, under which Maupin plays long tones. A bass vamp, soon with drums, becomes a collective improvisation featuring Corea, McLaughlin, and Maupin. Joe Zawinul emerges with soloesque lines through the second solo, and the vamp then fades in its final seconds into just bass and drums, providing a segue to the coda.

Comparative Structure

The structure imposed on "Bitches Brew" by Teo Macero is in an ABABA form: three repetitions of the introduction are wrapped around two series of solos. This approach was immediately abandoned in live concert during the fall 1969 European tour;[36] as evidenced in the recording, the opening section is followed by solos and then by a coda. The distinction is practical: there are fewer soloists and thus fewer solo segments to shape within the context of a coherent whole.

In neither case is a standard bebop head-solo-head form present. The opening and the coda do not provide a melody or chord sequence from which the solos take off, and the soloists spend little time reflecting further on the motifs as they solo on the seven-note bass vamp and metric beat. This format continues through the spring of 1970 and even at Freeport, Grand Bahama Island, in August of that year. The band returned to Macero's ABABA structure during the August 1970 dates at Tanglewood in Lenox, Massachusetts, and the Isle of Wight Festival in England. At those concerts, a repeated single note sometimes replaced the vamp.

"Bitches Brew" as an Impetus for a Shift in Musical Direction

"Bitches Brew" was a core part of the band's repertoire during its final year, through August 1970.[37] Rhythmic riffs and vamps were already on the mind of Miles Davis when his new band played the Newport Jazz Festival in July 1969. But the new kind of composition introduced with the tune "Bitches Brew" helped instigate a more open approach to performance. Davis had already experimented with minimalist composition in "It's About That Time." That tune introduced the idea that a Miles Davis composition could be based on a pulse, a bass vamp, and minimal melodic (or other) motifs. More than a vamp (such as "Miles Runs the Voodoo Down" or "Spanish Key"), "Bitches Brew" could be thought of as a series of moods or textures. It suggested a different kind of trumpet solo, pairs of stuttered notes or fractured lines strung together, with as much space between them as there were notes.

The studio performance of the material that became "Pharaoh's Dance"—the creation of many segments of constantly changing multilayered textures—seems to have particularly impacted Chick Corea. If his performance goal before this recording was more linear and in close relationship to the vamps, it now shifted to crafting changing textures and abstractions that could emerge from or be juxtaposed to those vamps. His performances necessarily became more deeply embedded within the textures collectively created in the moment by the full band, particularly the rhythm section.

The shift to a band with a single electric keyboardist, bassist, and drummer netted a very different sound from the recording, but the electronic qualities introduced by Macero's effects reappeared and were expanded when Corea adopted a ring modulator[38] to process his electric piano. The device generates from an existing sound, such as a guitar or electric piano, far more complex sounds. The result was a broader and more electronic sonic environment. The sound of the band moved even further in this direction during its final months, when in spring 1970 percussionist Airto Moreira was added (he had appeared on the studio recording, and his *cuíca* sounds blended well with the electronics), and finally second keyboardist Keith Jarrett joined. Also during this period, Dave Holland increased his use of the electric bass, often with wah-wah. Consequently, at this point half the band was playing electric instruments with electronic processing.

The instrumentation was new, but so was Davis's approach to performance. While the studio sessions were conducted piecemeal and assembled in postproduction by Macero, the live performances did not utilize the released recording as a template. The modular motivic approach to composition remained, but not the assemblage of larger structures that emerged from Macero's editorial razor blade: beginning with, repeating, and concluding with verbatim segments. While "Bitches Brew" opened and closed with elements selected from the same cluster of motifs, the exact components, their order, and their emphasis varied. The primary musical mission was the unfolding of an organic form, not a preconceived or standardized one.

"Bitches Brew" as a Live Performance Vehicle

Soon after the *Bitches Brew* album-recording sessions, the Lost Quintet moved into a new phase during its two-week European tour in the fall of 1969.[39] "Bitches Brew" was a frequent show opener, alternating with Zawinul's tune "Directions." Most apparent in those shows' recordings are Corea's highly angular, nonlinear, atonal solos and comping and, at times, open improvisation by the entire band. The electric pianist creates dissonant lines from patterns of major and minor seconds, far more rhythmic and percussive than melodic in character. Wayne Shorter's solos are less linear than before, seeking to explore endless variants of rapidly ascending melodic shapes. Their rhythms do not follow beats aligned on a grid, but are asymmetric and fragmented. Each repetition shifts the beat ever so slightly in a different direction, yet rarely aligned with a specific pulse. Dave Holland and Jack DeJohnette find a sense of balance, however unpredictable, and a particularly strong chemistry is developing between Holland and Corea.

Musical Example 3: Paris, November 1969

Chick Corea's percussive approach to the Fender Rhodes is exemplified within an electric piano and drums duet during "Bitches Brew" at the Salle Pleyel in Paris (November 3, first set). Holland's restless lines continuously stream in the background. Corea's repeated patterns of alternating tone clusters are reminiscent of Cecil Taylor. Later, fast-moving arrays of notes expand into further tone clusters. DeJohnette follows the entire enterprise very closely, intensely interlocking with the pianist's constructions. In the second set, Corea comps for Shorter with one complex, rhythmic chordal ostinato after the next. Soon, as if to underscore the rhythmic essence of the moment, he abandons the Fender Rhodes entirely, moving from piano to a second drum kit to add another rhythmic layer to DeJohnette's drumming. After a late Coltrane-esque sequence by Shorter, the two drummers and Holland continue alone as a trio, accumulating multiple layers of rolls all around the kit, with DeJohnette in the lead. Even after returning to the Fender Rhodes, Corea continues as if he were drumming, offering cascading tone clusters and abstract runs.[40]

Corea demonstrates another side of his skill set during Shorter's solo, where his playing is minimal (initially playing variations based on the "staircase" motif), followed by a section in which he lays out to leave space for Holland and DeJohnette to comp with more transparency. Shorter plays rapid runs, separated by pauses. Later, Corea exemplifies his close listening when he imitates

Shorter's rapidly repeated notes and then, as Shorter's solo builds toward its peak, moves into pointillistic and staccato articulations.

In Stockholm on November 5, 1969, Davis's solo is accompanied by drums alone and, for a brief period, bass, with Corea laying out.[41] DeJohnette's highly soloistic accompaniment is one of his most majestic moments with the band, enforcing the beat but adding a wealth of elaboration and filigree. Corea again lays out during Shorter's solo. DeJohnette outlines the pulse on cymbals, crafting variation upon variation. As Shorter's solo builds, the saxophone lines lengthening, DeJohnette's support grows in strength, featuring multiple rolls around the kit, and slashes at the cymbals. Shorter pays limited attention to the beat, while DeJohnette enforces that beat. As Holland plays on and around the vamp, DeJohnette's drumming continues and accentuates the vamp.

Solos without the Vamp—and When the Vamp Changes Shape

In Berlin on November 7, 1969, the band supports Shorter's solo without any sign of the tune's characteristic vamp. The result is harmonically ambiguous, leaving Shorter the space he needs to build a motivic solo. His solo begins with a four-note phrase drawn from the final moment of Davis's preceding solo (moving steadily upward, E♭–G–E♭, and then down to C).[42] Corea's solo receives a spare treatment from the rhythm section, accompanied by Holland alone.[43] The lack of harmonic expectations allows Corea to build a rapid series of lengthy phrases, sometimes highly pointillistic, drawing heavily from major and minor seconds. When he harmonizes his playing, continuing after the end of his solo, Davis comes in, playing a quiet, lyrical line above these chords, setting a mood that is melancholy and beautiful.

But When Does the Tune Begin?

When "Bitches Brew" opened a set, the point at which the tune begins was relatively obvious. "Relatively," because the sequence of sound events evolved, and showed some flexibility from performance to performance. But since the set list progressed from tune to tune without a break, the question arises nonetheless: How did the band know when and how to make the shift? Enrico Merlin refers to Davis's technique as "coded phrases."[44] He explored how Miles cued the next tune by inserting a representative musical gesture as the band was playing the current tune. The type of phrase reflected the characteristics of the upcoming tune: if it had a core melodic figure, he would play the "first notes of the tune."

If the core was a bass vamp, "the signal would be a phrase from that vamp; or if there was a core harmonic component, the signal would be 'voicings of the harmonic progressions.'"[45] "Miles Runs the Voodoo Down" could be cued either by the bass vamp or by the first notes of the descending trumpet melody. "It's About That Time" could be cued by alluding to the descending harmonic (chord) progression. In the recorded version of "Spanish Key," the code was a key change. This approach continued through the mid-1970s.

Testing the Waters

After the autumn 1969 tour, Davis seemed ready to explore a lineup of musicians different from that of the Lost Quintet. The *Bitches Brew* album would not be released until April 1970. In the months before that, he brought an expanded group of musicians into the studio between November and early February, playing a more groove-driven music (grounded in a cyclical rhythmic pattern suggesting a dancelike feel) and experimenting with the inclusion of Indian instruments.[46] The rhythmic feel was flavored in part by the presence of the pitched Indian drum, the tabla. Guitar-oriented and backbeat-driven sessions began in mid-February, with the recording that resulted in *Jack Johnson* taking place in early April.[47]

A *Tribute to Jack Johnson* was crafted as a film score about the world champion boxer much beloved by Davis. It is here that we first see full blown the trumpeter's fascination with James Brown, maybe heightened by Brown's appearance at the 1969 Newport Jazz Festival. Funk, particularly as championed by Brown and Sly and the Family Stone, would heavily influence Davis's work in 1972–75, but bass lines from their recordings have a strong presence on *Jack Johnson* and onward.[48] The April 1970 sessions were joined by Stevie Wonder's bass player, Michael Henderson, whose creative funk-oriented playing would help tilt the live band in that direction when he replaced Dave Holland the next fall.

But also on Davis's mind was the new band of his former drummer, Tony Williams. From a young age, Williams was an aficionado not only of the avant-garde and hard-bop approaches already noted, but also of British rock and roll—the music of Eric Clapton and Cream, the Who, and others. His new band, Tony Williams Lifetime, placed the electric guitar way out front, side by side with Williams's own hard-driving drumming and alongside the organ. It was a high-volume power trio akin to Cream or the Jimi Hendrix Experience. Drummer Lenny White observes:

In 1969, Tony had the idea to take a traditional concept—the standard organ trio—and put it on steroids. He formed Tony Williams Lifetime with John McLaughlin and Larry Young, and it became the new way, the new movement. I saw that group at Slugs when they first started—it was so great and SO LOUD. They were so good Miles wanted to hire Tony's band and call it, "Miles Davis introduces Tony Williams Lifetime." Tony said no, he didn't want to do that. So Miles went ahead and got Larry and John for *Bitches Brew*. Tony was not happy with that but I think he had definitely made the decision to go off on his own by then anyway.[49]

With Williams forming Lifetime, Jack DeJohnette became drummer of the Lost Quintet, with Billy Cobham, soon to join McLaughlin's Mahavishnu Orchestra, playing on *Jack Johnson*, which was released in 1971. In the meantime, *Bitches Brew* was newly available to listeners, and Davis was on the road with the Lost Quintet, which expanded to a sextet and then an octet, continuing to present its repertoire.

Up and Down, In and Out

As Chick Corea describes the flights of the Lost Quintet:

> We always took the audience on a roller coaster kind of trip. When Miles would play, everything would get very concentrated and to the point, and I'd see the audience come up because there'd be one line of thought being followed: Miles would play a melody, and then another melody that made sense after it, and suddenly a composition was being formed and there was an accompaniment that made sense. It would be happening, and the audience would get into it, and he'd stop playing, and the whole thing would blow up; and the audience would go down and not understand it.[50]

What Corea means here is that the audience's attention would wax ("come up") and wane ("go down") based on how directional and conventional the band's presentation was. When Davis played, his melodic focus, supported with an easier logic, would be easy for concertgoers to follow. But when Wayne Shorter or Corea stepped forward, the solos might follow a more abstract logic, and the rhythm section might go its own direction, juxtaposed to more than supporting the soloist in an obvious way. Audiences expecting a one-to-one correspondence between soloist and accompaniment would cease to follow the logic and could get distracted or even uninterested.

By "roller coaster," Corea is describing the general organizing pattern for the music that came about as the new band evolved. What it created was a more extreme version of what had happened in the 1960s quintet. Like the earlier band, the rhythm section developed a pattern of playing simpler, more beat-driven structures during Davis's solos, but would grow freer in his absence. In the previous lineup of musicians, Herbie Hancock recalls Davis complaining as early as 1963 that he wanted to be accompanied in the more complex, freer way that the group backed its saxophonist, George Coleman.[51] The result was what Hancock refers to as "controlled freedom": "He'd take the inherent structure and leave us room to breathe and create something fresh every night."[52]

In the new band, DeJohnette relates: "When Miles played, there was more of a beat to grab hold to, and then when Wayne would play, it would get more abstract, and then when Chick and Dave would play, it would get even more abstract."[53] There were times when, after a remarkably abstract segment with Davis, the trumpeter could return and play a lyrical, melodic solo line, as if nothing remarkable had happened moments prior. Or as if he were still playing in the previous band.

Writing in *Rolling Stone*, Langdon Winner offered a listener's perspective, in the context of his review of *Bitches Brew*. He compares the recorded Holland-DeJohnette "amorphous rhythmic patterns . . . a new way to cook, a way that seems just as natural and just as swinging as anything jazz has ever known," which supported soloists who "are fully accustomed to this new groove and take one solid solo after another," with a later, mid-spring 1970 performance of the Corea-Jarrett two-keyboard band, in which "fully one third of the audience at Davis's recent Fillmore West appearances left the hall in stunned silence, too deeply moved to want to stay for the other groups on the bill."[54]

Musical Example 4: Antibes, July 1969

As an example, in "Directions," the opening tune played at the Antibes Festival in Juan les Pins, France, on July 25 and 26, 1969, we hear the rhythm section shifting gears when Davis's solo winds down and Shorter's begins. First, DeJohnette's driving drums press Davis's energetic solo forward. As Davis concludes, Corea departs from a more strictly rhythmic accompaniment to reach for a rising, terraced series of chords, preparing for the transition to Shorter. Now, Corea and DeJohnette seem to move in opposite directions—as the drummer pushes rhythmically ahead, Corea plays a series of slower, syncopated, longer sustained chords. The combination of these opposing forces quickly increases tension, which is released a half minute later when Corea speeds up his repetitions and then plays a series of varied chordal ostinati, some multiply repeated and others rising in series.[55] Soon, toward the end of Shorter's solo and into Corea's, it is Holland who gradually changes speeds. The bassist alternates between a walk, sometimes unsteady, a series of rapidly repeated notes, and a groove.

Holland credits the eclectic approach he adopted to trend-setting bassists and other musicians he was observing: "What I did with Miles was influenced by the things that I heard around me at those times, what Jack Bruce was doing with the Cream, what Jimi was doing with his band and of course there was the influences of James Brown music and a lot of the other things that were going on at that time."[56] Holland's assessment is extremely modest. The genius in his playing with Davis in 1970 indeed incorporates techniques of his electric peers, but it is equally grounded in the open-improvisational approaches he learned and pioneered during his earlier career in London's free music scene. Thus, the abstraction of the Lost Sextet and Octet of 1970 is due in equal measure to the members of the bands' rhythm section, in which Holland played an integral and decidedly inventive role.

Who's in Charge?

The adventuresome nature of the rhythm section no doubt pushed the envelope on Miles Davis's musical conception. At Antibes and elsewhere during this period, he often remained onstage only while he played, moving offstage during everyone else's solos. From the perspective of Hancock's experience of Davis's nondirective leadership, the trumpeter's departure from the spotlight would seem to project a message to the band: "Go wherever your collective logic takes you." Holland explained Davis's leadership mode to Toronto-based drummer and artist John Mars in a 1975 conversation. According to Mars, "Dave said that all Miles would do is just say 'play C' or something, and those were the total instructions. Miles just ambled up onto the stage and started playing at the concerts, and everyone was supposed to just file in and begin"—something that Mars describes as "a baptism by fire."[57]

But one wonders whether the rhythm section had gone beyond the bounds of Davis's comfort zone. Shorter recalls that after he'd solo and join Davis offstage, the trumpeter would say to him: "What the fuck is going on out there?"[58] Yet when Corea and Holland left the band, it was at their own choosing, having been urged by Davis to stay on beyond the point when they had given notice.

There were exceptions to the template of "simple accompaniment for Davis, but then all hell can break loose." One of many moments of exquisite engagement between players came later, during a March 1970 show at the Fillmore East in New York City. In the midst of a solo by Davis, he and Corea lock "horns" until Davis breaks away to play a rising figure, only to land back in tandem with Corea. The interplay between the two is exhilarating: they take turns, one playing a line that lifts off while the other provides ballast, pulling it back down to earth with an incessantly repeated phrase. Then, as Corea and the rhythm section move into a prelude to the theme of "Directions," the band is off and running. And this is before Davis leaves the stage to make space for the intense, busy, abstract improvisations within the Corea-Holland-DeJohnette rhythm section, which promptly go their own mercurial way.

From Davis's perspective, at least in retrospect, as bandleader he was always in charge of organizing the music:

> Sometime you subtract, take away the rhythm and leave just the right sound. Or take out what you know belongs to somebody else and keep the feeling. I write for my group, for something I know Jack can do, or Chick. Or would want to do. What they've got to do is extend themselves beyond what they think they can do. And they've got to be quick. A soloist comes in when he feels like it. Anyway that's what he's being paid for. If it's not working out I just shut them up. How? I set up obstacles, barriers like they have in the streets but with my horn. I curve them, change their directions.[59]

Chick Corea acknowledges this:

> Miles had quite a lot of direction in what he did. It wasn't a free-for-all at all. When we were touring on the road, he would very often let the musicians play and play longer, because he knew that they were stretching out and experimenting. But, he knew what he wanted and he knew when the music was getting a little bit too self-indulgent and when it needed some form. He would walk back up to the stage and put some form back into the music redirecting the course of it with his horn. In the studio, he was very aware of what he was trying to get.[60]

From this perspective, Davis was comfortable when accompanied in the style he desired for his own solos, yet he allowed the band to play more abstractly when it didn't inhibit his own playing. As Dave Holland recalls: "Miles liked things to be kept fairly clear behind him. He liked the groove to be kept consistently, not messing with the groove or making it too elastic. And also, he adhered to the form of songs. Obviously there's a lot of freedom in his playing, but Wayne by contrast was just ready for anything to happen. We sensed that, and it gave us a sense of a little more freedom with Wayne in the music."[61]

There were times when Davis reined in his band members. Holland remembers Miles offering a constructive "reality check" on the young bassist's approach to his instrument. Within a year in the band, Holland began "feeling like I could do what I wanted to do. I started to maybe take too many liberties with the music as a bass player. So Miles just came over to me at the end of the concert and said to me, 'Hey Dave, you know you are a bass player.' That kind of gave me a reality check." This intervention led him to consider "how to maintain control of the bass and free it up somewhat so that it can have a freer role and a more interactive role with the band."[62]

Clearly, the music could be complex and volcanic. Corea remembers finding it difficult at times to find a role for his piano in what could be a dense morass—what he later referred to as "out in the ozone, but happily so." "Sometimes Wayne would be taking his solo and Jack and Dave's playing would become so vigorous that playing the piano wouldn't make much sense to me. So I'd jump on the drums, and Jack and I would both go at it, making all kinds of wild rhythms, creating even more energy. Jack and I had some fun with that for a few gigs, and Miles seemed to let it go for a while—he was willing to let anything go for a while—then he said, 'That's enough.'"[63]

We can see the two drummers, Jack DeJohnette and Chick Corea, playing during Wayne Shorter's solo and then moving into a drums duet, starting around seven and a half minutes into the filmed performance of "Bitches Brew" in the second set at Salle Pleyel in Paris on November 3, 1969. The duet leads into a driving but highly abstract electric piano and drums duet when Corea returns to his usual station. The activity calms substantially a minute later, when Davis enters with a somber muted trumpet, eventually returning to hints of the tune's opening section and building toward a brilliant, virtuosic, more linear trumpet solo. Following Shorter's solo on "It's About That Time,"[64] Jack DeJohnette takes a solo on the Fender Rhodes, accompanied only by Corea on drums. He begins simply but builds into a construction no less complex and abstract than what Corea might have played.

Continuous Evolution

As the quintet matured as an ensemble, its performances began to explore more fully the implications of the "new directions" promised by the studio recording *Bitches Brew*. This would include bringing the electronic—rather than simply electric—sonic exploration into live performances, and reconciling the central role of the beat in light of open form. In the band's first year, Davis had begun to consider how to square his conception of a beat-centered music with a highly exploratory group of musicians. Yet just as his interest in the beat was continuing to grow, so also was the band's interest in the freer elements. His test for the next year was how to reconcile the challenges of a beat-centered music with sonic and improvisatory complexity. This would remain an issue throughout Davis's work until his first retirement in 1975.

The premise of this book is that Miles Davis's Lost Quintet, even as it expanded in personnel, did not operate within a vacuum. It increasingly embraced but was not limited by the jazz, rock, and funk worlds. Its members were highly conscious of their more experimental predecessors and contemporaries. Then, during the height of the band's free-form and electric excursions, Chick Corea's and Dave Holland's more exploratory interests were heightened when they encountered a future collaborator, Anthony Braxton.

3

Anthony Braxton

Leroy Jenkins, Musica Elettronica Viva,
and the "Peace Church" Concert

Another European Adventure: Braxton and Jenkins in Paris

We now turn to Anthony Braxton and Leroy Jenkins, two musicians from Jack DeJohnette's hometown of Chicago, and both members of the Association for the Advancement of Creative Musicians. While neither was a member of the Miles Davis Lost Quintet, both men were integral to the aesthetic universe from which that group emerged. When Braxton joined with Lost Quintet members Chick Corea and Dave Holland (plus drummer Barry Altschul) to form Circle, he helped further the more exploratory side of the Davis band's legacy. Simultaneously, Jenkins cofounded the Revolutionary Ensemble, an important group of instrumentalists who inhabited a related musical space. Exploring the evolution of both these musicians can help us better understand the musical influences that shaped both the odyssey of the Lost Quintet and the musical world they all shared.

While the quintet toured Europe and the United States in 1969, a group of young, Chicago-born musicians affiliated with the AACM also had Europe on their minds and relocated to Paris. Since the 1920s, Paris had been a home away from home for African American expatriate artists, among them saxophonist Dexter Gordon and writer James Baldwin.[1] Despite a highly creative atmosphere in Chicago at the time, many musicians on the city's South Side were frustrated by the limited performance opportunities that had led to the founding of the AACM. Drummer Steve McCall led the exodus, soon joined by the core of the Art Ensemble of Chicago: Roscoe Mitchell, Malachi Favors, Lester Bowie, and Joseph Jarman. This cohort in turn was joined by three composer-performers who had formed a trio in Chicago: trumpeter Leo Smith (later Wadada Leo Smith),[2] violinist Leroy Jenkins, and saxophonist Anthony Braxton. They played as a quartet with the addition of Steve McCall. Upon Braxton's return to the United States in 1969 and Jenkins's in 1970, both men played pivotal roles in ensembles at the center of this book.

Leroy Jenkins

Leroy Jenkins began playing the violin as a child. George Lewis relates:

> When Leroy was eight or nine, his auntie's boyfriend Riley brought a violin to the house. Leroy was transfixed by the finger-busting classical marvels Riley played, and pleaded with his mother to get him a violin. Soon, a half-size, red-colored violin came from Montgomery Wards by mail order. It cost $25, which his mother paid for on credit. Leroy recalled that at first, he had "a terrible sound. I almost gave it up, but I figured I'd keep doing it and I'd sound like Riley."[3]

Born and raised in Chicago, Jenkins played in local churches as a youngster. He was accompanied by pianist-singer Dinah Washington, then named Ruth Jones, and also performed in orchestral settings.[4] Taking up the saxophone in high school, Jenkins became one of the budding jazz musicians mentored by "Captain" Walter Dyett, bandleader at DuSable High School on the city's South Side. Trained in a broad array of musical traditions, he played clarinet, saxophone, bassoon, and violin while attending Florida A&M, one of the historically black colleges and universities, where he completed degrees in music education and violin.[5] After graduation, he taught high school violin in Mobile, Alabama, and then in Chicago, where he returned in 1965 at the age of thirty.

Soon after his arrival back in his hometown, Jenkins discovered the AACM by attending a concert played by Roscoe Mitchell, Kalaparusha (Maurice McIntyre), Alvin Fielder, and other future colleagues. His college violin teacher—who had just played a gig with Muhal Richard Abrams—had brought him to the performance. Jenkins recalled that they "both were quite befuddled as to what was happening. But we liked it. It was very exciting, what they were doing." At some point during the concert, he brought out his violin and was immediately included in a collective improvisation conducted by Abrams. "Boy, that was really something to me, even though I was playing in a little more orderly fashion than I am now, or let's say a more traditional fashion. These guys were squawking and squeaking and making sounds and doing different things, and I was still playing little snatches of changes because I didn't know anything else."[6] Jenkins spent four years with the organization before leaving Chicago.[7]

His year in Paris performing with Braxton and Smith was exciting for him as well:

Archie Shepp [with whom he played] . . . everybody was there. Philly Joe Jones was there. It was great. I played with Philly Joe! I made a record with him. That was great. . . . Sometimes [the trio] was Anthony's group, sometimes it was my group, sometimes it was Leo's group—it was one of those kinds of things. But we were the first or second group of our type in Europe in 1969, and we raised quite a bit of Cain. [The Art Ensemble of Chicago, the best known of the AACM-affiliated groups] beat us over there by about a month.[8]

After moving to New York City in 1970, Jenkins played with Alice Coltrane and Albert Ayler. Kunle Mwanga (whom we'll soon meet) recalls: "People were calling Leroy for gigs. It was almost like Leroy was the first person to come up here and really circulate within the New York musical environment."[9]

Anthony Braxton

Anthony Braxton was raised on early rock and roll, as well as the music of the black church, the blues, and rhythm and blues.[10] He discovered jazz as a teenager, and while serving in the army in Seoul, South Korea, he came to appreciate the music of Ornette Coleman, Cecil Taylor, John Coltrane, Albert Ayler, and, in equal measure, Arnold Schoenberg, the composer credited with establishing the twelve-tone system in European art music. Schoenberg's explorations of atonality led him to recognize the limitations of that approach when composing

longer forms. He recognized the need for a new organizing principle to structure works of concert music that lacked a key structure.

Discovering Schoenberg helped Braxton claim as his own a larger musical
world than he had previously known. He recalls: "Until that time I had always
thought of Western art-music as something only relevant to white people; it
had nothing to do with me and my life. I played in the orchestra on clarinet,
I played my part, I played my Bach, but it never touched me. . . . Experiencing
Schoenberg['s piano piece Opus 11], however, suddenly made everything more
meaningful. . . . It opened up the next whole aspect of my life. It affected me in
as profound a way as anything has ever affected me."[11]

Braxton's musical vistas were also broadened at Wilson Junior College,[12]
where he became friends with Jack DeJohnette and Roscoe Mitchell (De-
Johnette of course would join the Miles Davis Lost Quintet in late 1968). Immediately upon returning home to Chicago from the army in 1966,[13] Braxton
made two of the most important connections of his musical life. First he met
Muhal Richard Abrams, then a bebop pianist who in the early 1960s had created an "Experimental Band" to explore the implications of the searching work
of Coleman and Coltrane. In 1964, Abrams cofounded the Association for the
Advancement of Creative Musicians as a way for black musicians to perform
original compositions and collectively create alternative structures to an oppres-
sive jazz business.

Also upon his return to Chicago, Braxton discovered John Cage's *Silence*,
an influential collection of talks and writings about contemporary musical aesthetics that had been published in 1961. Cage's ideas opened Braxton's eyes to a
world of musical sound beyond the conventional notion of pitches and metric
rhythm. He wrote: "There is no such thing as an empty space or an empty time.
There is always something to see, something to hear. In fact, try as we may to
make a silence, we cannot. Sounds occur whether intended or not; the psycho-
logical turning in direction of those not intended seems at first to be a giving
up of everything that belongs to humanity. But one must see that humanity
and nature, not separate, are in this world together, that nothing was lost when
everything was given away."[14] Recall, from chapter 1, drummer Billy Hart's recollection of having listened with Braxton to the music of Cage, Karlheinz Stockhausen, and David Tudor.[15]

In 1968, Braxton engaged in a burst of studio activity, recording one of the
first albums for solo saxophone, *For Alto*,[16] and his early ensemble recording,
3 Compositions of New Jazz. The following year, he was one of the younger members of the AACM who participated in the exodus to Paris.

Braxton's Parisian debut in his quartet with Jenkins, Smith, and McCall took place at the Theatre du Lucernaire, the scene of the Art Ensemble's premiere performance in the city. There, like the Art Ensemble, he was accorded numerous performance opportunities, and press attention. He met Ornette Coleman, who eventually became an important friend, and other American jazz notables. Being situated in a capital of the European avant-garde, he attended performances of the continent's new music, developing a particular affection for Karlheinz Stockhausen's work.

> It was Stockhausen who showed me the beauty and excitement of every aspect
> of music science. In my dark periods, in those times where I was wonder-
> ing how I could get through, his music would inspire me to keep doing my
> work . . . the philosophical dynamics of [Cage's] music would help me, as an
> African-American intellectual, to look into my own lineage and develop my
> own perspective. Experiencing the musics of Cage and Stockhausen would be
> the final part of my own equation, in terms of understanding what I wanted to
> do with my life. . . . . I discovered Schoenberg in the army; his music would be
> just as important to me.[17]

During this period, Braxton began to assimilate what he had learned from Coleman, Coltrane, Cage, and Schoenberg. The year before, when recording his landmark album for solo saxophone, *For Alto*, he composed his first notated works in a contemporary art music idiom, moving toward his unique synthesis of musical languages.

Braxton's early ensemble recording, 3 *Compositions of New Jazz*,[18] displays the musical eclecticism and experimentalism for which he was becoming known. On "Composition 6E" (the title of the work is represented on the album cover by a schematic diagram), he is joined by Leroy Jenkins and Leo Smith, two members of the group he cofounded, Creative Construction Company. The twenty-minute piece is simultaneously playful and serious, virtuosic, and abounding in complex juxtapositions of sound and emotional tone.

The work defies conventional expectations of genre and aesthetics, opening and closing with a "tra-la-la" vocal chorus complemented by whistling, and leading into Anthony Braxton's lyrical alto saxophone solo. His musical lines display a beautifully pure tone color, accompanied by harmonica, xylophone, hand percussion, and continued singing. Soon, Braxton is joined by Jenkins's violin and Smith's trumpet, all continuing in parallel play. Braxton's martial snare drum enters, as does hand percussion and vocals, while Smith's trumpet continues.

Jenkins's violin then returns with steady, mellifluous lines. Such is the opening six minutes of the work. As Chick Corea would later observe of Circle's *Paris Concert*, *3 Compositions of New Jazz* brims with "sharing, creating, loving, freely giving." Braxton was quickly absorbing everything he knew, all his influences, new and old, and shaping a distinctive personal musical voice. It was eclectic yet increasingly organic, clearly identifiable to the listener as Anthony Braxton.

The peril of open improvisation, with its lack of a clear organizing structure, is that it can be long-winded or become stale and repetitive. Many of Braxton's compositions from this early period in his work are conceptualized to provide new structures that can guide and inform the improvisational process, keeping it focused and fresh.

The score for "Composition 6E" specifies four sections. The first is a "basic use of voice with counterpoint like situation," followed by what Michael Heffley describes as an "extension of materials," a "whistle and pointillistic section," and a "repeat of first section," all within a context of open improvisation that makes use of little instruments and "with solo possibly inside."[19] "Little instruments" refers to the hand percussion and other miscellaneous sound sources often utilized within many AACM performances. The form of another of the pieces, "Composition 6A," includes patterns of accelerando and ritard, and changes from duple meter to 9/4. This piece and others in Braxton's "Compositions 6" series would later become part of the repertoire performed by Circle.

Braxton Meets Musica Elettronica Viva in Belgium

During the summer of 1969, as Miles Davis was preparing to record *Bitches Brew* and American rock fans were flocking to Woodstock, Braxton participated in an eclectic festival in Belgium. There he met Richard Teitelbaum, Alvin Curran, and Frederic Rzewski, members of Musica Elettronica Viva (MEV). Teitelbaum recalls:

> I met Braxton in 1969 in a cow pasture in Belgium, in a place called Amougies, at a big festival [Festival Actuel] that was one of the original attempts to bring jazz [musicians]—well, mostly rock, some free jazz, and a few wacky token electronic avant-garde types—to play in the same festival. Braxton played there with his trio with Leroy Jenkins and [Wadada] Leo Smith. The Art Ensemble of Chicago played there, an extraordinary performance; that was the first time I heard them and met them. MEV was part of that. [Before that] I had barely known anything about any of those [AACM] guys.[20]

Anthony Braxton speaks of the cow pasture as "something like five feet of mud in Belgium. . . . All of us were in our 20s, excited about music and the idea of music as a component to change the world. We were going to change the world with our work. We were idealistic and excited."[21]

Festival Actuel was a very different kind of event from the festivals where Miles Davis's band appeared.[22] It would be difficult to imagine an American or British rock event encompassing an aesthetic palate as broad as Actuel's, with its blend of rock bands, MEV, the Art Ensemble of Chicago, and Anthony Braxton. In contrast, Davis's Lost Septet's final show, in late August 1970, was an appearance before three-quarters of a million people at the Isle of Wight rock festival in England. There Miles shared a bill with Jimi Hendrix, Chicago, the Who, Sly and the Family Stone, Emerson Lake and Palmer, Joni Mitchell, and others. That spring, in a shift from jazz clubs, festivals, and concert halls, Davis had given three series of concerts at Fillmore East in New York City and Fillmore West in San Francisco. These were rock halls where his band was the opening act for rock groups.[23]

Calling the festival in Amougies a "daring project," Jane Welch wrote in *DownBeat*:

> Where Woodstock was a social revelation, the first Actuel Paris Music Festival was a musical revolution. This revolution was accomplished in the programming, which included all the kinds of music in which the new musicians and composers of today are involved. . . . The fact that it was a success (over 75,000 attended during a 5-day period) proves that audiences are ready to hear this type of music and, like the Woodstock masses, are willing to make sacrifices to take part in a musical milieu truly representative of their taste. The music was NOW, the audience was NOW and, despite all business or political opposition which attempted to abort the festival, the time was right and the baby was born.[24]

In addition to the nearly fifty groups performing individually, a jam session included Frank Zappa, Philly Joe Jones, Earl Freeman, Louis Maholo, John Dyani, Grachan Moncur III, and Archie Shepp.

The Festival Actuel shows in Belgium[25] were recorded, and additional sessions took place in Paris. Some of the musicians involved, most of them American, were already living abroad, and performed at the Pan-African Music Festival in Algiers. The result was a series of fifty recordings on the BYG label that represented some of the more important documentation of music from that period. Festival Actuel producers Fernand Boruso, Jean-Luc Young, and Jean Georgakarakos (more popularly shortened to Karakos) were the founders of BYG Records (the name was formed by the initials of the founders' surnames), and Anthony Braxton and the Art Ensemble of Chicago would each release recordings on that label.

The propitious meeting between Braxton and Teitelbaum at Festival Actuel brought together two musicians raised in very different cultural settings, but sharing key musical and philosophical sensibilities. Whereas Braxton grew up on the South Side of Chicago, playing rock and roll and later discovering a broader musical world in the army and through the AACM, Teitelbaum hailed from New York City. He attended Haverford College, where his

> main interests at that time were Stravinsky and Bartok. . . . And then I started getting interested in Schoenberg and Webern, more in graduate school [Yale University class of 1964]; and Stockhausen through having met him. And jazz. I liked bebop a lot. . . . I don't think I got really into Coltrane until 1960 or something like that. [I went to hear his] quartet, that's my recollection, Jimmy Garrison, [McCoy] Tyner, [and Elvin Jones]. But then I heard him several times in the period of "Ascension." . . . And then I also was getting involved with free-jazz stuff. I met Albert Ayler. I went to see him in the Village, and a friend who knew him took me up, shook his hand; that was kind of exciting.[26]

Then Teitelbaum went to Italy on a Fulbright Fellowship to study composition with Luigi Nono.

> When I got to Venice, I was still writing this instrumental piece, but I was hanging out with [saxophonist] Steve Lacy, [trumpeter] Don Cherry, and others—Ornette [Coleman]—and listening to more jazz, really, than to classical or electronic music. I still somewhere have some notebooks where I have pages where I did something like this [gestures in the air with his hand] when I was listening to Coltrane's *Ascension*. I was really quite obsessed with the notion that noise was a thing that was a common between the jazz of that period, such as *Ascension*, where there were twenty guys blasting away and ten of them were percussionists, and the others were just blowing their brains out, and noise music—electronic music. So, it was a very conscious awareness of the connection between improvised music, free improvised music, [and electronic music].[27]

In 1966 in Rome, MEV was cofounded by Teitelbaum, Alvin Curran, and Frederic Rzewski; all three were Ivy League university–trained American musicians steeped in post–World War II European avant-garde traditions. Curran and Teitelbaum had been graduate school roommates at Yale University, and Curran and Rzewski had met in Berlin. What they all sought was an alternative to the rigorously mathematical serialism of that world. While each musician came to Rome for different reasons, all were drawn to that city's musical and artistic vitality. Rome was the city of filmmaker Federico Fellini, and a home for expat American experimentalists like the Living Theatre and musicians Don Cherry, Ornette Coleman, and Steve Lacy.

MEV championed music that was collective, spontaneous, and participatory. Its members viewed their music-making as a revolutionary endeavor to empower people in the skill sets they would need during a time of social transformation. They envisioned a truly free society in which groups could function unconstrained by conventional, hierarchical political structures. Curran describes their endeavors as a "utopian challenge."[28] In works such as Rzewski's "Spacecraft" (1967), "Zuppa" (1968), and "Sound Pool" (1969), MEV thus drew from structures that allowed any number of participants, musically skilled or unskilled, to join in an improvisational experience. Curran writes: "What the group MEV[29] essentially did was to redefine music as a form of property that belonged equally to everyone and hence to encourage its creation freely by and through anyone anywhere."[30] For this reason, conventional musical skills could be constraining, as Rzewski notes: "Improvisation is a controlled experiment with a limited number of unknown possibilities. . . . The presence of too much theoretical or analytical knowledge in the conscious mind may interfere with the essential act, so that the perception of the thing being studied becomes distorted."[31] For Curran, musical improvisation was an exemplar of a generalized approach to life, "the art of constant, attentive and dangerous living in every moment."[32]

For Braxton, the late 1960s, highlighted by his sojourn in Europe, was "a very beautiful time. Teitelbaum and Frederic [Rzewski] were moving away from Stockhausen; more and more they were becoming interested in improvisation and the transAfrican restructural musics." He recalls hearing recordings of Stockhausen's Kontra-Punkte and Klavierstucke X (the latter performed by MEV pianist Rzewski): "I was very curious about the restructural[33] breakthroughs of the post-Webern composers. So we kind of met in the middle of this sector. I learned a great deal about the post-Webern continuum from Mr. Teitelbaum and Mr. Rzewski and Curran." Braxton refers to the members of MEV "as a part of this underground brotherhood-sisterhood that is permeated with love and respect—and of course, poverty! That's how I see my work. That is the proper context for my work. It's a part of the old underground."[34]

The musical values that Anthony Braxton affirmed at the time were in important ways sympathetic to MEV's call to arms, although maybe not as anarchic. In an MEV performance, social dynamics could unfold that were neither predictable nor always easy to manage. Curran observes:

> Anything could happen. . . . [There was] a generic problem that was happening in the MEV experience in those years, 68, 69, and 70. Because of, let's call it, philosophic necessity, we found that we had to open the music to anybody. When this went from a mere philosophical, conceptual idea to a practical one, the problems that arose were minor actually, were few. It was more like policing a rowdy crowd on occasion. Other times we're just sitting back and listening to this divine collective harmony that just happens spontaneously because we made it happen, or the people involved made it happen for themselves.[35]

Braxton wrote sympathetically, in 1968:

> We're on the eve of the complete fall of Western ideas and life-values. . . . We're in the process of developing more meaningful values and our music is a direct extension of this. We place more emphasis on the meaningful areas of music and less on artifacts, [today's] over-emphasis on harmonic structure, chord progressions, facility, mathematics, the empirical aspects of Art. Our emphasis is on the idea of total music, with each individual contributing toward it totally. . . . We're dealing with textures, now—individual worlds of textures. We're working toward a feeling of one—the complete freedom of individuals in tune with each other, complementing each other. This is going to be the next phase of jazz.[36]

In fact, Braxton's eclectic musical vision was just beginning to unfold. Six years after his prophetic statement,[37] he urged a younger musician to listen to Henry Cowell, Paul Desmond, and Charles Ives, referring to the latter as "Father" Charles Ives. And he spoke excitedly about various people whom he felt were "the most incredible ____ on the planet. . . . The direction he was trying to move into with his own music was composed music. Braxton didn't want to call it *classical*, just like he didn't want to call his other, small-group stuff with all the improvisation, *jazz*."[38]

At the close of the 1960s, the spirit of the time was being open to possibilities. There was a sense of living on the cusp of a new era of unlimited freedom, where responsible action would be based on mutuality and interrelationship. In this environment, MEV and Anthony Braxton would find shared sensibilities and impetus to collaborate. Chick Corea, Dave Holland, and Jack DeJohnette could push Miles Davis's band toward a greater openness. And soon, that common cause would extend to a musical partnership between Corea, Holland, and Braxton.

Braxton in New York

Although Paris afforded better performance opportunities than Chicago, Braxton decided to return to the United States in late 1969. While returning home might literally mean Chicago, New York City beckoned.[39] This was now the center of gravity for new music of all kinds. Braxton and Leroy Jenkins had met Ornette Coleman in Paris, introduced by an entrepreneur from Chicago named Kunle Mwanga.[40] This encounter occurred a decade after Coleman first arrived in New York City, keenly observed at the Five Spot by Miles Davis and John Coltrane. Mwanga's chance meeting with Coleman in London, the latter en route to Paris, led to Coleman's organizing a joint Paris concert with Braxton's Creative Construction Company, the Art Ensemble of Chicago, and Coleman's own group. The contacts were now in place for Braxton and Jenkins to reconnect with Coleman when they moved to New York. Once back in the States, Coleman invited Braxton to move into his loft, where Braxton remained for nine months.[41]

Ornette Coleman's Artists House

In the late 1960s, Coleman moved into the upstairs floor of a formerly commercial building at 131 Prince Street in lower Manhattan. The neighborhood's industrial base in small manufacturing had declined, and Coleman became one of a group of artists and musicians to find affordable housing among its abandoned buildings. His interest in welcoming fellow musicians and other friends over to his loft to visit led to the space's becoming viewed by some as an informal artists' hangout. Thus, it was only a matter of time that, at some point in the early 1970s, he took over the first-floor storefront in his building, naming it Artists House.

At first, Artists House was an extension of the saxophonist-composer's home and was a place for socializing; secondarily, it served as a rehearsal space.

By the early 1970s, it became to some degree an event venue. Revolutionary Ensemble drummer Jerome Cooper remembers: "He would give his parties, he would have his band, and he would let his friends rehearse there. I used to go to parties over there at the Artists House. I remember the bass player with John Coltrane—Jimmy Garrison—used to hang out there a lot. It was a great place." Artist Fred Brown observes: "I thought a loft was a hayloft and this place was like Shangri-la."[42] A *DownBeat* writer described Artists House as "quickly becoming a haven for some of our more creative musicians. The House presented the perfect atmosphere for music—African prints and paintings adorn the walls making for striking contrast between audio and visual. This is the type of setting where the music does the people and not, as it so often [is] the case, the other way around."[43]

Coleman served as an informal mentor and support to younger players. Vibraphonist Karl Berger, a member of trumpeter Don Cherry's band[44] and soon the cofounder, with Coleman, of Creative Music Studio, recalls: "We went a lot there in the late '60s. He had people coming over all the time. That's the first time I met Leroy [Jenkins] and a lot of other people who'd come there. And we were playing pool. He had a pool table. Always on the weekends there was a bunch of people there. Basically, we were there every weekend and also some weekdays."[45]

Cooper adds: "Leroy used to be at Ornette Coleman's house all the time, Sirone [bassist Norris Jones] used to be over there [too] and [so was] I—but I never talked to Ornette at that time. I used to hang out with Ed Blackwell. I remember the party he [Ornette] gave when he signed with Columbia and did *Skies of America* and *Science Fiction*. I went there and it was really nice."[46]

When Jenkins first arrived in New York from Chicago via Paris, he too moved into Artists House at Coleman's invitation, and he stayed for a few months. "We stayed downstairs at Ornette's Artists House, which at the time wasn't decorated. It was cold down there, where we slept. Ornette gave us a mattress but he didn't realize how cold it was.'"[47] Berger recalls that when he first arrived in the United States, "Ingrid [Sertso, Berger's spouse and collaborator] and I went to Ornette's loft all the time, and we discussed matters. He was the only one who made sense to me in terms of how he talked about music."[48]

Artists House would be the site of Braxton and Jenkins's rehearsals with Creative Construction Company in preparation for its concert appearance at the Washington Square Church (also known as the "Peace Church" due to its stated opposition to the Vietnam War), the first event sponsored by the Association for the Advancement of Creative Musicians to take place in New York.[49]

Coleman also hosted performances at the loft, among them those by his own group and shows by Julius Hemphill, Frank Wright, Sunny Murray, MEV, and, as Jerome Cooper remembers, Dave Holland and Jack DeJohnette (with a guitar player).[50]

The degrees of separation between present and former members of Miles Davis bands and Artists House were fewer than might be assumed. The Revolutionary Ensemble, Jenkins's new trio with Cooper and Sirone, whom we'll soon meet, would conduct rehearsals and hold a concert at Artist's House. A 1973 New and Newer Music series held there included works from various downtown musical worlds, combining music by Ornette Coleman with offerings by Carla Bley and MEV's cofounder, pianist Frederic Rzewski.[51] The following year, Creative Music Studio's first festival took place at Artists House.[52] Unfortunately, Coleman's space closed soon after that event.[53]

The informality and neighborly atmosphere of Artists House is captured in a session Coleman recorded in the space on February 14, 1970, released as *Friends and Neighbors: Ornette Live at Prince Street*. The spirit of the location is well captured by the buoyant, joyous title tracks that open the recording. Bassist Charlie Haden and drummer Ed Blackwell, members of Coleman's original quartet and reunited for the occasion, set up a rollicking, finger-snapping beat. The assembled crowd sings together: "Friends and neighbors, that's where it's at. Friends and neighbors, that's where it's at. Friends and neighbors, that's a fact. Hand in hand. . . ." Coleman wildly bows on violin, one of his new instruments, on top of which his old south Texas friend, tenor saxophonist Dewey Redman, plays a soulful solo, which dances around the melody. The chant returns, joined by Coleman's violin and the rhythm section. The audience whoops and shouts its approval before Redman continues his solo.[54] The recording offers an inside view of the communal spirit of the "jazz loft" scene, which would spring forth two years later, in 1972.

Joining Musica Elettronica Viva

Situated in New York City, Anthony Braxton was adrift. Kunle Mwanga, the entrepreneur who had introduced Braxton and Leroy Jenkins to Ornette Coleman in Paris (but who was living in New York), found Braxton to be uninterested in playing music. "As a matter of fact, he was playing chess a lot in the park." Mwanga would soon persuade him to play a reunion concert with Creative Construction Company, but throughout this period, he "was thinking about other things."[55] One of the first of these plans was another reunion, with his new friends from Amougie. As Braxton recalls: "I had the good fortune to be asked to join Musica Elettronica Viva, and in doing that, I had opportunities to meet American masters like Maryann[e] Amacher,"[56] along with Richard Teitelbaum, Alvin Curran, and Frederic Rzewski.

MEV's American Tour

I thought it was one of the best MEV ensembles that ever existed.

ALVIN CURRAN[57]

The tour was a success. I thought it was a really interesting group, actually.

RICHARD TEITELBAUM

By 1969 MEV continued to use Rome as a home base from which it actively toured Europe. For the concerts that concluded its time in Rome, the group consisted of its three core members (Teitelbaum, Curran, and Rzewski) plus saxophonist Steve Lacy, Franco Cataldi, and Ivan and Patricia Coaquette. Composer Guiseppe Chiarri joined for a concert in Palermo, Italy, where a work by Morton Feldman was on the program.[58]

Not long after meeting Braxton in Amougies, Teitelbaum and Rzewski prepared to return to the United States; Curran had decided to remain in Rome. Rzewski resettled in New York with his family for a few years.[59] One factor in Teitelbaum's decision to return was the influence of Morton Feldman. "Somewhere in there, I came back [to New York] and Feldman took me out to lunch at Chock Full o' Nuts. He was dean of the New York Studio School[60] in the Village. He kind of was urging me to come back. He said: 'This is your country' or something like that. I was pretty impressed by Feldman. I loved his music. I loved him. We had played a piece of his in Rome, at the Salon Casella."

The other factor influencing Teitelbaum's return to the States was his idea of developing a cross-cultural ensemble, which he called World Band.[61] The ensemble began rehearsing during the months leading up to MEV's tour with Braxton. Both endeavors joined musicians who had been raised in different musical traditions.

In late winter to early spring 1970, Anthony Braxton and sound artist Maryanne Amacher joined the three core members of MEV on an American tour.[62] Tour stops included a cluster of colleges and universities: Notre Dame, Case Western Reserve, Antioch College, and Bowling Green University, followed by Wesleyan College, Brown University, Haverford College, and State University of New York campuses at Stony Brook and Albany. Teitelbaum recalls that the group made money from the tour: "The pay was decent, I think. We might have gotten a thousand dollars for a gig. That was good for then. I'm guessing."

Curran explained the rationale for the tour to a *New York Times* reporter: "Our original music was based on friendship. We were all sort of sick of being composers abroad. Now, we are all very anxious to find out where we fit into the States. We have been in Europe six to eight years and things have changed a great deal at home, and we have changed a great deal. We could fall right into place, or we could flop right back to Rome."[63]

During that same period, Miles Davis was engaged in duo-keyboard and duo-electric guitar studio sessions in between tour dates with the Lost Quintet, and Wayne Shorter was making his final appearances with the group. Chick Corea and Dave Holland had begun playing acoustic duet music to which they would soon add drummer Barry Altschul.

The composition of the MEV group that toured the United States represented both a cultural shift and a new chemistry—in fact, a new formation that played together for the first time at its first show. Beyond the three core members, the personnel had changed from MEV's European tour.

TEITELBAUM: The core group was the same, [but] Maryanne and Braxton had replaced the Cataldis and Franco. [Braxton played (and transported!) a wide range of clarinets, saxophones, and other instruments, from contrabass on upward.]

CURRAN: Maryanne had her tapes . . . and her Revoxes [tape recorders].

TEITELBAUM: She had a heat sink and a bass bow. She had a mixer and, I guess, a contact mic, and she made these incredibly high sounds. I don't remember. She'd find stuff. I think it was at Antioch she had a bass. And she'd scrape the scroll of the bass against the wall and make this amazing sound. So she'd just have whatever. And these tapes, she had amazing tapes.

CURRAN: [The new composition of the band] changed everything. [But] when we found ourselves onstage when we played, there was absolutely no difference. And this was remarkable.

TEITELBAUM: Braxton and Maryanne had the commonality of Stockhausen, for instance, and Cage.

CURRAN: There were some clear cultural differences in the sense that what Braxton would play, you would hear there wasn't a moment when you weren't aware of the whole history of jazz behind him. But that didn't for one minute get in the way of his ability or the other MEV people's ability to integrate their sound with his.

I think there was one common musical space that people liked to get into. And it was that space of delirious energy, and that could be shared at any time. Someone would get on a riff or a high, screaming overtone, like Braxton, or radical blatting down in the lowest registers, honking like geese or something. . . . And so there were spaces between the cultures where one could enter at any time and just hang on to the immaterial material of pure sound. So there were certain energies and certain vibrations. They could have been of any shape or any size. As I say, there were very high-energy places. But they could have been very quiet moments as well. They were almost made of pure breath. Those kinds of places were extreme places, in both directions of speed and slowness and silence; [they] were places that were easy meeting grounds for all of us.[64]

First Stop: The Brooklyn Academy of Music

The MEV tour was organized by Saul Gottlieb, director of the Radical Theatre Repertory.[65] It was planned around four or five gigs, the fruit of letter writing by group members while still in Rome.[66]

First stop was the newly opened Brooklyn Academy of Music. Curran: "We did an MEV classic program, starting with a Feldman piece. And Feldman was there. We ended it up with Christian Wolff's 'Sticks,' and that was supposed to segue into this mass improvisation ('Soundpool'),[67] which it did."[68] The full program included Richard Teitelbaum's "In Tune," which translated brainwave activity into Moog synthesizer sounds; Wolff's "Sticks," a drone piece; Alvin Curran's "Rounds"; and music by Morton Feldman and Frederic Rzewski.

Curran recalls:

I don't know how we announced it or how it actually came out, but I do remember that there was a kind of a dreadful informality going on [once the Sound Pool audience-participation improvisation piece began]. Which was no longer a performance. The first part was a concert. And then the second part became this dissolution into a kind of this happy neighborhood anarchy. I personally felt that it didn't generate the kind of energy that other Sound Pools had generated.[69] And so therefore it failed. There was just the feeling that it didn't matter what was happening, who was there, or what. But somehow there was something that rode over everything to another experiential and existential level, [yet] it didn't transcend, it didn't go anywhere."[70]

New York Times critic Peter G. Davis concluded: "Contemporary music reached some sort of desperate nadir last night as the Musica Elettronica Viva displayed its wares. . . . If the shuffling aridities of this group of losers sounds like your cup of irrelevancy, it is giving a repeat performance at the Academy this evening."[71] Curran believes that the sheer size and sense of cultural importance of the Brooklyn Academy of Music, in contrast to the smaller venues MEV otherwise played, contributed to the difficulties.[72]

On the Road

After the Brooklyn Academy of Music kickoff concert, Curran recalls: "We packed in an old Oldsmobile car [a station wagon] that belonged to Frederic's [Rzewski's] father or mother. We all packed into one car. . . . We just barreled on rainy highways right from New York across Pennsylvania, into Ohio. It seemed like always with the radio going, playing Procol Harum. You know, the songs of those days. It's a kind of piece of history." Once MEV left New York, the tour went well. Curran's assessment: "Antioch, I thought, was one of the best concerts MEV ever played. The Albany concert was insane." Unfortunately, few recordings remain. But MEV's anarchic pieces, performed with American college students, were not without their challenges.

Curran recalls that the Brown University concert was pretty much a ruckus. "Everyone jumped into the howling collective fray with large tree branches— first used for 'Sticks,' then for the audience to play with—and things did, in fact, get out of hand, and left undeniable damage to Brown property: floors, walls, tables, chairs, etc. For this the University sent us a bill, which I recall we threw away as if it never had arrived—even me, the embarrassed Brown Alumnus."[73] Something similar happened at SUNY Stony Brook, maybe a year later.

Curran remembers the Midwest portion of the trip as passing through "some of the most depressed parts of America. . . . Well, it was remarkable to be at a Catholic college at that time and have so much upheaval and then at the same time we were in Ohio."

The Antioch College performance in Yellow Springs, Ohio, on April 6, 1970, stood out in Curran's memory as "like total freakout-ville." Teitelbaum remembers vividly that "while it was still going on, Braxton and I found ourselves outside, maybe having a smoke. And also I think because it was a 'Sound

Pool' [audience-participation improvisational piece]. Things got kinda wild. I was sort of driven out."

> CURRAN: I remember that. You got freaked.
>
> TEITELBAUM: I said to Braxton, "Braxton, do you like this music?" Or something. "Do you like this?" But I don't remember what his answer was. I think it was sort of ambivalent.
>
> CURRAN: I remember those kids jumped onstage. They started rocking. It was crazy. But it wasn't rock. I remember an electric bass, a guitar. I think someone was trying to push it in [a beat-driven] direction. That was a kind of loose, Sunday afternoon freak-out. That was the least interesting.

During the writing of this book, a recording of the Antioch College concert surfaced.[74] This was an unanticipated, wonderful discovery. The recording spans about an hour and a half of what must have been a longer show, given that the audience participation piece, "Sound Pool," is not documented on the reel-to-reel tape. The side of MEV in evidence here is stylistically diverse. Exploration abounds, and sometimes a rhythmic pulse evokes foot tapping. A panoply of musical improvisations ranges from textural sound collage[75] to unfolding melodic and rhythmically driven processes.[76] Four ensemble works[77] are complemented by seven saxophone solo improvisations by Anthony Braxton, whose distinct musical personality is evident throughout. These solo forays provide Braxton the space to present his own work; as an ensemble member, his playing is an organic and comfortable musical fit.

In the course of his solo pieces, Braxton traverses a broad range of textures and moods, from the lyrical and even romantic to the cacophonous. At times, spinning lines resolve in a harmonically grounded zone, underscored by warm vibrato; altissimo screeches, squawking, and honking; intense breath-long angular phrases; quiet trilling passages; serene phrases contrasting with sudden sonic outbursts. One of the solos reflects compositional ideas akin to "Composition 6F," described by Braxton elsewhere as "repetitive phrase generating structures . . . a phrase-based repetition structure that establishes a fixed rhythmic pattern."[78]

Among the ensemble pieces is a ten-minute work that juxtaposes Braxton's angular saxophone (and then bass clarinet) lines to spoken text, Richard Teitelbaum's atonal synthesizer phrases, a bass vamp (played by an Antioch student), and drums. The music then moves into a pentatonic, additive construction, played in unison by piano, Alvin Curran's flugelhorn, a trombone-tuba "patch" on a VCS3 (Putney) synthesizer[79] (together referred to below as "horn"), Teitel-baum's Moog synthesizer, and drums, reminiscent of Frederic Rzewski's "Les Moutons de Panurge" (1969).[80] A second ensemble improvisation opens with melodic saxophone lines, from which Braxton suddenly shifts into a musical explosion and, subsequently, elegiac moods, as he weaves in and out of the horn lines. A third improvisation combines Braxton's snarling sounds with a strong, backbeat-heavy drum pulse; the overall musical direction then shifts into an unfolding sound cloud drawn in part from Curran's assemblage of recorded bird sounds and spoken readings from an ornithology catalog, and Maryanne Amacher's dramatic sounds of a soaring airplane, combined with Teitelbaum's Morse code–like synthesizer patterns. Later, the listener encounters dense and boisterous collective sound clusters and Rzewski's expansive, cascading gestures on piano. Braxton, along with the horn gestures, emerges from behind a distant fog amid the building electronic and metallic textures.

MEV's Impact

While this configuration of MEV never performed together again, Anthony Braxton and Richard Teitelbaum's musical partnership has continued to this day. Braxton's participation in MEV exposed him to a broader circle of impro-vising musicians. Might that experience have opened him to the new opportu-nity, Circle, that would soon manifest? Had they heard MEV, might Braxton's future Circle-mates have been influenced by the group in their own views about intuitive improvisational structures or about their range of sonic possibilities? As Chick Corea simultaneously moved in an increasingly electric direction with Miles Davis's band, his future engagement with Braxton would be entirely acoustic. Had he heard MEV during this period, might its meld of acoustic and electronic sounds have influenced his thinking? Many ideas were percolating in Braxton's mind as his career back in the United States continued to unfold.

Kunle Mwanga Organizes Braxton's "Peace Church" Concert

Kunle Mwanga had moved from Chicago to New York in May 1968. Before traveling to Paris in 1970, he opened a store, Liberty House, in the West Vil-lage, where he sold works of African and African American art. Mwanga was inspired by the Association for the Advancement of Creative Musicians' model of self-sufficiency coupled with organizational and business acumen: "It was my contention that we had to continue to develop our own power to move ourselves. . . . The industry is in control. Yet we could be that industry ourselves had we stayed in control of ourselves. The power within: having to do with management, producing concerts, recordings and all administrative work, worldwide."[81] Mwanga found the New York environment at the time to be stimulating, as it seemed to him that there was no conflict between players representing differing musical styles and approaches. Thus, "it just seemed like things could happen if you wanted them to happen."[82] He decided to leverage his store income to produce a concert series at the Washington Square Church, the "Peace Church," that was Anthony Braxton's first performance in New York.

The May 19, 1970, concert featured Creative Construction Company, Braxton's group that had played in Europe, plus drummer Steve McCall. CCC— Braxton plus Leroy Jenkins and trumpeter Leo Smith—had played on Braxton's album 3 *Compositions of New Jazz*. Special guests also performing with the group were AACM cofounder Muhal Richard Abrams and bassist Richard Davis. All but Davis were members of that Chicago-based association. Mwanga found the Peace Church concert to be "one of the most exciting concerts I've ever been at."[83]

The performance was recorded thanks to Ornette Coleman, who, as John Litweiler reports, "arranged for an engineer to record the event. But Ornette's financial affairs were in flux, and a year later he offered Mwanga the concert tapes if Mwanga would pay the engineer; Mwanga eventually sold the tapes to Muse Records for their excellent Creative Construction Company LPs."[84] Braxton appeared with his trademark array of instruments (flute, clarinet, contrabass clarinet, soprano saxophone, alto saxophone, and orchestral chimes). Jenkins supplemented his violin and viola with recorder, harmonica, toy xylophone, and bicycle horn. The first set of the Peace Church concert consisted of Leroy Jenkins's extended, thirty-seven-minute work "Muhal"; parts 1 and 2 are divided over the two sides of an LP, followed by a return of the theme, titled "Live Spiral" on the recording.

The Music of the Peace Church Concert

A play-by-play description of the first half of the concert offers a flavor of the continuously changing, highly textural, yet periodically lyrical music that unfolded that evening. This is a music that depends substantially on close listening between players, an openness to building on what others are playing, and an instinct for when to lay out entirely.

The performance opens in a serene, spacious mood. There are two motivic statements, each repeated twice.[85] This sequence is followed by the main theme, played on violin,[86] which leads the group to a dense tone cluster.[87] After a pause, the second motif is presented by the full ensemble without piano; it is reminiscent of the opening of Richard Strauss's *Thus Spoke Zarathustra*. Next, Jenkins's gesture is more modest, yet affirmative. After a bass interlude backed by shimmering cymbal work, growing steadily in intensity, Jenkins returns to his thematic statement shortly after the two-minute mark. The motif is joined by cascading piano runs, over which Braxton—displaying a bell-like tone on soprano saxophone, followed by Jenkins and Smith and then all three in unison—echoes the theme.

Jenkins opens an expansive solo, with contrapuntal lines added by Braxton, and Abrams on cello; Smith punctuates Jenkins's playing with repeated trumpet notes and floral figures. Around five minutes in, Braxton's lines have moved to the forefront, and the entire ensemble quiets and pauses. The next section is far more textural in quality, blending Davis's harmonics and extended techniques on bass, Abrams's open harmonies on piano, Jenkins's recorder melodies, and Braxton's melodious saxophone, bells, and small percussion. After another pause, Davis plays a repeated G and then an E–D–E motif, which he embroiders, and Smith solos in the altissimo range.

A folksy Jenkins harmonica solo follows at the eight-minute mark, joined by bicycle horn. Jenkins then returns on viola, building a repeated note and then a double-stop motif—which he moves up and down the neck of his fiddle. Various squeaking horns and small percussion then come to the fore, the bass actively creating a bridge, joined by Braxton's rhapsodic solo on flute, backed by bass and percussion, and joined by viola, which then moves to the front. After the eleven-minute mark, the ensemble increases in energy level, with Abrams's piano figures, trumpet tones, intense viola gestures, and small percussion.

Nearing twelve and a half minutes, Jenkins's repeated strummed chord is imitated by Abrams and Smith and moves into a far-ranging solo; behind him there is growing activity on recorder, piano, bass, and percussion. Next, Braxton jumps into an energetic, spiraling clarinet solo, screeching and then ebbing and flowing. Jenkins returns with violin double stops. As the sixteen-minute mark approaches, he plays a solo line that builds in intensity and then slows down as orchestra bells are heard. These continue, joined by harmonica, bass harmonics, and sundry percussion hits as part 1 concludes, after nineteen minutes.[88]

The performance is a tour de force, a masterly work of ensemble playing. Points of cacophony are limited; the focus is on building a sense of group sound, from which emerge individual solos and, more often, small, collaborative, interwoven parts.

The idea of the individual within, among, and in tension with the group is in a sense a meeting point between Anthony Braxton's aesthetic and that of (Wadada) Leo Smith, who wrote:

> the concept that i employ in my music is to consider each performer as a complete unit with each having his or her own center from which each performs independently of any other, and with this respect of autonomy the independent center of the improvisation is continuously changing depending upon the force created by individual centers at any instance from any of the units. the idea is that each improviser creates as an element of the whole, only responding to that which he is creating within himself instead of responding to the total creative energy of the different units. this attitude frees the sound-rhythm elements in an improvisation from being realized through dependent re-action.[89]

Thus, in this concert we experience constant, dynamic movement between self-contained solo moments and group engagement.

Braxton Broadens His Horizons

The concert provided an opportunity for Braxton to connect and reconnect with other musicians who were living in New York City. This included a reunion with MEV member Frederic Rzewski, who subsequently introduced him to the noted minimalist composers Steve Reich and Philip Glass; he informally rehearsed with them during the summer of 1970.[90] Braxton observes: "By that time it became clear to me that I did not want to be remembered in only one context. I came to understand that I wanted to be involved in a broader area of creativity, Glass and as such, I didn't want to limit myself to just performing jazz. Not to mention I simply was curious and attracted to what people like Glass and [electronic music composer David] Behrman were doing."[91]

Also in the audience for the Creative Construction Company performance was Jack DeJohnette, Chick Corea and Dave Holland's Miles Davis bandmate, who knew Braxton from college. Later that evening, DeJohnette suggested to Braxton that they head over to the Village Vanguard, several blocks to the west. It was there that the propitious meeting leading to the founding of Circle took place.

4

Interlude

Musical Rumblings in Chelsea

The Chick Corea–Dave Holland–Jack DeJohnette trio within Miles Davis's band had traversed much terrain. If Davis's own solos represented a stabilizing force, the rhythm section was continually upsetting the cart. As a whole, and particularly after the addition of Keith Jarrett as second keyboardist, the band became even freer in its sonic conception. The musical bond between Corea and Holland grew particularly strong. The time approached when they would set off on their own path.

Corea recalls:

> While we were members of Miles's band, Dave Holland and I
> shared similar tastes in music and, of course, were playing a very
> free form of music with Miles. I think that Miles was letting us
> search out whatever we wanted—he was observing and waiting
> to see what happened—he gave us tremendous leeway. Only
> towards the end of our tenure did he begin implying that the free

form of improvisation was not where he wanted to be headed. . . . He actually encouraged us to form our own band—which we promptly did.[1]

Corea noted earlier: "Dave and I developed a concept together, and then when Miles wanted to go more into rock and a rock kind of a rhythm section, Dave and I really wanted to continue to pursue free playing."[2]

Even when they were not on the road, Corea and Holland crossed paths daily; they were living in the same building in Manhattan's Chelsea neighborhood, between Sixth and Seventh Avenues. The loft building at 138 West Nineteenth Street was becoming a hotbed of creative musical activity. It all began with saxophonist Dave Liebman[3] (who had graduated from NYU, majoring in history), who earned a living by working as a substitute teacher two days a week in the New York City Public Schools. By night, he played jazz-club gigs.

Liebman recalls:

> I had decided I didn't want to play any more club dates to make a living. I realized that I really had to be pure to get it right, but I had to make a living. That's when I found my first loft. It was January '69 when I moved into 138 West Nineteenth Street in a twelve-hundred-square-foot space . . . basically one room with a little toilet on one side and a small anteroom enough for a mattress as part of an open space, straight through. I set it up with a piano, got some drums, and knew that for me, the only way I was going to improve was to physically play a lot. So I had an open-door policy, which went on for the next few years. . . . I was playing and teaching, and eventually starting to work with [drummer] Pete LaRoca.[4]

Liebman would soon join the jazz-rock band Ten Wheel Drive; in 1971, he became a member of Elvin Jones's band, and in 1973, he joined Miles Davis.

Six months after moving into his loft, Liebman received a phone call from Dave Holland. The two had met in London in the summer of 1967.

> I wanted to travel across Europe. My parents gave me a thousand dollars, and a copy of the book *Europe on Five Dollars a Day*. It was one of those student travel things. The premise was to get cultured, visiting museums and so on, which I did, but of course I also took my tenor and looked for playing opportunities.[5]
>
> I flew into London. When I got there, I wanted to know what was happening in London. So I made some calls. Someone told me to go to Ronnie

Scott's [club]; everybody would be there. That's where I met Dave Holland and John Surman. They invited me to stay with them. After that, I traveled around Europe, came back to London and I stayed over with them again, and then came home.[6]

Now, in August 1968, "Dave [Holland] called to tell me that he got the gig with Miles and needed a place to live. I talked to my landlord on Nineteenth Street and asked about Dave. There were two apartments free. Dave moved in with his wife and young child. And soon after that, Chick moved in. He had been living in Queens but now divorced from his wife, needed a new place. When Chick came over he played me the master tapes of *Now He Sings, Now He Sobs.*"[7] Pianist Carl Schroeder also had a loft in the complex.

Corea relates: "Dave [Holland] and I practically lived together for a couple of years. . . . We were on the bandstand every night. We were talking about music all the time. So there was lots of sharing of ideas and concepts and so forth." Soon, "Dave Holland and I began to play together as a duet in my loft. I had brought from Boston the Steinway S that my mother and father bought for me when I was 16 years old."[8]

Chelsea as a Home for Jazz Musicians

The neighborhood of Chelsea, between Fourteenth and Twenty-Ninth Streets on the West Side of Manhattan, was an unanticipated home for jazz or other creative music-making. Although jazz clubs had proliferated in Harlem, Greenwich Village, and midtown Manhattan[9] since the 1940s, jazz musicians arrived in Chelsea only in the 1960s. Just as industrial decline brought artists and musicians seeking affordable spaces to the undivided factory floors of abandoned buildings farther downtown in SoHo, reconfigured as "lofts," a similar yet more limited process took place in Chelsea. It still remained a far cry from what the neighborhood has more recently become, home to art galleries and the Highline pedestrian walkway.[10]

The first to open a studio setting for jazz in Chelsea was *Life* magazine photographer W. Eugene Smith. From 1957 to 1965, Smith's five-story building at 821 Sixth Avenue (near Twenty-Eighth Street) had served as a meeting place for noted jazz musicians. Charles Mingus, Zoot Sims, Bill Evans, Thelonious Monk, Elvin Jones, Al Haig, Sonny Clark, Eric Dolphy, and future Chelsea loft resident Chick Corea all congregated and played in Smith's apartment.[11]

Two years later, in 1967, percussionist and composer Warren Smith[12] founded a studio at 151 West Twenty-First Street. Studio WIS became one of the longest-lasting musical spaces.[13] What he and his associates Coleridge Taylor Perkinson and Jack Jeffers were seeking in Chelsea was "a studio where we could practice and rehearse away from home. We were all in domestic situations [where] we couldn't play at night. We had children. We needed some place away from that to do what we did." Assisted by his former student Anton Reed, and an associate, Michael Henderson, Studio WIS incorporated as the not-for-profit Chelsea Performing Arts/Studio WIS. "It ended up being a living/working space for a whole bunch of people. Several people would come in and live there for months at a time. Julius Watkins, Howard Johnson. . . . We opened it up, started doing a regular series of [public] events. That's how people like Judy Nemack, Walter Thompson, and John Zorn came through, and they were trying to gain more exposure. We would charge maybe $2, 3, or 5 at the door and just put the money up. . . . People just came to us because there weren't any performance spaces available for alternative music."[14] Aesthetically, many of the performing musicians had musical affinities to Ornette Coleman, John Coltrane, and the Association for the Advancement of Creative Musicians, and thus are musically linked to the center of this book.[15]

Free Life Communication

> It was a great time. We were all young, and historically speaking, these were the hippie days in America, so we were all into that kind of vibe as well as free jazz. . . . It was the early '70s. Things were quite open. . . . There were a lot of people trying stuff. It was definitely a time to experiment in all kinds of ways, lifestyle, macrobiotics, Scientology, yoga, standing on your head, LSD, eat only rice, whatever. This is what you do. There was a core of people who were like-minded, and eventually many of us went on to become notable in the field, but this was the beginning.
> DAVE LIEBMAN[16]

Warren Smith's Studio WIS and the 138 West Nineteenth Street lofts building where Dave Liebman, Dave Holland, and Chick Corea lived were just ten blocks apart. Liebman's relatively small upstairs space had become the center of an active improvisational setting for a cluster of young musicians. He coyly observes that between the rehearsals in Corea's loft and constant sessions in his own space, "This building got pretty lively with things really happening, as you could imagine."[17]

Liebman says he treated his loft as an open performance space.

Anyone who wanted to play could play. My attitude was, "You ring the bell, I throw the keys down." It was like that. Bob Moses,[18] Steve Grossman, Randy Brecker, Michael Brecker, Lenny White, Al Foster, Bob Berg, George Cables, Ron McClure, John Abercrombie, guys like that would come up, and we would all play all the instruments. We were living that way . . . bohemian, hippie, artist . . . whatever you want to call it. Like I said, we were all in our early twenties, and on top of what was happening in the music scene. Besides free jazz, what was happening at that time is the beginning of fusion as a style in jazz. . . . I don't mean just rock influences, but also the beginnings of world music. . . . It was an exciting period when we were trying a lot of stuff, like electronics and synthesizers.[19]

Drummer Barry Altschul describes the scene as

a twenty-four-hour-a-day, free-jazz jam session experimental space in the building. . . . There were concerts thrown in the loft, and there was also a recording studio directly across the street run by a man named Tom DePietro [Upsurge Studio]. So, sometimes he let us have concerts there, and he'd record us. And there was another cat around at that time named Junior Collins, who was a French horn player—he's on the Miles Davis record *Birth of the Cool*. I heard him play with a trio—bass and drums. Man, it's fabulous. There was a lot of shit happening at that time. All the styles of music were going on at the same time.[20]

"Us" refers to Corea and Holland, who began rehearsing with Altschul in Corea's loft and at Upsurge Studio in 1970. Within their building, Liebman was also playing with Corea and Holland, usually in Liebman's upstairs loft. He and Corea also talked about music. Liebman recalls: "Chick was into [Thelonious] Monk and [Charles] Ives and Bud Powell at that time.[21] He'd stop by after his gigs with Miles to talk about what had happened that night. Miles came over for dinner one night and ate rice and beans."[22]

Liebman describes the music in his loft as "a lot of horns playing all the time, cacophonous, free-form jazz." In a 1980 conversation with Ronald Radano, he explained: "We played totally extemporaneously. There was very little talking about what to play. We never even set a starting note, we never set a tempo. We rarely played with a steady pulse. And there were many, many people playing at the same time. Sometimes five or six saxophonists would play, depending on who was there. We used any instrumentation, we switched instruments. The most important point is, however, that it was five to six hours of high intensity music."[23]

Liebman and his circle were profoundly influenced by John Coltrane's landmark collective improvisational work from 1965: "We played completely free in the language of [Coltrane's] *Ascension*,"[24] the probing, expressive, and at times fiery music that broke through inherited expectations about form, sound, solo versus ensemble, melody and harmony.[25] It is that combination of cacophony and highly focused solo playing that no doubt attracted Liebman's cohort. In his loft, upwards of six horn players would be playing at the same time. This was also the kind of music he played with Chick Corea, just as "it was the same music we were playing with everyone else who came through my loft."[26]

After a short period of private jam sessions, Free Life Communication sought a public. The first step was to develop an organizational structure, as Liebman recalls: "Bob Moses and I called a meeting of all these guys who had been playing in our lofts. I said: 'Guys, we gotta get out of the loft, just playing for each other, we gotta play for people. Somehow we have to get out there.' The point was to play for people this kind of free jazz, a hard call then or now. That was the motivation to form Free Life Communication." Saxophonist Bob Berg, another future member of a Miles Davis band, in the 1980s, coined the group's name during an organizational meeting. Liebman recalls Berg's explanation: "Free—free jazz; it's our life, and we want to communicate." Liebman's response in the meeting was "Okay, let's make an organization up. I'll take care of the business, let's do it."[27]

But for the young and mostly white musicians on Nineteenth Street, the cultural meaning of "free jazz" and *Ascension* was quite different from what it meant to Archie Shepp or to the Association for the Advancement of Creative Musicians. In place of black identity and economic/political self-determination, Free Life associated Coltrane's collective open improvisation with what Ronald Radano terms "a music for non-violent rebellion, for love and community . . . blending of the jazz avant-garde and the middle-class counter-culture."[28] These differences were underscored by a meeting the Nineteenth Street loft musicians held with two AACM members, Leroy Jenkins and Anthony Braxton. Seeking advice regarding musical collectives, the invitation came from Bob Moses, who had grown up, as Liebman recalls, a white musician surrounded by black jazz musicians "in a building where Elvin Jones and Max Roach lived uptown on Central Park West. [Moses's] godmother was Abbey Lincoln . . . talking pedigree!"[29]

Liebman describes the scene: "[At] the first Free Life meeting . . . we were twenty-four, twenty-five years old. There were about twenty of us sitting on the floor of my loft. . . . Leroy [Jenkins] basically said we 'can't do anything unless we got a reason, and you're all white so you don't have a reason'—kind of like that, which was a drag, as you could imagine. Then an hour later, Anthony came up with the 'peace and love' rap, and after he left we were inspired again."[30]

Whereas Free Life members sought a vehicle for shared musical and cultural affinities, they may not have fully appreciated the enormous political stakes involved in their predecessors' pioneering efforts. On the one hand, as a Free Life Communication member, pianist Richie Beirach, observes: "We were all swept up into Vietnam War protests and it was a climate of revolution. Free Life was a statement in support of that revolution,"[31] and an affirmation of values shared by the largely white youth counterculture. Free Life members also knew that their music lacked commercial potential and was not going to be welcomed in jazz clubs.[32] On the other hand, the premise of the AACM was, as discussed in chapter 1, grounded in "notions of self-help as fundamental to racial uplift, cultural preservation and spiritual rebirth [which] was in accord with many other challenges to traditional notions of order and authority that emerged in the wake of the Black Power Movement," as George Lewis points out.[33] Musically, the AACM was far more diverse than Free Life Communication.[34] Moreover, although both organizations sought to assert control of the circumstances of their performances, for Free Life the need owed more to the early career stage of its members than to the racism undergirding the jazz business, which led the AACM to separate from white-owned jazz clubs, booking agents, and record companies.

A recorded radio broadcast from the WBAI "Free Music Store"[35] on January 15, 1970, offers a window onto the nature of Free Life Communications jam sessions and performances. The band on that date included saxophonists Dave Liebman and—important to this story, because he would become the saxophonist in the Davis Lost band during four of its final five months—Steve Grossman, plus drummer Bob Moses; Gunter Hampel on vibes, bass clarinet, flute, and piano; and bassist Eddie Gomez. Other performers on that date but not on the recording were singer Jeanne Lee and bassist Miroslav Vitous (who briefly played with the Miles Davis Quintet, filling the gap between Ron Carter's departure and the arrival of Dave Holland and, later, Weather Report).

Like the collective improvisations of Coltrane and Coleman, these performances open with composed elements. These works by Bob Moses function as springboards for the open improvisations that follow. Indeed, the horns perform with relentless virtuosity in parallel play, contributing, along with the driving rhythm section, to an intense, dense texture. The players each craft freely flowing, steady streams of musical lines constructed by expanding, repeating, and varying phrases, sometimes with great frenzy.

Organizationally, Free Life developed as a democratic collective that conducted biweekly meetings in Liebman's loft.[36] Its first concerts were presented in art galleries, churches, and other borrowed spaces. It then became a resident organization at the Space for Innovative Development, a new arts center in a renovated church owned by the Samuel Rubin Foundation,[37] located just north of Chelsea.[38] Liebman describes the setting in this way: "We had one floor, while another group had another, et cetera. We were given two thousand square feet with a pristine wood floor and a grand piano which we could use as we liked, free."[39] The extensive and adventuresome programming included "double trios, six saxophone players, dancers and painters—we did it all."[40] The group worked well together: "There was a palpable feeling of unity, brotherhood, and of common cause," which was important, since "we knew we were avant-garde, we knew we were underground," during a period when "jazz was at the lowest point of its whole time, so a kind of 'bunker' mentality was evident."[41]

Free Life continued to present dozens of concerts each year through the mid-1970s,[42] undergoing changes in leadership and aesthetics after the departure of founders Dave Liebman, Bob Moses, Richie Beirach, and Steve Grossman. Moses tired of what he viewed as a lack of discipline and skill on the part of performers and an inability to curate with adequate quality control. The others returned to more structured musical forms, joining established bands directed by one leader: Grossman with Miles Davis and Liebman with former John Coltrane Quartet drummer Elvin Jones (and subsequently Davis's more Afrocentric 1973–74 band, after appearing on *On the Corner* in 1972). Beirach joined the Stan Getz Quartet (with Dave Holland and Jack DeJohnette) in 1972 and then Dave Liebman's Lookout Farm (with Frank Tusa and Jeff Williams) the following year.[43] After the closure of the Space for Innovative Development in 1974, Free Life moved to the East Village, where it collaborated with fellow downtown lofts, presenting jazz and open improvisation.[44]

Meanwhile, Downstairs in Corea's and Holland's Lofts...

The jam sessions in Dave Liebman's loft overlapped in time with Chick Corea and Dave Holland's duets in Corea's loft downstairs. At the same time, Miles Davis—in the studio without Corea or Holland—was increasingly exploring vamp- and beat-driven music (some of it appears on *Big Fun, Circle in the Round,* and *A Tribute to Jack Johnson*). As the music of the Lost Quintet/Sextet/Septet grew more and more abstract in its March–June 1970 concerts, Corea's loft became the launching pad for his equally abstract, yet budding acoustic trio with Holland and Barry Altschul.

Beyond Corea and Liebman's occasional private sessions, however, there was little or no overlap between Free Life and the new trio. Aesthetically, their goals differed.[45] While Coltrane had been an important inspiration for both sets of musicians, the intensity sought by Corea and company could be found in low-volume close listening, not in the thick-density juxtapositions of either Free Life jams or, ultimately, the high-voltage electric band of Miles Davis. The trio, particularly after expanding to become the quartet Circle, indeed journeyed into intensely complex thickets of small-group collective improvisation; but as we shall see, these moments of highly charged interplay could quickly lead to contrasting passages of simplicity and transparency.

But there were no purists among these musicians. Only one day separated the trio's April 1970 recording of *The Song of Singing* from Corea's and Holland's performances with Davis at the Fillmore West in San Francisco. Liebman's open collective improvisations coincided with his performances with the jazz-rock ensemble Ten Wheel Drive.[46] After the demise of Circle in 1971, Corea moved to Latin-inflected Return to Forever, while Holland and Altschul continued to pursue musical directions informed, in part, by the AACM, with Sam Rivers and Anthony Braxton.

Toward the New Trio

Corea and Holland declared their intent to leave Miles's band in late 1969, but agreed to stay on for a few final months following the release of *Bitches Brew*. Holland told *Melody Maker's* Richard Williams in June 1970:

> Chick Corea and I are planning to leave in October, after we've done six or
> eight weeks in California with the [Miles Davis] band, and we're going to form
> a trio with a drummer called Barry Altschul, who's been working with Paul
> Bley for three or four years. We're going to come to London and live and work
> there for one or two months, and then we'll be off to live in Europe. I'm hop-
> ing that Ronnie Scott will give us a couple of weeks in the club at that time....
> We had a recording session with Miles this morning, for the next album, and
> he asked us both to stay, at least until the end of the year, because the group is

more popular than ever and he wants to keep it together. So we may stay till the end of this year, but it's doubtful because we've done so much planning for the trio, and we've thought such a long way in advance, that it's difficult to back out of that now.[47]

Even though the music in Davis's band was quite free spirited, Holland and Corea had actively discussed the idea of forming their own group. In remarks that begin this chapter, Corea recalls that this process occurred organically. It made sense, as Holland told Bill Smith in 1973: "We both wanted to leave the group. I didn't feel that there was anything more to be done with Miles, for my own taste, for what I wanted to do."[48] The first recording of the new group was made in early April, right before the Davis band's appearances at the Fillmore West.

Holland articulated aloud some of his frustrations with the Davis band while he was still a member. After complimenting the bandleader—"Miles's music is very strong and has a fantastic dynamic quality plus a certain amount of magic which isn't really magic. It's just that he's such a strong person and has such a clear idea about his direction that he can draw people into it"—he added: "But playing as a sideman in that band is, for me, a little inhibiting. The premise on which Miles's music is built is still largely the old-fashioned one of a soloist and a rhythm section, which is valid and can still be very beautiful," but clearly not what Holland personally had in mind. He wished for "more of a group participation thing with each player concentrating on producing music that doesn't pinpoint one instrument, so that there's never a 'soloist' in the accepted sense of the term." He added that in his own music, he didn't see his role as "having the specific function of being the group's bassist. I prefer to feel like an independent voice, and the reason I'm leaving is just that I want more breathing space." He concluded that Davis's "direction at the moment is one way and mine is another."[49]

The distinction between the soloist-accompanist model and one that is more collective was an idea also taking hold within fellow Miles Davis alumnus Herbie Hancock's sextet. As it transformed into the Mwandishi band in the fall of 1970, the combination of a new chemistry between the players and the permissive attitude of their leader (a quality learned from Davis) contributed to an organic quality to their improvisations. As pianist Billy Childs characterized it: "They functioned almost like a chamber group, entirely dependent upon each other, but free from each other. They were free to do whatever, but what one person did affected the whole organism. It was like a living, breathing organism, like a representation of real life."[50] The desire for this kind of band is understandable.

Chick Corea: "Dave and I warned Miles that we would be leaving, and after that there was a transition period of some months. Miles did ask Dave and me to stay in the band and be part of the more steady, funky rhythm direction that he was moving into, but he saw that it wasn't our desire. Dave and I wanted to play free music. It was a very natural parting of ways. I sometimes regret leaving the band, but it still seems like it was the right thing to do."[51]

The trio in question was to be distinctively acoustic. Corea and Holland had been rethinking their interest in electric music. Holland told a critic: "The electric instruments we've been using destroy a large number of subtleties in the music."[52] Playing acoustically was becoming more satisfying and refreshing for them. When Corea returned to electric—and then electronic—instruments a few years later, it was with a simpler, more straightforward sonic and rhythmic conception. For Holland, there were stylistic concerns as well. Although he was part of a rhythm section that pushed the envelope toward open improvisation, he expressed the frustration that "Miles needs to control the band, he needs to mold us and give us roles to play so that all the music comes out as his conception. It's still very strong, but depersonalizing it in that way that stops it reaching its real peak."[53]

Holland sensed that Miles couldn't have it both ways: beat driven and disciplined, and freewheeling and substantially unpredictable. In 2012, he reflected on the internal process that should guide a close-knit ensemble that performs without a preset structure:

Nothing can be creative without some structural integrity. You have to just create it as you go. . . . You shape it and you use your instincts and experience to try and make a coherent musical statement. . . . What makes it work for me is that communication. You know, musicians playing in their own isolated spaces doesn't make a group for me. When I'm playing open-form music, I am still playing harmony, I am still playing rhythm. I think open-form playing presents a great challenge to the musician to really take responsibility for the entirety of the whole thing, the structure, the form. There needs to be a shared vocabulary. When you improvise with someone on the open form, you know you have to have some points of reference. For instance, what you share with the other musicians, those reference points are what you use to build the form of the music from.[54]

Eventually, Davis indeed chose a more unified path by replacing Holland with the more funk-oriented bassist Michael Henderson (no relationship to Studio WIS). In the meantime, Holland explored a middle ground between an electric bass with a wah-wah funk sound and his more open tendencies.

The roots of Corea and Holland's joint departure may be connected to their desire for greater experimentalism and a return to acoustic instruments. But the organic connection between the two players was apparent by the late July 1969 shows in Antibes, France, and as witnessed in our discussion of their moments as a duo during other performances. And their private duets at Corea's loft built on that partnership.

Becoming a Trio

To form the kind of acoustic trio they had in mind, Holland and Corea needed to identify the right drummer. Corea relates: "We decided that we would like a drummer that could roll with the free form direction we were interested in and also play with a sound that didn't interrupt the acoustic balance we loved with the piano and bass."[55]

In an interview with the author, Corea recalls: "Barry came in and fit the bill perfectly. . . . Barry was of our generation and liked the approach we were taking." As a drummer himself, Corea knew what he was after when placing someone else behind the kit. "I was always intrigued by the viewpoint of the drummer in a music group. An intimate connection with what the drummer was doing was always essential to making the music rich, tight, and whole."[56]

Becoming Barry Altschul

Barry Altschul, a New York native, arrived with substantial free-form piano trio experience from his time with pianist Paul Bley. He had learned to improvise as a child, as soon as he took up the drums. He would solo on his drum pad while his older sister, a concert pianist, practiced at home. Altshul recalls: "I wasn't keeping time, I was improvising—soloing, kind of, having a dialogue with what she was practicing at the time, whether it was Beethoven or Bach or whoever. . . . I did it all the time, to the television, to the radio. When I was listening to the radio and the big bands or something, I would keep time. . . . I didn't even realize that what I was practicing to my sister was my first introduction to a freer style of music. I didn't realize that until way, way later."[57]

Over time, Altschul brought an increasingly deeper sense of jazz roots and history, particularly bebop, to his playing:

> I was very fortunate to have been brought up in a neighborhood [in the South Bronx] that was full of musicians, wannabes as well as professionals. I grew up in a neighborhood that had, on Lyman Place, Elmo Hope, and on Teasdale Place was Donald Byrd. And all the musicians that came to visit them. Jimmy Cobb was living in the Bronx at one point, Junior Cook, Jimmy Lyons. . . . The neighborhood was full of mixed races and mixed cultures, so it was the true melting pot at the time. . . . They were very open with their information. You're hanging out at Elmo's house, and Philly Joe walks in, or Frankie Butler walks in, or [Thelonious] Monk walks in, or whoever. So you're getting to meet all these people, and I was very fortunate to have been taken kind of under the wing, in a certain respect, by Art Blakey and Philly Joe Jones.
>
> I was at Birdland almost every weekend, at least one night a week. The other place was the Apollo Theater. For a dollar you could go in at eleven o'clock in the morning, watch a movie, see the show, which was three bands and a comedian. I remember one show where there was Miles, there was Horace Silver's band, and there was Monk's band, and [vaudeville comedian] Moms Mabley. And you could stay until one o'clock in the morning for a dollar. You brought a hot dog for a quarter, and you were hanging out. So I went to see every jazz show that was at the Apollo.

His first important break came in a chance encounter with Bley:

> I was, at the time, a janitor at a recording studio. There was the recording studio that Phil Spector used in New York. It was called Mira Sound Studio, and Carole King and Gerry Goffin and all these industry people were using that studio. And I was the janitor and the button pusher—kind of like the assistant engineer. . . . So I'm a janitor in the recording studio, and Paul Bley comes in to record an album with Gary Peacock. I think Paul was on the date, and there was Don Ellis, the trumpet player, [whose music included] a lot of odd time signatures back in the '60s . . . so I was talking to Bley a little bit. Then he came in later on, maybe a year or so later, to do another record date with John Gilmore and the same rhythm section. And we had a long conversation at that time. We were really talking. And he found out I was really a drummer and this and that. And then [somewhat later], all of a sudden, out of nowhere—he

says, "You wanna play a gig?" I says, "Shit, yeah!" you know? I said, "Yeah." He says, "Okay, be at this place Sunday afternoon at such-and-such time, we have a gig." I said, "Great." That place happened to be what turned out to be the nightclub Slugs.

"Okay," so he says to me, "do you want to play some standards? Or do you want to play something that I'm into?" and I was an arrogant kid from the Bronx, because I was really taught by the guys. Not just the bigger guys, but my peer group were telling me things about what I should be doing, what I shouldn't be doing, what is a natural tendency for a white guy that might get in the way of the music, or this or that. All these kinds of things I was brought up with, I was told, out there. Everybody was very honest with me with that kind of a neighborhood, that kind of a group of people. Anyway, and I was appreciative of that, it was great. So I was an arrogant kid, so I said, "Play whatever you want!" And he did, and I just responded. This was David Izenzon, Paul Bley, and myself. And that was my first introduction to free music; the first time I ever played it. I tried to keep time to it, but it just didn't work! And then I found a way to play and respond, and did it; that all came very natural.

As time went by, Altschul would listen closely to the sounds of the city, the rising and falling of the sounds of the industrial era:

You grow up in New York, you listen to the train rhythms, you listen to the steam heat rhythms, and you're listening to all kinds of rhythms. The radiator and the trains. Which started me in what, I guess, has been termed wave music. And so I learned to play that from the actual waves. But no, I've always listened—car crashes, listening to when the hubcap flies, and it falls later than the actual crash, so there's extra sound coming. All those kinds of things I listened to. And eventually I listened to them to put them into the music.

He discovered ways to play more challenging aspects of Bley's music, Annette Peacock's compositions in particular, by listening, once again, to the world. This time, he was at the beach while on an acid trip, "sitting by the ocean and the waves; the tides started coming in. And the waves started coming and hitting and splashing against the rocks. And so the rhythm of the tide and the motion of the waves hitting against the rocks, the splashing effect—I heard all that shit. Because in the mentally induced state I was in, it broke it down to that level."

Also during this period, Altschul had significant experiences performing in Europe with many of the important beboppers: Johnny Griffin, Dexter Gordon, Kenny Drew, Jimmy Woody, Art Taylor, and Kenny Clarke. Chick Corea's invitation came after he returned from a second period of living in Europe. He had been playing with Babs Gonzales, the bebop singer in a band that included saxophonist Clifford Jordan. He had recently rejoined Bley.

Altschul observes: "I've always considered myself a jazz drummer. I don't consider myself an avant-gardist or a free guy. I would consider myself more free than avant-garde, because to me the definition of *free* is 'vocabulary.' The more musical vocabulary you have, the freer you are, depending upon your musicianship and how you use that vocabulary and where you use it and so on. [That is what] makes it feel avant-garde or free, because you're not just keeping a standing form, you're not keeping to the tenets of the jazz rules."[58] That is to say, Barry Altschul's roots are in bebop. His approach to that music draws from an unusually rich and varied sonic vocabulary. He uses the past as grounding and guide, but not as a directive. His strong listening skills support his ability to invent and respond freely in the moment. He can thus begin with a tune, but take it anywhere that his ears might lead him in the moment—within, around, or away from the tune. This is the quality in a drummer that Chick Corea and Dave Holland were seeking for their trio.

Drummer John Mars astutely breaks down Altschul's synthetic approach:[59]

> Barry's right-hand work on the ride cymbal was so intricate, and really interesting to me. In terms of the stuff he was doing with his left hand and his foot—[there were of course] the off beats and bomb drops. But then there was a dance-y, skippy right hand that Barry had, with a bop sort of influence but yet was entirely new. It just flew with those other "birds" in the band. Listen to Barry's quick responses to the twisting and turning of the other players, how they could all turn around on a dime and head in another direction. . . . At times, as the band fractures, so does Barry's right hand. But then in a way, it stays in that bop sound, too. Barry made up all kinds of new and interesting right-hand bop-influenced patterns. With a free-form drummer like Milford Graves, you don't hear bebop in there anymore; his drumming just floated, and I certainly learned my own sense of freedom from his astonishing example. . . .
>
> In Barry's playing, we hear bebop, but we can also hear the influence of John Coltrane's music and that of his drummers. . . . Rashied Ali, who I think was influenced by Milford's freedom and Sunny [Murray's] aggressive approach, must have influenced Barry, too. Albert Ayler's music, on which Milford played, influenced Coltrane very much at the end of his life. . . . During

the whole hippie LSD '60s period, when Albert and John were letting the rhythms get to this free-floating thing, there were also the sound-effect things that came from Pharoah Sanders and Roland Kirk when they weren't blowing their horns. This aspect came into what Barry did a little bit later, in the '70s: rattling bells on chains and blowing whistles and so on, and there was a Varèse aspect that I always heard in Barry's work; the incidental, staggered, percussive sounds played on things other than the drum set can have a very dramatic effect. When Dave Holland and Barry played together, you also heard some of those supersonic, fractured bebop patterns that were invented by Ornette's [Coleman's] groups. Although he was deep in a pocket with Dave, Barry was definitely also listening intensely to the notes that were flying from Anthony's [Braxton's] agile mind, mouth, and fingers, and his cymbal work was always responding to Anthony's genius for twisting and turning.[60]

In fact, Altschul joined Corea and Holland instead of accepting a tantalizing alternative offer that was already on the table: an invitation to join Jimi Hendrix's new band. The offer was more lucrative and would have guaranteed steady pay, something unusual for a jazz musician. And it was a chance to play with, well, Jimi Hendrix, who had jammed recently with saxophonist Sam Rivers (with whom Altschul would play after the demise of Circle). Rivers later spoke of playing with Hendrix as not unlike playing with pianist Cecil Taylor. Hendrix was putting together a more experimental group to follow the Jimi Hendrix Experience, and "Jimi wanted me to join his group while he was developing new directions."[61]

But Corea's offer was more musically intriguing to Altschul, who saw himself as "very idealistic at the time." Conceptually, the Corea trio was an expansion of Paul Bley's open-improvisational ideas, this time with a collective, and Altschul indeed viewed himself as a jazz musician, not a rock musician. The finances with Corea would be sufficient, so in either case, "it wasn't about the money. Playing with Chick—him and Dave coming out of Miles—the money would have been sufficient for me to support myself as a musician and not have to take day gigs. This was something which I did with periods with Paul Bley; we had to take day jobs, or stay in Europe."[62]

The new trio recorded *The Song of Singing* on April 7–8, 1970, immediately before Corea and Holland joined Miles Davis at the Fillmore West on April 9–12. Steve Grossman had replaced Wayne Shorter on saxophone, and Miles had added percussionist Airto Moreira.[63] Five weeks later, Anthony Braxton would sit in with the trio at the Village Vanguard for its inaugural moment playing as a quartet.

In June 1970, Dave Holland discussed the recording that the new trio had made, developed within the context of Corea and Holland's Nineteenth Street Manhattan lofts and Tom DePietro's nearby studio: "We all play regular acoustic instruments in the trio, and we've already an album for Solid State which is really very beautiful. That should be out before the end of the year."[64]

Oh man, I heard some of the freest playing coming out of that band. Man, with Keith [Jarrett] and Chick in the band, when Miles stepped off the bandstand, these cats went out, and not only that, they were switching instruments, because Chick and Keith played drums very well. Jack plays piano, Keith plays saxophone; so everybody was switching instruments. It was incredible, man.

BARRY ALTSCHUL[1]

5

Miles Davis's Increasingly Electronic 1970, and a Reflection on His 1971–75 Bands

An Increasingly Electronic Sound

Chick Corea found a solution to the difficulty of placing an electric piano within a dense, loud swirl of sound and distortion. Josef Zawinul's tune "Directions" opens the recorded March 7, 1970, performance of Miles Davis's sextet, *Live at the Fillmore East*, as it did most of the band's sets. Jack DeJohnette and Dave Holland prepare the ground with a circular groove of seven notes (four-and one-and-two-and-three . . . four-and one-and-two-and-three . . .), awaiting Corea's arrival. And what happens next is about neither the groove nor playing that is free of harmonic constraints. It is about the pure sonic experience. And it is wild and otherworldly. Even this repeated listener continues to experience surprise at being greeted by the harsh, maybe even shrill sound of Corea's electric piano.

The outlines of the narrative told by Herbie Hancock and Corea as to what led to their adoption of the electric piano are similar. Each of them, a year apart, arrived at a session with Davis

(Hancock's was in the studio, Corea's at a club date; Corea thinks it might have been the old Jazz Workshop, on Boylston Street in Boston).[2] Davis points to an electric piano and says in his whispery voice: "Play this!" Hancock skeptically plays a chord but becomes entranced by its lush, sustained tone. He remembers thinking: "'He wants me to play that toy over there?' I had heard about the Fender Rhodes electric piano from some other musicians, piano players, and they were saying: 'It's not an acoustic piano.' So I went in with that kind of skepticism, which was kind of negative. But I had never heard it. So I said: 'OK.' I turned it on and played a chord and much to my surprise, I liked the sound.[3]

Corea, on the other hand,

struggled with it for a while, because I really didn't like it. And I was struggling with it because I was with a maestro, a hero of mine; all of these guys were. And here I am with an instrument I hated the sound of. It just ate me up. . . . But as we continued to tour, I got more the idea of [what] Miles was doing. And the Fender Rhodes, I started to figure it out; started to see how to work it and how to bring it more into the sonic thing that Miles was looking for . . . the sound of youth; it was the sound of pop and rock, too. But yet I could play jazz on it.[4]

In an interview with Marc Myers, Corea recalled:

Before joining Miles, I had been pretty much a purist in my tastes. I loved Miles and John Coltrane and all the musicians who surrounded them. But I didn't look much further into rock or pop. I listened to a little bit of classical music, but that was it for me. When Miles began to experiment, I became aware of rock bands and the energy and the different type of communication they had with audiences during a show. I'd see young people at rock concerts standing to listen rather than sitting politely. It was a different vibe and more my generation. It got me interested in communicating that way. People were standing because they were emotionally caught up in what they were hearing. I related to that.

He [Davis] sensed early that something big was shifting in the culture. Miles didn't want to give up his form of jazz expression but he wanted to communicate with that new crowd, to a younger, more emotional audience. So the sound and the rhythm of his music changed. The band I was in with Miles starting in '68 was pretty wild. It was transitional in the fusion movement, and we were doing all kinds of stuff.[5]

When the first electric Miles Davis recording, *Filles de Kilimanjaro*, appeared in 1969 (recorded in 1968), audiences were already familiar with the electric piano thanks to Ray Charles and Joe Zawinul's work with Cannonball Adderley.[6] The warm, funky sounds of the Wurlitzer and later the Fender Rhodes were appreciated for both their sharp attack and their long sustain. The "attack" added a percussive quality, and the "sustain" offered a rich choral feel that could fill out the harmonic richness of an ensemble.[7] But Corea's sound on this March 1970 date was something of another order. The Fender Rhodes at first sounds like a bus honk, sharply articulated and insistently repeated. It is more an electronic than an electric sound, calling to mind more of the electronic music avant-garde than rock, pop, or funk. Its level of distortion is different in kind from fuzz guitar. Fuzz emphasizes a sustained albeit "dirty" sound; these articulations are brief and sharp edged.

One might think "synthesizer," but this was early 1970, when few audiences had heard that instrument in live performance. Early recordings featuring the Moog synthesizer, such as Bernie Krause and Paul Beaver's *Zodiac Cosmic Sounds* (1967) and Wendy Carlos's *Switched on Bach* (1968), were both melodious and created within the security of a studio. The first live synthesizer performance took place in 1965 at Town Hall in New York City, featuring Herb Deutsch and his New York Improvisation Quartet.[8] The first that was widely publicized, "Jazz in the Garden," took place before a packed crowd at New York's Museum of Modern Art Sculpture Garden. The August 28, 1969, event featured two quartets and relatively conventional sounds. Both groups included a noted jazz pianist, respectively Hank Jones and Hal Galper. Guitarist John McLaughlin, recently arrived from England and active in Davis recording sessions, was with Galper (Cris Swanson led the group).

The relatively conservative nature of the sounds is suggested by two critical responses. Bertram Stanleigh wrote in *Audio*: "These were real musicians playing real music, and it was clear that their message was getting to the audience . . . that was having too much fun to quit."[9] Allen Hughes of the *New York Times* observed: "Actually, not too much happened that really held the attention. Much of the time, the music sounded like a rather clumsy imitation of jazz."[10] A reprise jazz performance with a Moog synthesizer was given a year later by a quartet fronted by Dick Hyman,[11] around the same time as synthesizer events that captured a larger public: the premier performances by Emerson, Lake and Palmer in August 1970. ELP's eponymous album featuring the famous Moog synthesizer solo on "Lucky Man" appeared at the close of 1970. Emerson's sound highlighted the synthesizer's lyrical capabilities, but not its sonically outside-the-box timbres.

Emerson's and Hyman's performances occurred during the final months of Chick Corea's tenure with Davis. But already at the March 1970 Fillmore date, there was something distinctly novel and right in your face about Corea's new keyboard sound, unparalleled even by what larger audiences were hearing created on the Moog synthesizer.

...

Soon after Corea's surprising "sonic jab" in the performance of "Directions," we hear the clang of a sustained chord. In between the two is an angular descending musical line that cuts the air like a knife; then a pause, and a few tentative notes in response. The sound of the sustained chord shifts as it is played, revealing to the listener the source of the unusual timbre—a rising and falling wah-wah pedal. As we listen, we come to understand the root of the unusual initial sound of the Rhodes, the upward pivot of the pedal, which brightens the timbre. The intensity of Corea's articulation combines with the volume of amplification through the Fillmore's speakers and some feedback in the sound system, imparting a decided "otherness" to his sound. This effect is further heightened by his periodic use of a ring modulator.

Corea was growing in his ability to add variety to the electronic sonic environment. During an understated version of "Bitches Brew," he uses distortion as he adds filigree around the opening themes of the tune. The pianist's low Cs and the abstract web he weaves around Davis's elaboration of those themes create a cloud of sound. This is contrasted later in the tune by the clear, ringing, unprocessed sound of his electric piano as he comps for Davis and performs his own solo. Distortion returns during Corea's fast-paced solo in the next tune, "Spanish Key," meshing well with Dave Holland's electric bass. The electric sounds of the bass wind around and closely track the many thickets of Corea's distorted, spiraling passages, with both players building spiraling webs from brief ostinati.

The Fillmore East date was the start of a spring 1970 tour for Davis's group that included several shows at each of Bill Graham's famous rock halls, the Fillmore East in New York's East Village and the Fillmore West in San Francisco. The tour introduced a new saxophonist, Steve Grossman,[12] who replaced Wayne Shorter.[13] Moreover, the addition of percussionist Airto Moreira heightened the rhythmic dimension. Drummer Jack DeJohnette describes how he and Moreira worked together: "The role of the drummer at that time was laying down the groove, and also embellishing the groove. Keeping a steady pulse but changing and shifting it, making subtle changes in it; and providing the fire, stoking the fire, putting the heat on it. Airto was putting the colors on what I was doing."[14]

The strong rhythmic pulse throughout this set is heightened during its closing tune, "Willie Nelson," from the *Jack Johnson* album sessions. In addition, Holland's wah-wah electric bass drives "Bitches Brew," as he moves further forward within the mix than before.[15] The beat-centered approach could be a reflection of where Davis was heading musically, or of his desire to reach the young rock audience at the Fillmore East. The band's "look," as evidenced by photographs included in the 2001 CD release, suggests the latter possibility. In these photos, the musicians are dressed in less exotic, more informal rock-audience-friendly attire such as simple shirts and sweaters, and Corea wears a bandanna.

Ironically, Moreira's acoustic instruments served to heighten the electronic aesthetic. The high-pitched, squeaky sound of his friction drum, the *cuíca*, suggests a rather electric or even electronic *kind* of sound. The *New York Times'* John S. Wilson referred to Moreira as "the most provocative of the sidemen in this group," who played the *cuíca* "with devastating virtuosity . . . produc[ing] various gradations of cries, moans and whimpers." He appreciated the "brilliant counterpoint" Moreira offered "to some of Mr. Davis' solos and to provide startling accents in other passages."[16]

Between Corea's electronics, Holland's electric bass, and the percussion-boosted team of DeJohnette and Moreira, the band seemed to be heading more than ever toward a rock aesthetic. Composer Neil Rolnick, at the time a Berkeley graduate student, recalls of the Fillmore West concerts: "The free improvisation aspect was fascinating and beautiful, but I think the thing which really got me was Miles figuring out a way to put a real rock groove under the kinds of long lines I heard on the jazz recordings I was listening to, like Jackie McLean, Lee Morgan, Art Farmer, and the classic Miles Davis Quintet recordings with Herbie Hancock. At the time, I was playing in rock bands and folk-rock bands, and listening to these Blue Note records, *Bitches Brew*, and *In a Silent Way*."[17] The band was now synthesizing musical worlds, reinventing jazz traditions through a new rhythmic lens.

Anticipating the final three months of Corea's tenure in the band, Davis designated a keyboard replacement, Keith Jarrett. Following a stint with Art Blakey and the Jazz Messengers, Jarrett had made his mark as a member of Charles Lloyd's band, which had a strong following among young, white rock audiences. Miles Davis had now reunited two-thirds of the Lloyd rhythm section, Jarrett and DeJohnette.[18] The two keyboardists sat on opposite ends of the stage, each projecting very different kinds of sounds and textures, more juxtaposition than duet. The combined sound was distinctly electronic in texture.

1970 Performances of "Bitches Brew"—Increasingly Rhythmic and Electronic

In the band's recorded April 1970 appearance at the Fillmore West, Corea makes effective use of his evolving distorted wah-wah sound to create a more complex sonic backdrop.[19] He and Holland engage in a cat-and-mouse chase, joined by Moreira's tambourine in the midst of the section; Corea soon engages in call and response with Davis, joined by Holland's wah-wah bass and DeJohnette's drumming. Davis plays the "staircase" motif, answered by a dramatic, loud response from the rest of the band; and when Davis returns to it, Corea, Holland, and DeJohnette play a pointillistic accompaniment that builds in intensity.

With Jarrett in the band as a second keyboardist, the texture of the rhythm section's sonic mix grows in complexity and internal contrast and tension. At the recorded Fillmore East performance on June 17, Jarrett can be heard playing sustained organ chords that are juxtaposed to Corea's boisterous and dramatic use of wah-wah and ring modulation. On June 19, the "sound" of the low Cs is shaped by heavy wah-wah and distortion. Corea's filigree—the electric piano phrases he wove around the motifs back in 1969—has expanded into a multi-layered web, with each player moving at his own rate. Here, the section ends with a collective open improvisation that draws from elements of the various motifs, moving through a range of textures and moods. Swirling keyboards create a rich sonic tapestry during the "Coda" on that date.[20]

At Freeport, Grand Bahama Island, on August 2, Jarrett's sustained organ, shaped by a wah-wah, creates a pedal point. The rhythm section periodically accents the low Cs, and moves into a pulse on which Davis solos before returning to the opening motifs. At Tanglewood in Lenox, Massachusetts, on August 18, and at the Isle of Wight Festival in England on August 29, Corea creates abstract electronic sounds with his ring-modulated Fender Rhodes; the pitch shifts as he turns the modulating frequency dial. Jarrett adds a layer of a much thinner-sounding RMI electric piano, providing a disjunctive combination. At Tanglewood, Davis and Holland play overlapping staircase motifs.

Turning On the Funk

During the June evenings at the Fillmore East, Davis solos over the steady vamp and many wah-wah sounds, and layers of organ and Fender Rhodes. On June 17, the first of those shows, his second solo is played over the bass vamp and Jarrett's wah-wah organ comping; Corea's arrival heightens the funky environment before the concluding section of Davis's solo, which becomes an elegy over sustained chords. In Freeport on August 2, 1970, Corea's playing is as highly rhythmic, tied to the vamp, as his ring-modulated sounds—angular, atonal, with seemingly quasi-randomized pitch—are electronic in timbre.

During the band's final performances at Tanglewood and the Isle of Wight (August 18 and 29, 1970), the vamp during Davis's solos will become highly minimal. What remains is a repeated single pedal note, played on Holland's wah-wah bass, Jarrett's RMI electric keyboard,[21] Corea's ring-modulated Fender Rhodes, and, locked into a groove, DeJohnette's drums. At Tanglewood, the comping has become heavily rhythmic. The two percussionists, two keyboard players, and the electric bassist, with lots of wah-wah, function like a cluster of drummers. Davis's second solo at Tanglewood returns over regular vamp.

Davis had previously explored the idea of a bass line pivoting on a single repeated note in the band's treatment of "Spanish Key." On the studio recording, starting around the three-minute mark, the drumming varies in its subtle details, fills, and layering. Variety is created through adjustments in the dynamic range of the drumming to suit each soloist.[22] Tension is built through the repetitive (multi) electric piano ostinato, Corea's imitation of soloists, between-the-beat conga beats. A lively and funky rendition was performed as an encore on June 19, 1970, at the Fillmore East. Ironically, it was not included in the original recording of the concert, but can now be heard on *Miles at the Fillmore* (2014).

Collective Improvisation

Open-ended improvisations were a regular feature of the Fillmore East shows in June. One striking moment within the opening-night performance of "Bitches Brew" (June 17) features a highly textural, free-form trio improvisation consisting of Steve Grossman's flute, Airto Moreira's chimes, and Keith Jarrett's organ. This grouping emerges from a Chick Corea solo that seems to undergo a structural collapse.

Steve Grossman's solo on June 19 unfolds into a multilayered madhouse of rapid streams of notes. The proceedings speed up and slow down; bass and drums move at multiple tempi, part of an amorphous sound mass. Jarrett's wah-wah organ and Moreira's bells match timbre. The keyboardists play faster and faster, not quite in sync. As the textures slow and thin out, the performance calms, leading into Davis's sparse solo. While the accompaniment becomes quieter and more clearly synchronized, it remains no less playful than during the collective improvisation, in part thanks to Moreira's squeaks. Soon, the keyboard wah-wah sounds of Jarrett's organ ramp up the energy level.

On June 20, the final evening of the Fillmore East stand, the distinct sounds made by each of the two keyboards maintain their unique identities. Then, out of a thicket of sound, the two—Jarrett's organ and Corea's ring-modulated Fender Rhodes—somehow, though uneasily, coexist, or we might say collide, within the same sonic space. Open improvisations occur elsewhere within these shows; "Directions" was regularly a vehicle the band used for this approach.[23]

Sometimes in the absence of open improvisation, seemingly unrelated sounds could be juxtaposed. During saxophonist Gary Bartz's solo at Tanglewood on August 18, the mood of Jarrett's organ accompaniment is elegiac, while Bartz is playing in an earthier and more blues-based realm. (Bartz[24] had replaced Grossman shortly before this show.)

And abstraction and funk could coexist as well. At the Isle of Wight, the various layers in the rhythm section behind Bartz's solo begin to move out of sync. Only Jack DeJohnette holds the pulse, to which Bartz remains tied, allowing the groove to continue unabated. Jarrett moves at a different clock, Holland's bass slows, and Corea plays abstract sounds that are distorted by the ring modulator. Jarrett remains slightly out of time sync during Davis's solo. The rhythm section's accompaniment is quite spare. Despite all the abstraction, though, the overall feel reflects the funky beat. When the band is locked in together rhythmically, we hear a clear sense of where Davis was heading: toward an Afro-futurist blend of funk, electronic sounds, and abstraction. His future direction would be a groove with swirling electronic sounds.

Final Months of the Lost Quintet (plus Two)—through Summer 1970

In early April, Chick Corea and Dave Holland recorded their own acoustic session, released as *The Song of Singing*; Jack DeJohnette also made a record. A few days later, the Miles Davis band performed at the Fillmore West from the tenth through the twelfth. Corea's sound on the set opener, "Directions," is highly distorted and percussive on the recording, including during most of Davis's opening solo, although less so when new saxophonist Steve Grossman is playing. If an electric sound was not Corea's preference at the moment, it certainly is not apparent in this show. His comping for Grossman is more active, utilizes more ostinati, and is responsive to the abstraction of the saxophonist's angular lines. Yet his sound becomes more distorted once again during his own solo.

"Bitches Brew" appears late in the set. Here Corea presents an abstract introduction, leading into a cat-and-mouse duet with Holland that is soon joined by DeJohnette and Airto Moreira. When Corea lands on a chord, he distorts it, again creating a cloudlike sonic event. Grossman's solo becomes another display of intersecting lines, this time between him and Corea. There are moments of intense abstraction at the Fillmore West, but they occur in the context of a rhythmically simpler presentation.

By early August, Corea and Holland were engaged in further recording sessions, now as a trio with Barry Altschul. Through the rest of that month, Anthony Braxton joined them for the first sessions as Circle. By now there were just two more engagements for Corea and Holland to fulfill with Miles Davis: at the Berkshire Music Center at Tanglewood, and at the Isle of Wight Festival.[25]

At the Isle of Wight Festival, a major rock event with an audience of several hundred thousand, the show opens with a rhythmically driven version of "Directions." Holland and DeJohnette are locked into a solid groove, with growing levels of abstraction flying around them. In both that tune and "Bitches Brew," Corea creates abstract electronic sounds with his ring-modulated Rhodes; Jarrett seems to be playing a much thinner-sounding RMI electric piano, resulting in a disjunctive combination, but one where the distinction between instruments is clearer. The band moves into a simple vamp for Davis's solo, with everyone more in sync than usual.

This pattern of groove plus swirling electronic sounds ushers the septet through the end of the engagement and the conclusion of Chick Corea and Dave Holland's tenure with the band. A door had already opened for Corea and Holland to explore open improvisation in a more collective setting. Another door now opened for Davis, with Keith Jarrett and soon to be joined by Michael Henderson, to create some mighty creative funk—yet funk not as dance music but as the ground for further creative exploration of unconventional ideas, still under the umbrella of jazz.

Placing the Lost Quintet in the Context of Davis's 1970s Electric Bands

With a new keyboard player and bassist in tow, Davis's sextet settled in for four nights at the Cellar Door, a club in Washington, DC. Thanks to the release of a collection of complete sets from that week, we can listen in on how the band progressed during its public unveiling.[26] With the exception of "It's About That Time" from *In a Silent Way* and "Sanctuary" from *Bitches Brew*, the repertoire was new. "Yesternow" from *A Tribute to Jack Johnson* was joined by new tunes, among them "Funky Tonk" and "What I Say." The most dramatic change from the previous band is the rhythmic anchor provided by bassist Michael Henderson, particularly on tunes like "What I Say" and "Inamorata." Henderson keeps an impeccable pulse, but his patterns subtly shift and gradually morph. He interjects a variant for a few cycles, and then returns to the previous ongoing pattern. All the while, he never loses a tightness of groove.

Henderson's solidity offers DeJohnette great flexibility to play on and around the beat. He can lock squarely in the beat, building the intensity by reinforcing Henderson's downbeat. When Jarrett's solos are square on the beat, however lengthy their phrasing (for instance on "What I Say" during Thursday night's second set), Henderson and DeJohnette are right there, providing metric grounding against which Jarrett can push. The rhythmic counterpoint set up between Jarrett's off-the-beat ostinati and Henderson's and DeJohnette's emphasis on the "one" in the first two minutes of "Directions" in Friday's third set (repeated several times) in turn sets up each of the solos. DeJohnette makes use of the leeway he gains from Henderson's metrically solid riffs to create endless variations of rhythmic patterns. The continuous invention the drummer achieved in the Lost Quintet continues, but the knowledge that Henderson will always be there on the beat allows DeJohnette to exercise even more freedom of movement. We hear this in his many fills and rolls during Gary Bartz's solo in "What I Say" and throughout "Inamorata" in Friday's third set.

The solid pulse from his rhythm section enables Davis to construct within his own solo brief jabs and longer phrases that remain rhythmically tight within the context of the bass line. The same is true for Bartz's solo playing (on "It's About That Time" during that same set), in which variants of short blues-inflected phrases can be placed within a regular metric reference point. When his phrases lengthen, we can feel the coming downbeat on which he will eventually land being provided by the rhythm section. In an interview with Ted Panken, DeJohnette observes: "Miles liked me because I knew how to anchor. I could be as abstract as I'd want to be, but I knew how to lay out a groove, and Miles loved to play with the grooves I laid down. So I had the technique and imagination that he wanted, but he also wanted something that was going to be rock-steady."[27]

By this time, Davis had begun to play trumpet with a wah-wah, obtaining a more percussive, more electronic sound. The *New York Times'* Ben Ratliff observes that now "Davis was scraping off the outer levels of the sound that made him famous, masking and distorting his instrument. . . . Suddenly he wasn't making the trumpet sound like a trumpet. . . . As much as Davis alters himself, you hear his phrases, and even his tone, at the core of that changed sound. It's still him."[28] Jarrett, on electric keyboards, often plays the role of third (actually fourth, when including Moreira) percussionist. But when his playing grows more abstract, Henderson, often in tandem with DeJohnette, provides a rhythmic container, holding down the beat. Jarrett's improvisations, interspersed throughout the sets, provide space for greater abstraction not tied to a beat.[29]

By the time of the extensive October–November European tour, Jack De-Johnette had left the band, replaced by Ndugu Leon Chancler. Percussionists (James) Mtume (Forman) and Don Alias (from the *Bitches Brew* sessions) stood in place of Airto Moreira. DeJohnette recalls: "I just wanted a change of scenery. I wanted to play a little freer. Miles was moving into a more specific thing that he wanted from the drums. Not as much freedom to elaborate. He was going into the groove, but he liked the way I played grooves."[30] Davis subsequently returned to the studio in the spring of 1972 (for the first time since 1970) to record *On the Corner*. DeJohnette returned for those sessions.

On the Corner, and Beyond

The sessions that produced *On the Corner* took place that June. This was another three-keyboard project. Among the players were returnees Chick Corea, Herbie Hancock, and guitarist John McLaughlin. Davis also paired the drummer from Hancock's Mwandishi band, Billy Hart, with Jack DeJohnette and Davis's two current percussionists. Two Indian instruments, the sitar and the tabla, add variety to the texture. The saxophonist is now Dave Liebman, with Mwandishi band member Bennie Maupin on bass clarinet.

The recording functions on two layers: a relatively static, dense thicket of rhythmic pulse provided by McLaughlin's percussive guitar attack, the multiple percussionists, and Henderson's funky bass lines, plus keyboard swirls on which the horn players solo. Segments of tabla and sitar provide a change of mood and pace. Aside from "Black Satin," most of the material consists of intense vamps and rhythmic layering.

Scholar-musician Michael Veal describes Miles Davis's approach to the construction of this work by invoking the influence of German composer Karlheinz Stockhausen.[31] Davis had found at least two concepts of interest in Stockhausen's work:[32] the electronic processing of sounds, present in *Telemusik* (1966) and *Hymnen* (1966–67),[33] and formal structures created through rules-based expanding and subtracting processes, found in *Plus-Minus* and related works created between 1963 and 1974.[34] Thus, the concept of layering, of adding and subtracting musicians and sounds, drawn from Stockhausen's compositional ideas provided a conceptual framework to construct gradually changing active participants and thus sound densities. This structure allowed Davis to square concepts of jazz performance, contemporary art music composition, and, as Veal points out, beat-driven dance music to create *On the Corner*.

By the September 29, 1972, show documented on *Miles Davis in Concert: Recorded Live at Philharmonic Hall, New York*, it is clear that *On the Corner* indicated Davis's musical destination. The show displays a dense layering of interlocking rhythms (with Al Foster now on drums, plus Mtume on percussion and Badal Roy on tabla), a funk-oriented electric guitarist (Reggie Lucas), a haze of synthesizer washes (Cedric Lawson, soon to be replaced by Davis playing electric organ), and a soprano saxophonist (Carlos Garnett here, but later Dave Liebman).

Davis's bands in 1973–75 would undergo further changes in the number of electric guitarists (up to three) and in repertoire. Mainstays would be drummer Al Foster and Chicago-born guitarist Pete Cosey, a master of techniques spanning rhythm and blues, distortion, and Association for the Advancement of Creative Musicians–oriented open improvisation. In his autobiography, Davis explains that Cosey "gave me that Jimi Hendrix and Muddy Waters sound that I wanted."[35] *New York Times* writer Ratliff described a typical scene: "Sitting in a chair behind a row of guitar pedals, with dark glasses, tall Afro and long beard, he used original tunings, sometimes on a 12-string guitar, chopping through the dense rhythm with wah-wah and downstrokes, pushing his solos toward ghostly delicacy or scrabbling arias striped with reverb and feedback."[36]

The unexpected conceptual mix of Hendrix and Muddy Waters points to Cosey's melding of traditional urban and rural blues with new technologies, invoking sounds of the late twentieth century: missiles, traffic, and electric power. A new tonal sensibility is invoked, replacing the assonance-and-dissonance binary with a pitch-to-noise continuum. When Davis drew from vamps by James Brown, Sly and the Family Stone, and Jimi Hendrix, the band with Cosey in the mix could dip into a deep well of funk sensibility and repertoire. With the addition of the percussionists and sometimes a second (or third) guitar, the listener experiences a constant haze of sound from which the various soloists emerge. Each soloist can also sound like a percussionist.

The late pieces, both in the studio and particularly in the live recordings *Agharta, Pangaea*,[37] and *Dark Magus*—Davis's concerts recorded in Japan, in

June 1973 and January 22–February 8, 1975—are marvels of intensity, surging rhythms, high volume, distortion, and duration. Ratliff describes them as "strange, forbidding obelisks, sometimes prescient and exciting, sometimes interminably dull . . . yet within these large blocks of music there were wrenching shifts of tempo and mood. Oddly, the music seemed to be about stasis and quick change at the same time."[38]

Greg Tate beautifully captures this bountiful palate when discussing "Calypso Felimo" from *Get Up with It* (1974):

> Cosey's staccato guitar simultaneously functions like a second set of congas to Mtume's, a second rush of cymbals to Al Foster, a second steel drum simulacrum to Miles's gnostic organ, a second rhythm guitar to Lucas's, and as one of the three solo voices . . . his [Davis's] trumpet and Cosey's guitar *improvise* a swinging infinity of new colors, lines, lyrically percussive phrases, and needlepoint-by-laser stitchings out of the given melody . . . and because Cosey and Miles can continually solo, and enhance rather than rupture the communal fabric of the calypso, they celebrate jazz as a way of life and as an aesthetic model for the human community. [Davis's final 1970s band presents] an entire band of improvising composers onstage creating a pan-ethnic web of avant garde music locked as dead in the pocket as P-Funk.[39]

The titles of Davis's compositions, such as "Zimbabwe" and "Calypso Frelimo," evoke African liberation themes, helping culturally situate the band within the revolutionary politics of its time at least in allegiance if not in action.

Miles's 1971–75 Bands, in Light of the Lost Quintet

What do Davis's bands, beginning with the Michael Henderson–Keith Jarrett–Jack DeJohnette (and subsequently Ndugu Leon Chancler) configuration and culminating in his final 1970s group with Al Foster, Michael Henderson, and Pete Cosey, tell us about the Lost Quintet? Does the later music suggest that the Lost Quintet should be viewed largely as an entry point through which Davis traveled en route to the later bands? In a sense, we must answer yes. Beginning in 1968, Davis was seeking ways to inject a heavy, steady beat into his music and to engage a contemporary and popular black musical sensibility. From this perspective, he had to experiment—as he did with the Chick Corea–Dave Holland–Jack DeJohnette band, to which he later added Airto Moreira and

Keith Jarrett to form a septet—to find his way. From this perspective, we could say that the replacement of Holland and Corea with Henderson and Jarrett was a course correction.

However reasonable this analysis may seem in hindsight, it oversimplifies the creative mind and eclecticism of Miles Davis. The Henderson-Jarrett-DeJohnette band was not simply a vamp-plus-solos jam band that leads to its successors but a complex framework designed to offer substantial room for exploration and discovery. On another occasion, when DeJohnette reflected on the changes the band was beginning to go through before he left, he noted: "The music was getting more restricted and more predictable. I left, because I wanted to keep doing freer, exploratory things."[40] Clearly what DeJohnette appreciated about playing with Davis was the mixture of groove and freedom, but in his judgment the music was changing. The final evening of the December 1970 Cellar Door engagement shows us how the Henderson-Jarrett-DeJohnette band, as it rapidly matured through an intense week of long nights, combined a strong beat with a high level of abstraction. This suggests strong continuity with the Lost Quintet, no less than the Lost Quintet had continuity with the 1960s Miles Davis Quintet including Herbie Hancock, Tony Williams, and the others.

Listening just as closely to the 1972–75 recordings, this listener is struck by not just the intense rhythm and volume but also the high level of abstraction crafted by Davis: the organ "haze," the sonic distortion, and the open manner in which the musicians navigate this backdrop. These, too, were bands functioning on a very high musical level, driven by the beat but also by much more. There are tremendous differences between the first ensemble of Davis's electric period, the Lost Quintet, and the final band, with Pete Cosey. Yet the two groups bookend an enterprise that contains shared sensibilities. Each represented a unique angle on collective musical enterprise that engaged both beat and abstraction. Each was capable of tremendous heights of musical intensity and focus.

The Lost Quintet was not simply a way station for Davis. Both the 1960s Miles Davis Quintet and the Lost Quintet that succeeded it were experiments through which he sought to balance his musical values, those already established in his work and those emerging. *Filles de Kilimanjaro* (1968) represented a pivot point, including segments from Davis's 1960s quintet and the new electric band (before Jack DeJohnette replaced Tony Williams), offering a steady beat within the context of the fragile, open-improvisational environment of the 1960s quintet. The recording *Bitches Brew* and the Lost Quintet's performances from the fall of 1969 through the summer of 1970 introduced greater abstraction and open forms within a more beat-driven and electric environment.[41]

The Henderson-Jarrett-DeJohnette band more intensively explored a steady meter, yet did so in the context of rhythmic complexity and an open-improvisational sensibility. Davis's subsequent bands explored multiple layers of dense sonic material and beats within the context of changing intensities, sound, and an Afrocentric cultural milieu. The genius of Miles Davis lay in his ability to take in multiple influences—from African, to African American funk, to open improvisation and beyond—and shape those materials within his own sensibilities and in light of his chosen musicians, who listened closely, ever adjusting and composing in the moment. It was music that thrived on a strong beat, yet also on exploration, albeit of varying kinds.

What changed for Davis was an increasing awareness of black identity, his own and that of the younger generation he wanted to reach. At the point he hired bassist Michael Henderson, he realized:

> Black kids were listening to Sly Stone, James Brown, Aretha Franklin, and all them other great black groups at Motown. After playing a lot of these white rock halls I was starting to wonder why I shouldn't be trying to get to young black kids with my music. They were into funk, music they could dance to. It took me a while to really get into the concept all the way. But with this new band I started to think about it. . . . I wanted the drummer to play certain funk rhythms, a role just like everybody else in the group had. I didn't want the band playing totally free all the time, because I was moving closer to the funk groove in my head.[42]

Figure 1. An intimate moment is captured between Miles Davis and pianist Herbie Hancock in 1967, the time of Davis's second great quintet. Photograph by Jan Persson. Used by permission.

Figure 2. Founding members of Musica Elettronica Viva pose for a photograph in 1974 at the Kitchen, downtown New York City. *From left:* Frederic Rzewski, Richard Teitelbaum, and Alvin Curran. A Putney synthesizer is to the left of the group. From the personal collection of Alvin Curran. Used by permission.

Figure 3. Anthony Braxton sits amid the multi-sensory "noise" of Gordon Mumma's "Communication in a Noisy Environment," part of the Intermedia series on November 19–20, 1970, at Automation House, New York City. Photograph by Amanda Lagare, from the historical archive of Gordon Mumma. Used by permission.

Figure 4. Anthony Braxton focuses intensely while performing in duet with Dave Holland in March 1975 at A Space, Toronto. Photograph by John Mars. Photograph © 2015 by John Mars / johnmars .com. Used by permission. Mars notes: "The director of the gallery, the poet Vic d'Or, asked me to point the lighting for the stage area, since I am also a visual artist. I made it very harsh and all-white light, and so I was able to get away with using Kodak Tri-X at 400 ASA, again with no flash. As a result, Anthony is seen just slightly in motion, blowing very furious 'sheets of sound.' That photo somehow exhibits some of the off-kilter aesthetics that I use in my oil paintings."

Figure 5. Anthony Braxton plays bass saxophone at a 1974 studio session. The instrument was but one of several saxophones he would play during a set, and not even the lowest in register. Photograph by Jan Persson. Used by permission.

Figure 6. The rhythm section of Miles Davis's Lost Quintet in 1969, deep in a musical thicket: Chick Corea (sporting a headband), Dave Holland, and Jack DeJohnette. Photograph by Jan Persson. Used by permission.

Figure 7. Miles Davis Lost Quintet drummer Jack DeJohnette in 1969—a study in intense focus. Photograph by Jan Persson. Used by permission.

Figure 8. A fashion-conscious Miles Davis in 1969, dressed in the latest "mod" clothing. Photograph by Jan Persson. Used by permission.

Figure 9. Wayne Shorter wails on the soprano saxophone, surrounded by the Lost Quintet's intently engaged rhythm section, with Dave Holland on bass and Jack DeJohnette on drums. Chick Corea's Fender Rhodes electric piano is slightly visible to the left. Photograph by Jan Persson. Used by permission.

Figure 10. Chick Corea absorbed in his performance at the keyboard of his Fender Rhodes electric piano; the cover has been removed, exposing the tines. With the Miles Davis Lost Quintet in 1969. Photograph by Jan Persson. Used by permission.

Figure 11. Looking very 1970 in the Bay Area, the Miles Davis Sextet in Berkeley, California, in April of that year. *From left:* drummer Jack DeJohnette, Miles Davis, percussionist Airto Moreira slightly behind, Dave Holland on electric bass, wearing a poncho, Chick Corea with electronic devices on top of his Fender Rhodes electric piano, and Steve Grossman on saxophone. Photograph by Veryl Oakland. Photograph © 2015 by Veryl Oakland. Used by permission.

Figure 12. Barry Altschul looks up from his drum kit while performing with Anthony Braxton and Dave Holland in December 1974 at Trinity Church, Yorkville, Toronto. Notice the whistles decorating his embroidered Indian shirt. Photograph by John Mars. Photograph © 2015 by John Mars / johnmars.com. Used by permission. The photographer relates: "Braxton, Dave Holland, and Barry Altschul were in town to play a concert. It was supposed to be the Sam Rivers Trio, but Rivers couldn't make it, so they brought in Braxton. I just took a very few pics with available light, using Kodak recording film at 2000 ASA. I always compose my photographic art by framing it through the lens; no cropping afterward. The winning shot was one of Barry. I was really glued to what Barry was doing, and feeling the music spiritually while I was at the concert. The music and especially Barry's playing were making me feel similar to the way Albert Ayler's music always makes me feel—like my own special version of going to church."

Figure 13. Violinist Leroy Jenkins with drummer Jerome Cooper, members of the Revolutionary Ensemble, reunited in 2005. Photograph by Larry Fink. Used by permission.

Figure 14. Revolutionary Ensemble bassist Sirone, waiting for the moment to respond to violinist Leroy Jenkins, who is deep in a musical reverie. Photograph by Larry Fink. Used by permission.

Some of the free music that was being played [in the sixties] was not just a need to break rules to try new things, but it was also an assertion that we have the *right* to do this. . . . And I was definitely a part of that movement, without a doubt, and so when Dave Holland and I hooked up in Miles' band we shared like minds on that idea. Then we formed our first trio and began to experiment by freely improvising—basically the modus operandi of Circle was to freely improvise. We would have nothing set, we would have no songs set and we would go on the stage and play a complete concert—beginning to end—by just improvising.

CHICK COREA[1]

6

Circle

The Trio Becomes a Quartet

On the night of May 19, 1970, when the Chick Corea, Dave Holland, and Barry Altschul Trio performed at the Village Vanguard—the same evening as the concert by Anthony Braxton, Leroy Jenkins, and Leo Smith of Creative Construction Company, at the Peace Church—they played opposite drummer Roy Haynes's band with trumpeter Freddie Hubbard.[2] Peace Church concert organizer Kunle Mwanga recounts: "After we did that concert we all went down to the Vanguard where Chick Corea and them were playing and Braxton sat in with them. That's when that connection was made with Anthony to deal with Circle."[3] As Altschul puts it: "Then Chick invited him up to play."[4] Braxton sat in, on the heels of his intense playing at the Peace Church, and a pivotal new connection was made.

Altschul recalls that after the Vanguard show, "Braxton and Chick started playing chess together. They're both way into chess.

So I don't know what kind of conversations they got into while they were playing, but then Chick brought the idea that Anthony join the group, that is the way
I remember it." Chess was at the time a central part of Braxton's life, as he has
recounted: "The beauty of chess for me is that it gives a wonderful opportunity
to look at structure and relationships, and intentions, and target strategies, and
the relationship between target strategies and variables and objectives, and ful-
filling objectives. The beauty of chess also extends into physics and pressures....
As far as I'm concerned, chess demonstrates everything."[5]

Braxton wasn't the first saxophonist that Corea and Holland had considered
to supplement their trio. In June 1970, *Melody Maker*'s Richard Williams asked
Holland about a "rumour that Evan Parker, the English saxophonist who was
with him in the Spontaneous Music Ensemble would be joining the new band."
Holland responded: "There are no definite plans, because I haven't really talked
to him about it yet, but he's definitely one of the people I'm going to be playing
with when I come back [to England].... Chick's heard some tapes of Evan that
I have here in New York, and he's very interested and has expressed a desire to
play with Evan. I'm hoping that we'll be able to do something soon."[6]

But Braxton was ultimately their choice, as Holland recalls: "Anthony came
over to talk to us and so we got together a few days later and did a few gigs. We
did a concert in Baltimore.... The music was so strong."[7] Corea: "I remember Dave bringing Anthony to the loft to meet me and play. It was an instant
match. Anthony brought a 4th dimension to the band and, a compositional/
improvisational approach that gave us more material to work with along with
the compositions that Dave and I were bringing in."[8] Holland adds: "We all
came from very different directions. Anthony Braxton came from the Chicago
school, with Cage's music and the theatricals.... And of course Chick came
from quite a melodic Latin kind of thing and I came from England, with all that
stuff that's going on there, and Barry was from New York, and had played with
people like Paul Bley. There's quite a wide variety of viewpoints that came to me
in the music which is why it has got such a lot of attention, and I figure that we
had many different directions going on."[9]

Corea, Holland, and Altschul were really just coming into their own as a unit
of three. Altschul observes: "Deep down inside I would have liked for the trio to
stay together a little bit longer, as a trio. I loved Circle, but I was finding another
place, kind of, during the trio thing, and I just really wanted to continue with
that for a little more. It worked out fine [as Circle!]." Later on, in January 1971,
Corea, Holland, and Altschul did record one further trio album, in the midst of

an active period for Circle. This came shortly before Circle's famous Paris Concert on February 21, 1971, only three months before its demise.[10]

First Quartet Sessions

In a 1973 interview, Holland described the new quartet's first experiences: "We did a lot of playing in the loft that Chick had and the first music we played was very experimental. We really just opened that up, we just broke down all the barriers and said OK, 'we'll just play with any sounds that we can find.' We used things from the kitchen, and bellows and shouting and singing and whistling, we did all kinds of things, just to find out how far we could take it. And then it started to get more defined. We started to try and get a bit more precision into the music."[11] These sessions took place in early August 1970.[12] The band began recording immediately, on August 13, 19, and 21, in Tom DePietro's studio near Corea and Holland's Nineteenth Street loft building. Altschul describes the time in the studio as "a totally improvised thesis. We were playing and everybody had lots and lots of improvisational ideas. They were just flowing out of everybody. The musicians we were made the music. We made that into a music."[13]

During the same period, on August 16 and 25, Corea and Holland played their final dates with Miles Davis. The shows at Tanglewood in Lenox, Massachusetts, and the Isle of Wight Festival in England, respectively, were among the most volcanic, technologically electric, and funk infused of their tenure with Davis's band. Sonically, these concerts—high volume, with ring-modulated electric piano and wah-wah bass—contrasted dramatically with the freely improvisational acoustic quartet in New York!

Expanding an existing trio, even one recently formed, into a quartet meant making space for the new member. Corea recalls: "Circle definitely began as a duet with Dave and myself. Our first trio recordings were with Barry—and I always felt that trio as a partnership. Of course, when 'the new guy' comes in an already established setting, he's the new guy for a while until he's a full-fledged member. This never got really discussed but I think was tacitly felt. The same occurred when Anthony was briefly the new guy but certainly Circle was a cooperative music-making group."[14] Clearly, the chemistry expanded to incorporate its fourth member rather quickly and organically.

Two sets of brief duo improvisations were recorded during the quartet's first formal recording session on August 13. The first pair was played by the original duo of Chick Corea and Dave Holland. The second set, by Anthony Braxton and Corea, was titled "Danse for Clarinet and Piano" (No. 1 and 2),[15] and makes clear the new group's terms of musical engagement: open improvisation; changing moods; stylistic and textural diversity, at times tonal but next atonal; and free use of extended performance techniques.[16]

In its August 21 studio session, Circle recorded three improvisatory works, "Quartet Piece 1, 2, and 3," comprising most of the *Circulus* album. These improvisations are exploratory, the ensemble work governed largely by intuition. Each musician creates phrases and patterns that imitate and/or contrast with his fellow musicians. Often, what they all are responding to are the nature of the sound itself and the contours of melodic gestures. A detailed description of some of the improvisations offers a window into how the band members began to explore their possibilities as a group. We can see how quickly they grew comfortable with one another's aesthetic sensibilities and performance techniques. It is difficult—without some description—to explain the ways that musicians use sounds to engage in dialogue.

The opening of "Quartet Piece #1" is textural; each player selects sounds that are similar in timbre: a spinning small object, fragile bowed cello, and bowed cymbal, followed by altissimo sopranino saxophone, cello harmonics, quick piano phrases in the upper register. Sustained saxophone notes are followed by brief, interlocking, rhythmic ostinato patterns on cello and piano. These patterns grow in speed and intensity as Braxton plays a slow series of sustained notes. The textures become more atonal, pointillistic, and energetic.[17] Braxton's solo is accompanied by piano and bass; the three musicians continue the theme of matching the kinds of sounds their instruments make.[18]

The concept then changes from similarity to difference when Braxton's solo picks up speed. Holland plays rapidly bowed, angular bass figures, with Altschul adding quickly muted cymbal and rapid-fire drum and cymbal hits. Next, with Holland at the fore, Altschul contrasts the arco bass with a thunder sheet and a panoply of percussion sounds. Corea's tinny string-muted piano is met by Altschul's vibraphone and temple blocks, leading to a duet for atonal piano and percussion that grows in intensity as Corea uses the entire span of the keyboard. A more lyrical, pastoral section follows, with Braxton returning on sopranino saxophone. But the next thing we know, the quartet shifts to a fevered pitch. Braxton fires off rapid, angular lines, punctuated by Holland's walking bass, Altschul's soloistic drumming, and Corea's piano tone clusters and then celeste. Repeated-note bass figures and steadily streaming drumming accompany the final section of Braxton's solo, and the piece closes with ringing bells.

"Quartet Piece #2" is a free-for-all on a vast array of instruments,[19] with "Quartet Piece #3" showing equal sonic diversity.[20]

What is most striking about these three quartet pieces is the breadth of sonic possibilities deployed by each musician and the collective sensitivity to sound, texture, and mood. Substantial technique is brought to bear, yet always in the service of the collective musical effect. The pieces move from section to section, mood to mood, always intuitively and without advance plan. The total spontaneity that emerges in this early session, quite full blown, presages the collective expression awaiting the band throughout its brief but illustrious life on concert tour.

It is tempting to describe Circle simply as a furthering of the Corea-Holland trends within the Miles Davis band. And in fact, many of the kinds of textures and give-and-take between the duo reflect ideas they had begun in that setting. Circle's tendency toward open collective expression did extend the work they achieved in dialogue with Jack DeJohnette, but their choice of Barry Altschul and Anthony Braxton as partners set a much freer course. Altschul's drumming was oriented more toward sheer sonic experience than was DeJohnette's, although both were firmly grounded in a solid beat when desired. Braxton was oriented less toward narrative and was more explorative of sound and gesture for their own sake than was Wayne Shorter. Particularly when viewed against Miles Davis's steady move toward beat-focused music, Circle pulled the duo from the Davis orbit and directed it toward music influenced by the Association for the Advancement of Creative Musicians and late John Coltrane.

The Impact of Marion Brown's "Afternoon of a Georgia Faun"

One possible influence on the new quartet—particularly its textural and coloristic explorations—may have been Corea and Braxton's participation on Marion Brown's album *Afternoon of a Georgia Faun*. This work was recorded on August 10, less than two weeks before Circle's sessions at Tom DePietro's studio. Like Braxton, Marion Brown was a saxophonist who had recently returned to the United States from Paris. During the early and mid-1960s, he had been a fixture in New York's free jazz scene, playing with Archie Shepp and on Coltrane's *Ascension* (1965). Calm and filled with evocative sense impressions, "Georgia Faun" the tune shows Brown employing instruments and textural improvisations associated with the AACM. Braxton was thus an excellent choice to participate. For Corea, the recording was an opportunity to explore sonic possibilities in new ways, in tandem with Braxton as his new musical partner. They are joined by percussionist Andrew Cyrille; Bennie Maupin on tenor saxophone, alto flute, bass clarinet, and percussion; singer Jeanne Lee; and others.

"Georgia Faun" opens with a "forest" of tapping sounds produced on wood blocks and other instruments, and sounds of water. Whistling is briefly heard. With a title that invokes Debussy's *Prelude to the Afternoon of a Faun*, Brown describes his composition as "a tone poem. It depicts nature and the environment in Atlanta . . . a percussion section that suggests rain drops . . . the second section is after the rain."[21] Indeed, we can imagine the sound of the woods in spring—birds whistling and woodpecker beaks knocking on trees.[22]

At the four-minute mark, we hear bell ringing, sounds of metal, and clanging cymbals. Soon, a quiet humming voice appears in the distance and then the call of a hunting horn, answered by flutes and winds. Shortly before seven minutes, a soprano saxophone calls out, heralding the beginning of a strikingly simple piano solo, which begins with the scraping of the piano's bass strings, a lovely chorale in quartal harmony. These passages alternate with more pointillistic plucked strings and playing on the keys, followed by a return to the chorale. Jeanne Lee's *sprechgesang* (quasi-pitched speech song) joins the pointillistic piano, and soon her coloratura soprano vocalization pairs with a lyrical flute line.

Energy levels and density of sounds increase; piano, flute, and soprano call and respond within the dense mix. Tension builds with high pitches and rapid runs, immediately returning to quiet. Lee offers angular lines, giving way to Corea's chromatic harmonies and, in a different key, a dramatic flute solo. Piano and flute engage in a call-and-response dance, the duet giving way to a return of the busy wood knocking, clicking, and whistling. Voices join and the density of sounds increases, gradually quieting down as the piece concludes.

Overall, the music is lush and evocative, presented with conviction by musicians sensitive to the nuance of open improvisation. The spare, textural qualities of the improvisation reflect the kind of heightened mutuality and sensitivity to sonic and gestural nuance characteristic of Circle in its finest moments.[23] The band's more textural treatments of Braxton's composition, variously titled "73 degrees Kelvin" or "Composition 6F," discussed below, provide examples.

Circle: Open Improvisation and Musical Form

The spontaneous organic nature of Circle's music was at the core of its musical endeavors. This was no doubt one of the reasons that more traditionalist critics found its music challenging. Chick Corea observes: "To me, Circle was a pretty straight-ahead experiment and joy in improvising new music—music with little or no pre-arranged form. The results had their absolute highs and lows."[24]

Each of the band members had core experiences to draw from regarding how to engage musically with others in an intuitive manner. Barry Altschul had performed with Paul Bley and Anthony Braxton with various AACM groups, including his own. Chick Corea and Dave Holland drew from their experiences with Miles Davis. Corea:

> Miles, with Herbie [Hancock], Ron [Carter], Tony [Williams], and Wayne [Shorter], had already established ways of breaking the song form down into little pieces or no pieces at all. It was very refreshing and inspiring to the rest of us—and always will be. The freedom to play a set way or to not play that way was and is the ultimate freedom of choice and freedom of expression. Miles had already demonstrated that he wanted to free himself up from "forms." So when Dave and I joined the band, songs like "Dolores," "Agitation," "Paraphernalia," and even the standard ballads like "'Round Midnight" were all being treated very, very freely. With Dave and Jack [DeJohnette] and encouraged by Wayne, we took it even further "out."

When the initial trio—and then quartet—began its first sessions, it was with an open mind as to what might unfold. Corea recalls: "At first, Dave, myself, then Barry, then Anthony made no decisions on form at all. The decisions were to begin playing—then end playing." Slowly, basic ideas regarding how to guide musical direction emerged. Corea: "After doing this for some time, we began to impose some loose forms to differentiate one 'piece' from another. Sometimes they were just a set of verbal directions—an idea of how to change tempo or start or stop a section."

One excellent example of the band's use of open forms is the first quartet piece included on the album *Circling In*: Holland's "Starp," recorded on August 19, 1970. This piece opens with a theme constructed from several long phrases, each separated by a brief pause. The four musicians play at a rapid clip, synchronized closely in rhythm. Some brief parallel play between Corea and Braxton leads to a winding piano solo. Corea moves easily between extended lines and brief phrases, which suggest being caught in a thicket yet always finding an escape route. A brief transition crafted by Corea and Holland leads to Braxton's solo.

Altschul remains in constant motion as Braxton plays, as Holland contributes steadily energetic angular lines—some of them repeated two- or three-note figures. Holland changes speed suddenly and with urgency, at times building tension by creating a holding pattern through insistent repetition, then releasing it with a rapid stream of notes. After staying briefly out of the fray, Corea returns behind Braxton—alternately matching and contrasting in force and energy—with a kaleidoscopic array of tone clusters and chord fragments played in alternating hands, expanding into cascading gestures, before again withdrawing. Holland solos, backed largely by Altschul, who playfully tosses the bassist's rhythmic patterns back at him. A sustained note by Braxton leads to isolated rhythmic strikes by Corea, and then a very spare Altschul solo, which abruptly concludes the piece.

The opening segment of Braxton's solo (beginning at 1:08) demonstrates a tight, intuitive structural logic within the saxophonist's playing. Note the alternation of three types of motifs: an opening phrase that functions like a call seeking a response, a grainy gutbucket saxophone sound ("growl"), and five angular phrases, sometimes incorporating a sustained note, that serve as the response to the opening call. The solo subsequently continues until 3:15, increasingly enmeshed with the playing of his partners.

The opening segment of Anthony Braxton's solo in "Starp," 1:08-1:35

1:08-1:10—Braxton "call" phrase—lyrical gesture ending w/upward leap

1:11-1:15—atonal "response"—angular phrase #1

1:16-1:17—growl #1

1:18-1:20—angular phrase #2

1:20-1:23—sustained note with timbral inflection and angular phrase #3

1:24—growl #2

1:25-1:28—angular phrase #4

1:28—growl #3

1:29-1:32—angular phrase # 5, more frenzied and winding

1:33-1:35—growl # 4, transitioning into a sustained tone

The quartet's approach to collective improvisation demanded everyone's complete attention. In many cases, one of the musicians would generate a melodic or rhythmic cell, which is open to examination and exploring for its implications. Implicit in the kind of musical gestures a musician would play is a series of "questions" each band member would need to unconsciously ask at every moment: What kind of support or challenge should the others provide? Should additional material be offered or exchanged? Does an evocative moment require punctuation? Is there a space to fill, or, alternately, a silence to respect? Band members indeed held discussions following their performances. Yet these kinds of questions require no explicit discussion; they are the bread and butter of a successful performance: while an individual might instigate activity, tension and release is built communally. Mysteriously and effortlessly, the music all comes together, intuitively and in the moment.

In essence, the band's name embodies its process orientation, as John Mars observes: "I think of Circle as like a round table with the four of them all around it. You put each guy at his place around the circumference of this table . . . all facing each other. . . . Decisions were made in a 'conference,'[25] in a hair trigger of a second with all those groups. When you play like that, there's a little wire hooked up between your heads."[26]

Indeed, Circle functioned as a collective. This was a value strongly felt by the entire band, as Corea relates: "I like to be in a group where everyone is free to express themselves freely—musically and otherwise. It's an ethic that matches the 'equal rights' aspect of the music I love to be a part of." Altschul notes: "We would discuss the music the minute we came off the set. We went into the back room, discussed the music, and then left it alone. But we talked about what we did, what we didn't do, what's happening, what wasn't happening, all that kind of shit. That was the height of the music, and the tapes show it. Fabulous. . . . It was everything collective. Everyone had a job to do in the band: librarian, busi- ness . . . we were also kind of a commune. We were on the road together with our families—those who had families—and we cooked, we had little cookers with us, bought fresh vegetables and brown rice and shit. And anyone who wanted to eat meat, that's what they did, but still, we were all like a family. So, we were very tight."

As Circle continued to develop, an unpredictable logic arose from the shared chemistry and history. Altschul:

When you're playing music where you're relying on each other for the forms that the music becomes, an E.S.P. develops. And the more you do it, the more it develops. It's like any other method. So what then comes into play is your musical vocabulary, and how many places you can go to and how many moods you can set up. We went to Dixieland! There are places where we jumped into some Dixieland shit. You know? So whatever we went. Everyone had a vast musical vocabulary, and everybody was familiar with each other's vocabulary, because everybody's vocabulary, a lot of it was the same. Not necessarily the same concept of the vocabulary, but the vocabulary. . . . We tried to play fresh every time. The only thing that would have been a kind of a form, though it wasn't thought of as a formulated thing, was within the concept of tension and release. The release used to seem usually to fall into a time thing.

One of the band's conscious goals, whether playing off of composed tunes or more freely, was to avoid habits and clichés. For Chick Corea, this had been a priority in his career up to that point: "The direction that I was headed was upwards to a way of being and creating that was free of categories and analysis. When I heard the music of Bud Powell, I was inspired by his musical freedom—he seemed able to become the music when he played. Monk was the same—he expressed a complete freedom of personal expression. The same with Bartok's compositions—the way they broke new ground and fused new elements together." Barry Altschul had incorporated this way of thinking into his own playing: "As a matter of fact, as part of my development as a drummer, there was a period where if I was to play a Philly Joe Jones lick in my playing, I would say to myself, 'Oh that's Philly Joe, that's not you—change it.' So, I think it was the same kind of approach. It was, 'Oh, I used a cowbell on a place—on a texture like this—let me play something else.' I didn't think it, but it was an instinct."

The Miles Davis Lost Quintet also placed a high value on spontaneity, but might we view Circle's difficult-to-attain ideal of "if you've done it before, don't repeat it" as taking this a step further?

Circle's Use of Compositional Materials and "Tunes"

Early in the band's history, written compositions were adopted, at least as boosters to spur improvisation, "almost from the beginning of the formalized band," as Altschul notes. "Everybody started [composing]—that was a lot of the rehearsals, getting people's concepts of their compositions down. I was the only one who didn't write, and they all encouraged me to write. I started writing after Circle. But they all encouraged me to write. Everybody was writing, always, from the beginning." Corea adds: "We always [throughout our time playing together] occasionally used a written composition—as in a series of notes and/ or harmonies—as a start point."

Soon, the band began to integrate more of a metric pulse into its improvisations, to complement the more rhythmically free music of the early sessions. At this point, compositions became useful to spark improvisation, as Corea recalls: "In our desire to have more form in terms of variety of melodies, variety of rhythm, and especially in the desire to have some music begin to groove again, we brought in the program some song forms. It was fun to approach these, at this point in the band's development, from the other direction—coming from playing free-form music to music with a form. As you can hear, our approach to these songs was extremely loose."

Altschul clarifies: "In other words, when the tunes were written, it wasn't so much to adhere to a structure, to a form of a song. There was not a song form; it was improvised to the concept that this melody or rhythm conjures up." Nonetheless, "we were very well rehearsed, we were very tight, and at the time, how we improvised just fit together in that style. It just was." Even when an improvisation began with a conventionally organized tune, those structures could break apart from that pretty quickly. Elements of the tune's melodic or rhythmic structure remained in the minds of the players and would resurface, as Altschul comments: "If you listen to it real close, no matter how out everyone goes—maybe they'll come in on the two instead of the one, or something like that—the form is back there somewhere."

This freewheeling approach to tunes was witnessed by composer Neil Rolnick during one of the band's spring 1971 performances:

I heard Circle at Jazz Workshop in Boston. The first night, I was so blown away that I came back for the next five nights or so and heard every set they played. What amazed me was the seamless integration of clearly rehearsed and worked-out heads with what seemed like completely free improvisation. They would play very angular, fast, well-coordinated tunes, then seem to drop off into outer space, and then ten or twenty minutes later (or so it seemed) drop back in for a recap of the head. It was just completely mysterious to me, and I loved it.[27]

The concept of "improvised to the concept that this melody or rhythm conjures up" articulated by Barry Altschul was also a feature of Miles Davis's Lost Quintet. The compositions would segue from one into the next when Miles played a snippet from the latter as a cue to move on. Some tunes began with a recognizable opening: the melody of "Sanctuary," the bass and drums vamp of "Directions," or the thematic motif of "Miles Runs the Voodoo Down." "Bitches Brew" could begin with one of several of its elements described earlier: Chick Corea playing the repeated low Cs or Davis playing the "staircase" motif. Once a tune was under way, the ensemble could treat these materials freely, particularly during the final year of the band. The sonic events of "Bitches Brew" were the most malleable. Vamps such as the "Miles Runs the Voodoo Down" theme evolved over the months. Circle continued the notion that arose in Miles's band, that fragments of materials could be used playfully during improvisations. But, as we shall see, it took the concept even further.[28]

Throughout their days on the jazz club and concert circuits, Circle's set list also included tunes drawn from the broader jazz repertoire. These were used more as instigators for improvisation than to provide formal structures for organizing those improvisations. The two main tunes of this kind are "Nefertiti" and "There's No Greater Love."

"Nefertiti" was a regular piece in Circle's repertoire.[29] First recorded by Corea and the trio on *The Song of Singing*,[30] it is a Wayne Shorter composition from Miles Davis's 1967 album *Nefertiti*.[31] The Marty Symes-Isham Jones standard "There's No Greater Love" was a favorite vehicle within the Circle repertory, showcasing how malleably the performance of a jazz standard could move between straight-ahead playing, free-ranging solos, and highly textural abstraction. It received highly extended treatments, from seventeen and a half minutes at the conclusion of the Paris Concert, to twenty-five minutes at Hamburg.[32] A twenty-one-and-a-half-minute version at Iserlohn, Germany, from November 28, 1970, runs the gamut of possible ways this band could address a jazz standard, from remaining close to the chord changes, invoking them, ignoring them, and using the spirit of the tune as a departure point for open improvisation. Corea, Braxton, and Holland deliver extended solos, followed by a saxophone and drums duet, each its own composition, yet serving as one portion of a larger, integrated whole.[33]

New Beginnings

The idea wasn't to start out and play free; the idea was to play this music. It wasn't about playing free, or playing avant-garde, or anything. It was that there's this concept of playing music, and we are going to write music to stimulate those concepts.

BARRY ALTSCHUL

For Anthony Braxton and fellow Circle members, the second half of 1970 promised to be a heady time. The saxophonist looked forward to his new musical associations, and Circle was to open new creative opportunities. As he later recalled: "The most fundamental axiom that I grew up with was the importance of finding something of your own, and when that happens, either everyone can hear it or they can't. Fortunately for me, many of the musicians and percussionists I hoped would be open to my music were, in fact, open to it."[34]

Circle's initial recording sessions bore fruit, and it began performing in public in the fall of 1970. The "jazz pedigree" of its two recent alumni of Miles Davis's band paved the way for bookings across the American and European jazz club circuit. Barry Altschul: "We had an agent in America who was out in California, and she booked the circuit. She was getting us gigs. We consider ourselves jazz musicians, [who played] on the circuit. At that time, I'm not sure if Braxton did or didn't consider himself [a jazz musician], but we were on the jazz circuit. We played the circuit, and we were asked back. We played some concerts too."

Altschul continues:

[Chick's presence was helpful in the booking of the band.] Yes, we knew his name power was stronger than ours. Chick himself wanted to make it Circle, where his name wouldn't seem that [out front], because it was a cooperative band. But yes, we all were aware of his publicity. He was out there. I mean, he was with Miles at the time. A lot of attention was on him, let's put it that way. So sure, we talked about it, we said, "Yeah, let's use it," of course. Chick and Dave—'cause when they were playing together—people were wondering what was happening; what happened after Miles. So we were aware of that.

Indeed, as we will see, Corea and Holland's reputation was a double-edged sword. Their association with Miles Davis brought opportunities to Circle, but often led critics to place highly conventional expectations on the band. This is of course ironic, given the unconventional nature of the Lost Quintet; in the popular imagination, Davis remained the trumpeter who created *Kind of Blue* in 1959 and, maybe, the 1960s quintet. There was little relationship, in other words, between what critics were looking for and the actual highly unpredictable, open musical presentation that Circle offered. It treated tunes that critics expected to hear, whether from the Miles Davis repertoire or jazz standards, no less broadly than it did its own members' compositions.

■ ■ ■

The band traveled with a large amount of gear, suited to create a wide range of musical sounds and textures. Altschul recalls: "We had two cars. We drove. There was a time I was carrying almost twenty cases of instruments. That was just the percussion shit—not counting the bass, the cello, the guitar, and all the saxophones."

Among Circle's early shows was an extended stand at the Lighthouse, in Hermosa Beach, California, from September 29 through October 11, 1970. These concerts coincided with the first tour of the retooled Miles Davis band: Dave Holland had been replaced by funk-oriented bassist Michael Henderson, with Keith Jarrett continuing on electric keyboards, Gary Bartz on saxophone, and Airto Moreira on percussion (supplemented by Jumma Santos). A couple weeks earlier, Chick Corea had made a studio recording, *The Sun*, with Holland and two former colleagues from Davis's band, Jack DeJohnette and Steve Grossman.[35] Circle's Lighthouse appearances were followed by a jazz workshop it held at the University of California, Irvine.[36]

While Circle had many positive experiences during its tours, the Lighthouse shows were neither well received nor well attended, as a *DownBeat* reviewer reported: "The Lighthouse reported a noticeable drop in business as the Chick Corea Quartet, known as Circle, followed Joe Henderson. The diet seemed to be too avant-garde for the Hermosa Beach crowd."[37] Remaining on the West Coast, the group appeared at the Both/And in San Francisco on October 17–24. A month later, Anthony Braxton performed without his bandmates as part of a multimedia performance, "Communication in a Noisy Environment," in New York on November 19–20.[38]

In late November, Circle embarked on an extended European tour that took it to Germany, the Netherlands, Belgium, and France.[39] A November 28 show in Iserlohn, Germany, was recorded by German radio for broadcast and released on a Japanese label as *Circle 1*. Following these quartet dates, Braxton made a piano recording, and in early January played his own concert in Paris.

On January 11–13, 1971, the original trio without Braxton recorded *A.R.C.* for ECM Records. The album's title is a term in Scientology that means "affinity, reality, communication," said to be the components of understanding. Corea had recently become involved with Scientology and took inspiration from its founder, L. Ron Hubbard.[40]

In early February 1971, Braxton recorded *The Complete Braxton*, which included three duets with Corea; Holland and Altschul appear on three other, quartet tracks (with trumpeter Kenny Wheeler, but not Corea). Also included on the album are two solo saxophone pieces, one multi-tracked, and a work for five tubas. The recording, made in London on February 4 and 5, represents the beginning of Braxton's string of LPs on the Arista Freedom label. The compositions are drawn largely from Braxton's 6 series, which may also be found in his repetoire with Creative Construction Company and Circle. *Complete* simultaneously represents a summation of his earlier work and an opening to what was to come in the next decade.[41]

Circle's only widely released recording, *The Paris Concert*, was made later that month, on February 21, at Maison De L'ORTF. The concert had its logistical challenges, as Barry Altschul remembers:

> We went through an aggravating time just before that. . . . They wouldn't let us in, 'cause we didn't have our badges with us. We were standing next to our posters saying, "Look, it's us! It's us! It's us!" and the security wouldn't let us in. Finally, the promoter came looking for us—and I think he fired that security guard—because eventually the concert was forty-five minutes or an hour late, by the time we started. And then we had guests with us. We had people from America that were with us and we had a guest list and everything, and they didn't let the guests in. Security—the same thing. So we went onstage and we announced to the audience the situation, and we're not gonna play until we see our guests sitting in the audience. So this was while we were on the stage just before we started playing. So that's how we approached that concert. And that was supposed to be the concert everybody talked about.

The band was back in Germany in March 1971. Shows documented by radio broadcast and recording include concerts at Jazzhaus in Hamburg (March 4, Norddeutscher Rundfunk [NDR]) and in Bremen (March 5, Radio Bremen). A third German concert may have taken place, followed by shows in Italy. A March 19 performance at Third International Jazz Parade at Bergamo was both radio broadcast and recorded. I have heard only a fragment of the Bergamo show, a recording of "Nefertiti."[42]

In April 1971, Anthony Braxton performed in Paris while Chick Corea made his own solo piano recordings for ECM.[43] Circle was back on tour and in the studio at the end of that month, including the Jazz Workshop in Boston in early May; the Village Vanguard in New York; a recording session for the multisection, extended work *The Gathering* at Upsurge Studios in New York;[44] and a stand at Slugs, the East Village jazz club.

The band returned to California for its final shows in the summer of 1971. Two of these took place in early July at the Both/And in San Francisco[45] and in early August at Shelley's Manne Hole in Los Angeles.[46] Not one to spare criticism of the group, critic Leonard Feather observed: "Their voyages of discovery are liable to create singularly hypnotic moments of unity, followed by atonal passages that are notable more for the intuitive intergroup communication than for their comprehensibility." In summary, while impressed by the virtuosity, Feather expressed disappointment: "Circle's music represents a certain eclecticism, a straining for totality of sound experience that loses some of its emotional impact in the process."[47]

Endings

The life of a touring ensemble is rarely a long-term affair. Circle and the trio that preceded it had a yearlong run, a respectable length of time for a band that brought unconventional music to mainstream commercial venues. According to Corea, "It ran its course as so many high-spirited and creative groups of artists do. We had a good run and made some memorable recordings. There came a point where our musical goals went in slightly different directions."[48] For him, "Circle was a deep and meaningful part of my life. My musical association with Dave has always been dear to me. We seemed to spur each others' inclination towards musical discovery and freedom of musical expression. There was always a great joy in our duet improvisations. This was the spirit that became Circle with Barry, then Anthony."[49]

Perceptions between band members often differ, and such was the case with Circle. Altschul: "There was tension toward the end, yes. The music that we were playing, we wanted to continue to play; Me, Dave, and Anthony, but Chick was changing. We didn't realize at the time. There was just tension in the band. But when it [the music] was happening, it was really great. We had an audience, and for us at the time, it was enough. We would have liked bigger audiences, but the Jazz Workshop was full up every day of the week when we played there."[50]

Braxton believed that some level of conflict is an inherent and unavoidable part of musical life: "We already have some very interesting music and it's very nice to work with Chick. It seems to me . . . that once we started travelling and touring we lost something. Relationships in different situations tended to have too much stress, the personal relationships, but with this band we seem to have good personal relationships and this is very important when you're travelling. We have a desire to understand each other—seemingly, and it's important. I mean, it definitely wouldn't 'hurt' the music if musicians liked each other!"[51]

Interpersonal challenges may have contributed to Circle's demise, but these are more the concern of a gossip magazine than the present musical study. Whatever the exact source of Corea's changing interests and sensibilities, his musical plans were changing. After a stint with Stan Getz, he formed the first Brazilian-tinged Return to Forever. The pianist's interests were in transition to a simpler presentation that was more accessible to audiences. Dave Holland continued to keep one foot in the aesthetics of Circle, joining Sam Rivers's band, and the other in more straight-ahead jazz, joining Stan Getz in 1975 (along with Jack DeJohnette and pianist Richie Beirach).[52]

Holland felt that were it not for the conflicts, Circle could have continued musically and economically:

> Well, that particular group [Circle] I think could have survived had we stayed together. You see there were enough people who knew who the people in the group were, so we were assured of a certain number of people coming to hear us. With the right kind of handling of a group of that kind, and with enough traveling, you could cover yourself between albums that you might do. You could go to Europe for the summer, doing concerts over there, coming back to make it to a university, doing things like that. We had a very large following from young people, partly from the fact that they knew Chick and I from Miles, and had heard some of those albums, and wanted to come and find out what we were doing on our own. And the music seemed to appeal to them, it wasn't just the idiom that we were using, it was the feeling that we produced as a group.[53]

But it was not to be. Holland and Altschul became two-thirds of Sam Rivers's band, and for a time worked as Braxton's rhythm section. Altschul:

> So Anthony goes back to Chicago and then I think goes back to Europe. I go back to New York, and Dave goes up to Seattle for a while and then his wife was pregnant, so they went up there for a while, and then they came to New York. While I was in New York for the first year I was there, I got a gig—I took Billy Cobham's place with the Paul Winter Consort. I'm on their album *Icarus*. It was before [Dave Holland's] the *Conference of the Birds*.[54] And it was a great gig because they only went to colleges on weekends. So that was good for what was happening in my life at the time. And I was also playing with Sam Rivers, but I couldn't really leave town at that time, so the weekend thing was cool. And Sam Rivers's thing included Cecil McBee playing bass. So then Dave comes back to New York, and eventually I hook Dave up with Sam, and that becomes the trio.[55]

Altschul continues: "And then Anthony comes back [from time in Chicago and then Paris], and says he wants to form a quartet with me and Dave and Kenny Wheeler. And we said, 'Okay!' So we are working both ends [simultaneously with Rivers and Braxton's bands] at the same time." What was first called the Sam Rivers, Dave Holland, Barry Altschul Trio was renamed the Sam Rivers Trio, a collective improvisation ensemble in which "whoever had the most creative energy could dictate the direction. . . . We gave up our egos to the music. . . . Any given night there were no compositions, nothing, just the trio improvising. Everybody was a composer." Ultimately, Holland and Altschul felt the need to choose between Rivers and Braxton, "and we both decided to go with Sam . . . because it was closer to more of our musical experience. Braxton's was more written out, more compositional. . . . And then Braxton went and became *Braxton*; he was already Braxton—he became more Braxton."

Braxton and Holland would again cross paths with Jack DeJohnette when vibraphonist-educator Karl Berger formed Creative Music Studio[56] and began to run workshops in Woodstock, New York, in 1972. The organization was established in conjunction with Ornette Coleman. Berger, Braxton, Holland, and DeJohnette, all living around Woodstock, were among its core master teachers.[57] Berger developed a curriculum based on his experience teaching at the New School. The principles similar in spirit to Circle's: improvisation that was not limited by genre or stylistic concerns.

Looking back on his experience with Circle, Holland concluded:

And this is something that I've noticed happened with the music, is that no matter what kind of music you play, it doesn't matter what the style, if the spirit is in the music, if there's really a spirit in the music, it communicates to people. The people sense that, and we really had a unified feeling going on for a while, and people immediately caught fire because of it. They saw what happened on the stand, which made them feel good just by virtue of the fact that they could see that kind of closeness and communication and love between people was possible. The music kind of represented that, and so that took them beyond the idiom that we were working with, whether we were using strange or common sound, it didn't seem to matter, it just could relate to the feel of it. So in that sense, I think survival means that, survival means flowing. Survival means doing, and I think Circle was doing and was flowing while it existed.[58]

But long-term musical survival also engages economic issues. Circle was never going to be able to inhabit the economic world of Miles Davis's bands.

Chick Corea's change of direction had economic implications in that it gradually moved him into a more mainstream position in the music business. Anthony Braxton's, Barry Altschul's, and Dave Holland's choices solidified their connection with a more informal, less commercial and thus economically marginal musical enterprise. Examples of musical collectives that have remained economically viable for longer periods of time are rare. The Art Ensemble of Chicago will be discussed briefly in the pages that follow. The Revolutionary Ensemble, one of the most economically marginal yet long-lasting groups, is the focus of the next chapter.

7

The Revolutionary Ensemble

Musical freedom is relative. The Miles Davis Lost Quintet was a model of a band fronted by a relatively nondirective leader who allowed his musicians substantial leeway to play as they wished. Circle took this model even further by beginning with the idea of a leaderless group that generated musical form even more substantially from interactions between its members. In Circle, individual freedom was balanced with the maintenance of group musical cohesion. The Revolutionary Ensemble expanded Circle's approach: individual and group configurations were malleable constructs, one giving way to the other without so much as a moment's notice. Collectivity could just as soon feature simultaneous and multiple individual initiatives as it could musical togetherness. Construction of a cohesive whole was constantly subject to instantaneous negotiation. Some might view this approach as anarchic, but the three musicians of the Revolutionary Ensemble functioned like a musical high-wire act, sounding sometimes like one voice and at other times like independent individuals coexisting in the same sound space.

Introducing the Revolutionary Ensemble

Among Anthony Braxton's most significant collaborators during the late 1960s in Chicago and Paris was violinist Leroy Jenkins. The two were members of the Association for the Advancement of Creative Musicians[1] who, in search of greater support and performance opportunities, joined a 1969 European sojourn led by drummer Steve McCall and the Art Ensemble of Chicago. Braxton and Jenkins were among the first AACM members to settle in New York City upon their return from Paris in 1970. Creative Construction Company, their collectivist ensemble that they founded in 1967 with Leo Smith, reunited, and performed a concert on May 19, 1970, at the Peace Church.

Then Braxton began to pursue his collaboration with Chick Corea, Dave Holland, and Barry Altschul—after touring the United States with Music Elettronica Viva—and Jenkins formed a new improvisatory trio, the Revolutionary Ensemble. The group included bassist Sirone (Norris Jones) and percussionist Jerome Cooper (who replaced founding member Frank Clayton). Despite its limited public performance opportunities, the band became one of the most vibrant open-improvisation vehicles during this era of dynamic, expressive music-making.

Jenkins and Cooper first met in Chicago, albeit briefly. Cooper recalls: "[Pianist] Ahmad Jamal opened a club in Chicago called the Alhambra, but the club folded. The reason it folded was because he wouldn't serve alcohol, and you gotta have alcohol in Chicago. Me and a friend of mine went there for a jam session and a lot of the AACM cats were there. Leroy, Muhal [Richard Abrams] . . . a lot of cats. I played, and Leroy played, but I couldn't hear Leroy because Leroy played violin and he had no amplifier. And I spoke to Leroy, and that was it."[2]

Jerome Cooper

Fourteen years younger than Leroy Jenkins, "multi-dimensional drummer"[3] Jerome Cooper grew up in Chicago. Like Jenkins (and many other AACM members and notable jazz musicians), he was an alumnus of "Captain" Walter Dyett's jazz program at Jean Baptiste Point DuSable High School. His studies continued at American Conservatory and Loop College. Then, while in his early twenties, Cooper performed with Oscar Brown Jr. and Kalaparusha Maurice McIntyre.

He recalls having been invited to join the AACM at the time, but declined to become involved. Cooper joined the European exodus of Chicago-based musicians, first arriving in Copenhagen and then Paris. Among the notables with whom he played during this period were Steve Lacy, Rahsaan Roland Kirk, the Art Ensemble of Chicago, Alan Silva, Frank Wright, and Noah Howard. After a while, Cooper decided to move to New York City, where his association with Jenkins took off. He recalls:

> I was working a lot in Paris, but Paris around 1970 started to become a drag, and everybody was leaving and I was close to Roscoe [Mitchell] in those days. And I dug the idea, what I liked about the Art Ensemble [of which Mitchell was a member] was their cooperative effort, you know, everyone equal. And so I said, "Roscoe, you know, I'm going back to New York. Who should I call? Because I'm interested in being part of a cooperative group." And he gave me Leroy's number. . . . Meeting Leroy that one time [in Chicago] was the only reason that I had enough nerve when Roscoe told me to call Leroy, that's the only reason I called him. I thought, "He seems pretty cool," so I called him up when I came back to New York and I went over his house, and he took me over to Sirone's [bass player Norris Jones, the third member of the band].[4]

Sirone (Norris Jones)

Sirone was raised in Atlanta, where he played as a teenager with saxophonist George Adams. Early in his career, he also played with Sam Cooke and Jerry Butler, and his broad musical background prepared him well to play a wide array of musical forms, including

> the gospel . . . but the other music that I was introduced to early in high school was classical music. In some way or another if you are going to study music from a technical point of view you have to have the experience of European classical music. But I was very fortunate because my first teacher was a trombone player with a Dixieland group so I got on the job training. . . . I was listening to all sort of music, even hillbilly music . . . in Atlanta the group that we had at this point, and this was in my latter teenage years was called "The Group" and we would be the opening band for all the main New York bands.[5]

Upon moving to New York City at the invitation of Marion Brown, Sirone co-founded the Untraditional Jazz Improvisational Team with pianist Dave Burrell and saxophonist Byard Lancaster. In the late 1960s, Sirone performed and re-corded with Brown, Gato Barbieri, Sonny Sharock, Pharoah Sanders, and Ben-nie Maupin before joining the Revolutionary Ensemble.

Founding the New Group

At the time, in 1970, all three musicians were living downtown in New York City. Cooper: "Leroy was living on Bedford Street in Manhattan, in the West Village. And Sirone was living on Bleecker Street in the West Village, a hop skip from Leroy's house. And I was living across the street from the Fillmore [East]. I lived on Sixth Street, between Second and Third Avenue. During them days there weren't any lofts, meaning commercial lofts where they would have per-formances every week."[6]

Sirone recalls that he and Jenkins had been playing with a larger group of musicians, some of whom he thought were not up to the task.

> We had some players that weren't hitting [playing well enough] at all and Le-roy and I was walking and talking about music and I said "Listen man, I have no problem playing with you but those other cats, you gotta get rid of them, they're not there, you know." And he said, "What are you talking about, what are you thinking?" And I said "Let's have violin, bass and drums" and that's when he almost fainted and Leroy said "What do you think about the name" and I said, "I dunno man. I dunno about the name" and he said "What abut The Revolutionary Ensemble" and I thought *he* was crazy; three cats, but it worked.[7]

The ensemble's first rehearsal was at Artists House, Ornette Coleman's com-bination home and studio, where, according to Cooper, Jenkins was already spending a good deal of time. They also rehearsed at artist Fred Brown's, "going back and forth between there and Ornette's."[8] Brown was a noted painter, whose loft at 120 Wooster Street in SoHo became a meeting group for numerous cre-ative artists working in a variety of media. The year 1970 was pivotal for Brown, as he mounted his first solo exhibition in Chicago. Poet Felipe Luciano remem-bers Revolutionary Ensemble's rehearsals at Brown's loft. Luciano, cofounder of the Latino activist group the Young Lords, had recently joined the spoken-word ensemble the Last Poets.

> As I'm coming in the door [to Fred Brown's loft], Leroy Jenkins, Sirone is go-ing "doom-doom-doom . . ." not 4/4, 8/8, and Leroy's going "eh-eh, eh-ehhhh,

ehhhh . . ." and I'm not "beam me up Scotty" and Jerome plays with his face in your face; all I saw was his fingers. That was the first poem I wrote with Fred Brown. It was called "Fingers Moving." After that, came the other poems, jazz poems. I remember Fred had inspiration; he would actually elicit poetry. That loft had the ability to take whatever spiritual energy you had, that you thought you had suppressed and Fred would squeeze it out of you.[9]

The context of downtown lofts as a setting for the Revolutionary Ensemble's rehearsals, and some of its performances, will be explored below.

The "Jazz Loft" Scene in Context

Leroy Jenkins, like Anthony Braxton, was at the vanguard of musicians moving to New York in the early to mid-1970s. Many were members of the various African American musical collective organizations that had formed in the 1960s, including the AACM in Chicago, Black Artists Group in St. Louis, and Underground Musicians Association in Los Angeles.[10]

These musicians' frequent encounters with clubs that refused to book artists who engaged in open improvisation were replicated in New York, so they began to take matters into their own hands. We've already seen how young, largely white musicians in the New York neighborhood of Chelsea banded together in informal settings away from clubs. A broader move was taking place among black musicians, just as it had in Chicago. Bassist William Parker explains: "People were finding storefronts, lofts, and creating and producing their own concerts because the established clubs were not that receptive to hiring them. So you had all of these musicians who instead of staying at home, came out and created work for themselves, performing and recording their music."[11]

Music presented in the lofts tended to feature players dedicated to innovation and expression whose work was not constrained by marketplace demands. The commercial infrastructure that helped promote Miles Davis, including promoters like George Wein, the jazz press including DownBeat, and record companies with substantial budgets, was rarely accessible to loft musicians. Davis's Lost Quintet may have been an anomaly. While that band shared some aesthetic similarities with groups playing the lofts, it attracted attention and compensation due to Davis's personal reputation. It was not dependent on popular acceptance of the specific music it made.[12] Lacking both the Miles Davis name and the interest of club booking agents, bands playing the lofts had barely gained traction within the jazz economy. This disparity in access to monetary sustainability meant that the economic gulf between these bands and Davis's exceeded their aesthetic commonalities.

Lacking the organizational strength and sophistication of a true anomaly, the Art Ensemble of Chicago,[13] the Revolutionary Ensemble perpetually found itself on unsteady ground. It turned its vulnerability into an asset, however, as it furthered its connections with an informal community of (mostly) black musicians in downtown New York City.[14] A galvanizing event in the development of the loft scene was the 1972 New York Musicians Festival,[15] which took place across multiple venues in the city.[16] One of the key festival venues was Sam and Bea Rivers's Studio Rivbea at 24 Bond Street.[17] A saxophonist and composer, Rivers had mentored Tony Williams in Boston in the early 1960s and was briefly a member of the Miles Davis Quintet before Wayne Shorter joined. Rivers moved to New York City in time for the 1964 October Revolution in Jazz concerts, and opened Studio Rivbea in 1969 originally as an informal space focused on family and friends. It was at first a rehearsal space, replacing a public school Rivers had been using near his Harlem apartment. Beginning with the NYJMF, Studio Rivbea began to offer ongoing public programming.[18]

Jerome Cooper was a denizen of the Riverses' loft. "I used to go at three o'clock in the morning. Sam would always be up. I went back into their living area. The children were really courteous and nice. I really believed it was the love between him and Bea and their children. That's why the place was so hip." He sums up the relationship between Rivers and the musicians with whom he played: "The reason I used to go there was about love. It was total love."[19]

Unlike many of their peers, the Revolutionary Ensemble did not use Studio Rivbea as a performance venue. Yet the environment and circumstances under which musicians struggled to perform was something they shared.

Revolutionary Ensemble's Performances

In its early years, before the mid-1970s, the Revolutionary Ensemble performed infrequently. Cooper:

> [To arrange] concerts, the few that we did—we would go up to the Public Theater, just walk in there, and walk upstairs and say we want to see Joe Papp. I'll never forget Novella Nelson was the secretary there, and she introduced us to Joe Papp and I don't know if he liked us, but he said: "I'm going to let you rehearse over at the Annex." Across the street from the Public Theater, Papp had the other building up the street; he called it the Annex, and he let you rehearse

there a couple weeks. And then he gave us a concert at the Public Theater. He didn't give musical performances at that time, very rarely. There were some musical performers that I heard, but not on a regular basis. This is 1971. The only loft we played a concert was at Ornette Coleman's place, and it was jam-packed.[20]

It is not clear why the group did not participate more fully in the loft scene, like other musicians within its circle.

One of the first Revolutionary Ensemble concerts, and a rare extended engagement, took place at the Mercer Arts Center on Broadway. *Rolling Stone* described the center as "a kind of supermarket of entertainment containing five theatres, a video-tape room, an actors workshop, a bar and boutique. In its short history it housed several Off-Broadway productions, including Ken Kesey's 'One Flew Over the Cuckoo's Nest' and 'The Proposition,' a satirical review."[21] The venue would soon become the first home of the Kitchen, a multimedia arts center. Cooper continues:

We played four weeks there, in 1971 or 1972. It was our first really extensive [series of] concerts. The owner [Seymour Kaback] was a guy who owned an air conditioner company. He hadn't had music in there; just plays. He was a very nice person. He owned buildings. He liked us and just let us have the space. We played in the Oscar Wilde room. He said: "Come here and do your thing." We did our own advertising. What happened was we had friends, and they gave us the money to deal with posters. First week at Mercer Arts Center, nobody was there. Second week, two or three. Third week it was half packed. The fourth week it was jam-packed. We used the [Mercer Arts Center] poster later for the cover of our record *The Psyche*.[22]

The group's 1972 performance at Artists House was heralded in *DownBeat*: "The music literally swirled and smoked right before the spectator's eyes, truly a devastating study in group unity." Critic Roger Riggins described the Revolutionary Ensemble as "a unique, utterly contemporary unit of extraordinarily talented players who possess a *world understanding* of what 'organized sound' is all about."[23]

Building an audience proved to be a ground-up operation for the group. As it lacked professional promoters, "our own advertising" meant extensive interpersonal networking and posting flyers. Cooper explains:

[In terms of jazz clubs], we worked the Five Spot; at that time it was on St. Marks Place. It had moved from Fifth Street to St. Marks. I think we had a weekend or maybe two weeks, and [the owner] asked us if we wanted to buy the Five Spot! We did play the Village Vanguard one Sunday afternoon. The audience was small, but the main thing was Max Gordon. Max sat down and talked with us the whole day, and just told us the whole history of the Vanguard. He gave us a Sunday afternoon performance. There weren't that many people there, but what I remember was Max Gordon talking. One night, Leroy and me tried to get a gig at Slugs [a club on East Third Street]. It could have happened, but Slugs was going out.[24]

Slugs had been one of the few clubs in New York City whose programming spanned a sufficiently wide range of aesthetics to include the Revolutionary Ensemble.[25] Much farther to the west, the Village Vanguard was a mainstream club that stretched its aesthetic boundaries in May 1970 to welcome the Chick Corea Trio with Dave Holland and Barry Altschul. Lacking the name recognition of Miles Davis sidemen, a primetime or repeat performance by the Revolutionary Ensemble was unlikely. Similarly, jazz pianist Paul Bley's edgy 1969 synthesizer performance at the Vanguard proved to be his final show at that club.[26]

Another place where the Revolutionary Ensemble would perform was the old St. Marks Theater, where it recorded its album *Manhattan Cycles* on December 31, 1972. Other engagements included a recorded concert released in 1972 as *Vietnam*, and a show at the Jamaica Art Center in Queens, New York, in 1973.[27] Cooper adds: "We did radio interviews on WKCR and WBAI. Verna Gillis had a radio show called *Soundscape* [*Soundscape: Music from Everywhere*]. I used to do that show a lot. She later produced the Revolutionary Ensemble concert out in Prospect Park."[28]

A Short-Lived Record Contract

In the mid-1970s, the trio gained greater recognition and began to appear at festivals. It also received a recording contract with A&M Records during the brief existence of that company's Horizon Jazz Series directed by John Snyder. Sirone recalls that the Revolutionary Ensemble remained a source of controversy with the company after landing the contract. Herb Alpert, A&M's cofounder,

> wanted to impress Quincy Jones [the company's musical director] with the new catalogue for Horizon. They were having dinner and he put on the Revolutionary Ensemble's *The People's Republic*. He probably put on the first cut called "The People's Republic" and it opens with voices and Quincy said

to Herb Alpert that he has been conned; that it wasn't jazz *or* music and blah blah blah. Mr. Jones did miss the point. If he wanted to enquire a little more about it, the point of the piece is that everybody can sing, you may not like the voices but *everybody* can sing and at the very end of the composition we played that line [sings the line] and that is the transition from the voice to the voice *through* the instrument.[29]

The People's Republic actually represents an excellent entry point for listeners unfamiliar with this band, and post-Coltrane improvised music more generally. Recorded in a studio in Burbank, California, on December 4–6, 1975, the parallel voices of the trio are presented with clarity. The music is exceedingly diverse, from Leroy Jenkins's beautiful ballad "New York" (that very elegantly begins and ends with its theme) to the texturally diverse and at times cacophonous "Trio for Trio." The violin and bass duet in "New York" lies in the middle ground between counterpoint and parallel play, punctuated with great subtlety during the second half by Jerome Cooper's drumrolls and bugle calls. "Trio" is laced with inferences from the European avant-garde and a Stravinsky musical quotation.

The diversity of this recording continues with the catchy melody of "Chinese Rock," from which a violin-led open improvisation unfolds; Cooper organizes his drumming into a loosely constructed beat, on which Sirone lays down an infectious dance riff. The title track offers a kalimba-led multi-percussion display featuring bells and vocalizations. The recording concludes with the multi-sectional "Ponderous Planets," which begins with ringing long tones, yet after a poignant, extended trio fantasia and percussion extravaganza, culminates in a section that swings, breaking apart into a freer section guided by Jenkins's breath-length phrases.

●●●

After its two initial recordings, the band released *The Psyche* (1975), followed by a studio album, *The People's Republic* (1976), its most widely circulated recording. The final recording during the band's initial period together was *The Revolutionary Ensemble* (1977); private recordings exist of contemporaneous shows at Tin Palace, September 26, 1976, and April 9, 1977. The band reunited more than a quarter century later, producing the studio recording *And Now . . .* (2004) on June 18, 2004, and a live recording documenting a May 25, 2005, concert in Warsaw, *Beyond the Boundary of Time* (2008). Additional live-performance recordings are in private circulation.

Clearly, access to the Revolutionary Ensemble's music was limited to those who witnessed its live performances and the few who heard its recordings. From an economic perspective, the band lived on the margins, playing together for the sake of making music its members loved.

Musical Form and Structure

Jerome Cooper comments on the group's distinctively cohesive playing:

> When we were really together we were really together. It was almost like a basketball team! We played a concert once—someplace in Cologne—and people wanted to keep the tape and run off. And bam, I went here and Sirone went there. I remember we had grabbed the tapes.
>
> People didn't know what had happened [we were so in synch]. Musically, we were totally in tune. Totally. We didn't have to look at each other. Another thing is we never played a bad concert. We might go to a concert, fighting it out, screaming and yelling, and once we'd hit that bandstand, all the stuff would just go away. We never played a bad concert.[30]

The unique nature of the Revolutionary Ensemble can be first detected in its instrumentation: violin, bass, and percussion (sometimes supplemented by bugle, piano, viola, and harmonica).[31] Trios without a piano are rare outside classical chamber music, no doubt because instruments that can play multiple notes add density to the spare instrumentation. One thinks of Ornette Coleman's 1960s trio with bassist David Izenzon and drummer Charnet Moffett (with Coleman doubling on violin and trumpet). Even saxophonist Lester Young's trio, which had no bass, included a piano, plus drums.

The strength of a two- (or three-) melody-line trio is the ability of its instruments to interweave phrases, if not play counterpoint. If there is a harmonic foundation, it is subtly implied rather than spelled out. This was why the piano-less trio and quartet formations were excellent vehicles for Coleman's harmolodic approach, where melody lines are semiautonomous. Pianist Paul Bley sought similar results in his free-improvisation trios, where the piano's function was to provide an independent melodic voice rather a conventional harmonic foundation. The flexibility of the trio format was well suited to the dynamic approach of the Revolutionary Ensemble, as evidenced throughout the band's first two recorded performances, *Vietnam* and *Manhattan Cycles*.

On *Manhattan Cycles*, the importance of the instrumentation is immediately apparent. We first hear the sound of strings and wood—unmistakably connecting these sounds to their source in the physical instruments. The musical action unfolds quickly: Sirone rapidly sets the stage by playing a rapidly repeated high C, first arco and then pizzicato. Jenkins adds textural pizzicato sounds and then a melody that morphs into an upward arpeggio. His whimsical gestures lead to a rising and falling arco run, from which flows a melodic exposition. Moving into the upper register, Jenkins plays a double stop, repeatedly sliding up and down the neck, as Jerome Cooper enters with quiet taps on the side of a cymbal. Sirone's sonorous arco bass emerges from a brief silent pause. Jenkins joins with lightly bowed figures, and then the two string players race furiously upward, reaching a note that they rapidly repeat, at the top of their ranges. Cooper taps a cymbal in support, and Jenkins adds harmonics as filigree. Sirone returns to his opening figure, which again closes out the section in silence. Next, the band mixes lo-fi sounds of a barely audible recording of Billie Holiday with Cooper's light tapping sounds, to which Jenkins juxtaposes a quiet melody, variations on the song Holiday is singing, now louder, "Lover Man."

Parallel Play as a Mode of Musical Engagement

The balance of the first half of *Manhattan Cycles*, part 1, represents a shift from foregrounded solos with accompaniment to parallel play,[32] in which the three musicians match energy levels and rates of change, but rarely intersect in unison or display conventional harmonic relationships. This is the kind of interplay and group dynamic at which the Revolutionary Ensemble particularly excelled—its own realization of Coleman's theories of intergroup dynamics, simultaneously individualized by each musician while joined together in ensemble. The group creates a breathless speedy gesture that becomes a shared leitmotif, with each player freely expressing variants. Throughout the second half of part 1, all three musicians are fully engaged, listening closely to one another, yet contributing in a manner that betrays little obvious conventional musical dialogue. Instead, there is a shared energy level, evidence of a cooperative construction. Even when vigorous and forceful, the musical glue has qualities that are more inchoate and magical than they are the product of rules governing idiomatic jazz or classical music. Parallel-play construction continues to govern *Manhattan Cycles*, part 2.[33]

A second example of parallel play is in evidence at the opening of *Vietnam*, after a pentatonic melody is played in unison by the strings, repeated, and then extended with a coda. From there, the floodgates open and out flows an energetic violin and bass duet based on the melody, lightly accompanied by Cooper on shimmering cymbals. Jenkins's and Sirone's lines move sometimes in parallel, counterpoint, or parallel play, often sharing aspects of all three. Five minutes later, Jenkins's lines continuously flow forth new material, adding twice- and multiply repeated double stops and scalar runs, while Sirone sculpts continuously unfolding, cascading bass lines, never resting long in one spot. Cooper presses the ensemble's thick, dense energy forward. Near the end of the twenty-three–minute-long part 1, after many ebbs and flows of parallel and sometimes imitative play and an extended bass solo, the trio is back in its trademark integral yet parallel-play ensemble mode.

Parallel play was an approach found to a limited degree in Circle and even less so in Miles Davis's Lost Quintet. The Revolutionary Ensemble had no leader looking in from outside the hub of activity, no Miles Davis to limit musical forays from continuing until their logical end, however anarchic the journey.

Integral Role of the Bassist

Sirone's understanding of his function as the group's bassist is another important feature of the Revolutionary Ensemble. In idiomatic jazz, the bassist's role is to anchor the harmony, keep a metric pulse, and solo when it is time to do so. These distinctions often lose their meaning in the setting of this band. A superficial listen to its recordings might suggest that Leroy Jenkins's violin is the lead instrument, supported by a rhythm section that doesn't seem to keep much rhythm. Certainly, Jenkins's obvious virtuosity is constantly on display. Yet a closer listen clarifies that the band is an integral group of three that, as we have seen, sometimes plays in parallel, with the bassist as an equal partner.

Sirone rarely plays a conventional supportive role, in that he constantly invents and generates new melodic, rhythmic, and textural ideas. In an ensemble dominated by parallel play, distinctions between solo and support can sometimes be obscure. Throughout his solos, Sirone constructs continuously unfolding gestures built from a collection of articulations, performance techniques, and idiomatic elements. Among them are walking melodic lines, often jagged and angular and sometimes stop-start, along with arpeggiated motifs, repeated notes, hints of ostinati, harmonics, double stops, portamenti, and metrically changing lines. Literal repetition is rare, but gestures are treated as material for endless variation and extension. A phrase suggests its antecedent, although the relationship between the two may not be linear or obvious. Stream of consciousness can suddenly give way to surprise turns in direction.

In *Manhattan Cycles*, part 2, the start of Sirone's solo overlaps with Jenkins's. After a while, Sirone's melody briefly suggests qualities of a folk tune, but quickly returns to a more abstract, stop-start, stitched-together alternation of lines and repeated notes and octaves. Later, harmonics lead to a more textural section where Sirone's partners scratch and tap rhythmic patterns as the bassist plays high-pitched portamento lines. Twelve minutes later, Sirone's solo continues unabated, focusing on high pitches and harmonics while the others make further tapping sounds. He then revisits the musical figures that opened part 1, playing a rapidly repeated, high-note arco. Jenkins adds intense, rapid bowed figures, supported by Sirone's fragmentary lines and Cooper's drumming. All three fade out, and a brief segment of recorded instrumental music returns to conclude the performance.

At ten minutes into *Vietnam*, part 2, Sirone provides a five-note bass ostinato, from which he periodically draws while constructing a continuous, forward-moving line. He is joined by Jenkins's fluttering violin and then Cooper's tom-toms and cymbals. He offers glimpses of the ostinato figure along his hesitant walk. Then the drums and violin lay out, leaving him to solo, which he constructs from harmonics and widely angular arco phrases, and then pizzicato articulation. Sirone plays an energetic phrase, pausing to reflect, and continues, next ferociously strumming the strings, before he returns to a more spacious construction, which builds in energy despite the pauses between phrases. High-register double stops are followed by intense melodic phrases and then a return to a more angular, repeated gesture approach. Sirone's solo concludes with strummed strings before shifting to walking bass, joined by Cooper's steady cymbal-ride pulse and then Jenkins's stop-start phrases.

Listening to Sirone is akin to reading James Joyce, where sound, diction, and grammatical construction work in tandem, obscuring familiar roles and expected emphases. With Sirone, the listener should expect invention and surprise.

Texture as a Musical Feature

A third key aspect of the Revolutionary Ensemble's musical approach is attention to texture, the use of sonic qualities as a musical device. A clear example of this is found in *Vietnam*, part 2. Following Jerome Cooper's drum solo, we hear quiet harmonica phrases in the background. In the foreground, Sirone plays sharply articulated, highly amplified fragments of a musical line. Then Leroy Jenkins steps forward with a delicate, harmonic minor solo line, which leads us to the sounds of bird whistles in a forest. Within that sound event, Jenkins plays a melancholy lyrical line, at times echoing the birdlike gestures. A happy/sad harmonica quietly joins Jenkins in a duet, disturbed only briefly by a gong. A bugle phrase appears ever so fleetingly before Sirone enters on arco bass, above which Jenkins hints at the opening melody.

The band's textural interests and the physicality of its instruments come together not only in the spontaneous improvisation but also in the players' choices regarding musical form. Cooper comments:

> My music was based more on what I would call "structured and patterned," because as a drummer I don't rely on B-flat and C-sharp. I have to rely on colors. I would write out a letter A, in which I might say at letter A, I want you to play viola, Leroy—improvise. And we'd move into letter A1, where Sirone would come in with trombone, and then we'd move to letter B, which would be the written-out song—things that would be really written. Then we'd go into letter B2; it would be a variation of, maybe, B. It would be like that.
>
> When I first [started] writing, I used to write my tunes in the old bebop way, meaning you write a melody and improvise off that melody and play the melody and end the song. It wasn't musical from a drummer's point of view. If you took away the harmonization and just left the drums there, it would be totally unmusical.

In its place, Cooper offered structures and instrumentation, reflecting his coloristic interests.

Each of the three musicians composed, and often the works presented unique challenges. Sirone describes the preparation for a reunion concert in 2004: "Leroy had this incredible piece that we didn't even use. It was changing rhythms, damn, every four bars and sometimes every two bars and I'm not talking common 4/4 rhythms. I'm talking about 9/8s, 7/4, 5/4." His reflective conclusion was that "each one of our compositions is very different. But the beautiful thing about it is the freedom to create; get that color; that sound; that expression; that motif, and it comes from the raw spirit; from the soul."[34]

The Revolutionary Ensemble really constructed collective sound paintings. Whether playing a melody, a rhythmic pattern, or a more abstract sonic gesture, the varying qualities of sound itself were central to the band's musical inventions.

Endings

Cooper remembers how tenuous the existence of the Revolutionary Ensemble was: "When we got together—we had no work from 1971 to '75—what kept us together was the music. The Art Ensemble, them cats worked. Air [another AACM-related improvisation ensemble] used to have a lot of gigs. I don't know. Maybe it's because we weren't like a trio. We were three individuals playing. A lot of times, people would come up after the concert and say, 'Leroy, I really like that song you wrote.' And it would piss Leroy off, because it would be my music."

Cooper's observation that the Revolutionary Ensemble was "three individuals playing"—unlike a conventionally conceived band—is a helpful guide to understanding this group. Its music, like everything else about it—its internal process as a group and its face to the world—was informal and collective. This was collaboration in the purist sense. Although compositions could be tagged to individual composers within the group, the spirit of the Revolutionary Ensemble was that of the revolutionary anarchist. As I recall strongly from my own experience seeing the band perform, there was no formal presentation: the band just got up and played. There also was no discernible business plan, because the band played for the sake of making music, doing its best to go from club to club in search of gigs, but often happening into them. And the timing proved right, for a very brief time, for the music of the Revolutionary Ensemble to fit within the vision of a record producer, resulting in a major-label record contract. Yet the band had no marketing scheme, just an ad hoc affixing of posters to light posts, walls, and bulletin boards.

The collaboration was sustained despite strong wills, as Cooper recalls: "So me and Leroy—a lot of people think we argued—we did argue, but we argued about how we were going to go about something, so you've got to get your point across. I loved Leroy. Leroy was really cool." Well-formed musical personalities aside, there was also no front person representing the band. There was just . . . the Revolutionary Ensemble. Sirone's observation about the band's focus and work ethic, that "we rehearsed three days a week: Monday, Wednesday, and Friday—four hours a day, and in-between we'd be looking for jobs, so it was every day, really," is summed up in his conclusion: "But the first thing we thought about was the music."[35]

Love of shared music-making was not enough to keep the Revolutionary Ensemble alive, however, and the group disbanded in 1977. As Cooper recalls, this happened for "a lot of reasons. The main reason was we didn't have no work. There was no work. And the other reason, musically, we were going in different directions. I was going into more of a shamanistic journey. I was hanging out with this Mexican, pre-Columbian drummer, Antonio Zapata. And Sirone was going into theater and moving to Berlin. Leroy was going into a more notated European music." Sirone's interest in the theater continued throughout the rest of his life.[36]

Six years was nonetheless a substantial duration for a band. While the Art Ensemble of Chicago remained together for decades, the Miles Davis Quintet of the '60s lasted five years, Herbie Hancock's Mwandishi band for three, Davis's Lost Quintet for a year and a half, and Circle for less than a year.

Leroy Jenkins passed away in 2007, followed two years later by Sirone. Yet even in the years after the demise of the Revolutionary Ensemble, Jenkins and Cooper's musical bond remained strong. Cooper recalls: "After we broke up, me and Leroy kept playing. We did the Chicago Jazz Festival together as a duet. Leroy would hire me as a composer for his European classical stuff. So I could play through his connections." The drummer's admiration for Jenkins has never faded: "Leroy didn't show off. Very undercut. His shit was really—you know what I mean—he wasn't no show-off cat. He could play his ass off, and he wasn't a show-off." His death came as a shock: "When he passed away, I just got back from Burma—something told me to come back, and Roscoe [Mitchell] called me up and said, 'Leroy died.' I said, 'What?' He said he died of lung cancer. And Leroy didn't smoke that much. That's crazy."

Sirone sums up the experience of all three members of the Revolutionary Ensemble: "It was very difficult even to be alive for the three of us, and it's a miracle in itself playing this music; the dedication that we put towards this music . . . having the rare opportunity to write music like that and have musicians to honestly approach it. That just don't happen every day."[37]

The daily miracle experienced by Sirone very much defines the Revolutionary Ensemble. Yet it is not distant from the ever renewing and evolving musical journeys of Circle and the Miles Davis Lost group. For all three bands, every musical moment was filled with surprise and spontaneity. At the same time, the Revolutionary Ensemble was a far less economically sustainable organization than either of those peer groups. With limited financial expectations, the band played for the sheer joy of making music, seizing whatever opportunities might emerge. Despite its inability to build a listener base beyond its largely informal network of listeners and fellow musicians, the band remained vital for a number of years. And twenty-five years later, it returned for a final, energetic bow.

8

Ornette Coleman's Children

Comparisons and Contrasts Inside and
Outside the Jazz Economy

One goal of this book has been to challenge the oft-perceived aesthetic distance between the early electric work of Miles Davis (often termed "jazz rock") and musicians associated with open improvisation (often termed "free jazz"). In this chapter, I summarize the evidence of shared musical and aesthetic sensibilities between three bands I refer to as "children of Ornette Coleman": the Miles Davis Lost Quintet, Circle, and the Revolutionary Ensemble. The band Circle is presented as an aesthetic bridge between these worlds, while operating, just barely, within the commercial economy of mainstream jazz.

A second goal has been to call attention to the way that the musical economy distorts what would otherwise be shared sensibilities between musicians. From this perspective, what distinguishes the Miles Davis Lost Quintet from music that is often understood to be a world apart (such as the Revolutionary Ensemble) is less connected to musical ideas than to the subculture and economy that each inhabited. In this chapter, we begin with aesthetic comparisons, and then move to economic and cultural distinctions.

Comparative Musical Dynamics: A Summary

The lifeblood of all three bands was collective improvisation and spontaneous invention. A schematic layout of each band's core elements can help elucidate similarities and differences between how these musical values came into play.

Unrestrained Musical Invention

A signpost of all three bands is how strongly each one valued spontaneity. From its inception, the Revolutionary Ensemble privileged free flights of the imagination. It did so within the context of compositions, drawing from unstated rules of engagement that emerged organically through the members' experience of collective improvisation. Circle's early rehearsals and performances were also highly spontaneous, only gradually introducing melodic or rhythmic compositional material as an instigator for improvisation. The rhythm section in Miles Davis's Lost Quintet, the cauldron from which Circle emerged, increasingly moved toward spontaneous generation as the band developed.

The latter two bands, with Chick Corea and Dave Holland (plus their respective drummers) at their collective improvisational centers, bore signifiers of a bebop lineage in at least superficially beginning each segment of playing with compositional elements. To the more conventional listener, this might have sounded like head-solos arrangements, except that the directions the antecedent improvisations took might have followed an internal logic only nominally connected to the "tune" with which the bands' excursions began.

Individual Abandon while Maintaining Group Cohesion

The Revolutionary Ensemble excelled at a dynamic best described as parallel play. This is a performance mode in which all three musicians pursued their own direction while contributing to a shared overall construction. The "glue" for such performance is a combined energy level, density, texture, and sense of shared purpose. Moments of a solo, duet, or trio flight—like a flock of birds traveling in the same general direction, or a swarm of bees moving through space—can be exhilarating, particularly when players dramatically sprint out of the gate with great velocity and intensity, as if the world depended on it. Yet this description oversimplifies the matter, since it might require a very distant vantage point to see each individual musician's playing as part of the larger whole. The whole group functions as a container for the boundless, multidirectional energy projected by individual members.

Such moments of restless individual abandon also can be heard in the Lost Quintet, albeit to a lesser degree. Corea could be heard distinctly going his own way during collective free-for-alls in the rhythm section during the band's late period. Yet Corea, Holland, and Jack DeJohnette, particularly the former two, can also be perceived as deeply interconnected, as if by a tether. Each musician was constantly responding to the smallest rhythmic, melodic, or textural articulations offered by his partners. Each paid close attention to timbre, to subtle changes in sound. The bassist or the drummer might slowly speed up and then slow down, or play double or half time, creating the perception of changes in pace far more dramatic than actual.

The relationships within the Revolutionary Ensemble were equally synergetic, although the specific connections between players are at any given instant more difficult to perceive. The key is to listen for rates of change and energy levels, or how fragments might fit together like a jigsaw puzzle. The "sprint" moments make the interconnections easier to discern. All three bands excelled at close listening and response, be that response obvious or extremely subtle. More than anything, these were deeply listening bands.

Motivic Development, Ostinati, Melodic Contour, and Texture as Structural Devices

Soloists in all three bands tended toward motivic development. This is well within the traditions of John Coltrane, Ornette Coleman, and Cecil Taylor, but also Ludwig van Beethoven. A brief phrase or fragment could be spun upside down, turned inside out, elongated, sliced, and diced. From small amounts of existing material, the soloist sought out opportunities to generate novelty and variation. The first saxophonist in the Lost Quintet, Wayne Shorter, excelled at this method.

Ostinati were a common currency in all three bands. A fragmentary phrase could turn into a repeated figure, which then morphed into something new. Corea built ostinati from notes, chords, or tone clusters. Holland could begin with an ostinato, turn it into a walking line, and head back, only to generate new material that suddenly traveled with a different trajectory. Revolutionary Ensemble members crafted material that could be repeated and varied, but often in an even less predictable manner. In the Lost Quintet, an ostinato could serve as a rhythmic anchor, but this occurred far less frequently in the two other bands.

Literal repetition was less often found within the Revolutionary Ensemble than in the other bands. Beginning with the Lost Quintet and progressing to Circle and later the Revolutionary Ensemble, we find increasing foreground-background relationships between the soloist and the rest of the band. This is distinct from the soloist-accompanist dynamic, where the job of the latter is to support (or at times challenge) the soloist. Corea, Holland, and DeJohnette were gifted accompanists, but as time moved on, their roles moved toward free-wheeling juxtapositions to soloists. Corea and Holland (and Barry Altschul) accomplished both roles with aplomb. The Revolutionary Ensemble, in contrast, was more a parallel-play collective than a group of accompanists for a soloist.

The melodic contours—the shapes of phrases—played by these musicians were often quite angular, and less frequently melodic in a conventional, lyrical manner. Miles Davis is of course an exception, although his playing in the later days of the Lost Quintet and in his subsequent bands became more staccato, sparse, and percussive. The angularity of phrasing was in part an aesthetic movement away from conventional tonality (or a further development of the angularity of bebop), but also an expression of each musician's virtuosity. Every one of the musicians in these bands was capable of profound technical brilliance, but this was across the board, and rarely deployed for display or to impress. Virtuosity—the use of the fullest potential of each instrument—was manifested in sudden changes of melodic shape, tempo, mood, or sonic color, as well as in extended instrumental techniques, and the sheer velocity of notes and density of sounds made manifest at any given moment.

Texture was of profound interest to all three bands, albeit accessed in different ways. Listening to their recordings, we become aware of the players' consciousness of the sound of their instruments—the literal materials from which instruments are constructed (wood, gut, metal), and the sonic possibilities (shimmering cymbals, plucked violin strings, finger-muted piano strings struck by the piano hammers). The sonic palate was always broad: Revolutionary Ensemble members doubled on trumpet, harmonica, trombone; Circle's registers and percussive sounds ranged widely (smallest to largest saxophones, whistles); and in the Lost Quintet, electronic treatment of the electric piano and bass steadily increased, changing the sonic qualities of the group's music.

Despite their differences, the three bands are linked through interconnective musical tissue, chiefly the groups' priority given to sound, texture, spontaneity, and close listening, and their dynamic collective engagement, flexible use of compositional materials, angularity of melody, flexibility in the treatment of time, and motivic development. All three were fundamentally process-oriented groups. The title of Herbie Hancock's Mwandishi composition (and the title of my book about that band),[1] "You'll Know When You Get There," aptly expresses their shared core theme.

The Revolutionary Ensemble

The band may be understood as a combination of three integral, coequal voices engaging in spontaneous invention. It presented a dynamically changing presentation of melodic and textural material and ideas.

Modes of engagement

Parallel play in which one to three players simultaneously explore ideas— matching energy levels and rates of change rather than melody. Rarely are there unison passages, melodic intersections, or conventional harmonic relationships.

Model for solos is foreground-background rather than soloist-accompanists; minimal referencing of harmonic relations or overt metric pulse

Duo or trio "sprints"—simultaneous non-unison rapid playing, sometimes in stop-start manner

Cooperative stitching together of phrases; each player sequentially interpolates fragmentary material to create a whole fabric

Whimsy as a musical value; changes in mood, feel, texture

Spontaneous improvisation; sometimes compositions serve as a starting point for improvisation

Use of ostinati, sometimes just hinted at; changing and odd rhythms such as 9/8, 7/4, 5/4

Musical materials

Texture: emphasizing sounds of the physical instruments—sounds of strings and wood, plucking and bowing, shimmering cymbals, skins

Motivic development: melodic figures or fragments treated as material for endless variation and extension; slow morphs into new, related phrases; limited literal repetition

Multiple instruments: trumpet, harmonica, trombone, in addition to violin, bass, and percussion

Juxtaposition of recorded source material (such as Billie Holiday's "Lover Man" in *Manhattan Cycles*) on which the players offer musical commentary

Broadly exploiting the virtuosic potential of each instrument

> Leroy Jenkins: a wide range of bowing techniques, rapid movement of fingers on the neck, double stops, portamenti
>
> Sirone: asymmetrical, jagged and angular walks, sometimes stop-start and changing rates of speed; arpeggiated figures, repeated notes, harmonics, double stops, portamenti
>
> Jerome Cooper: wide range of percussive sounds—shimmering cymbals, tom-toms—and techniques—rolls, fills, combinations, phrases

Circle

Spontaneous organic improvisations; "open-mind," intuitively unfolding forms; simple instructions used as a guide (tempo changes, endings of sections); compositions used as jump-off points for improvisation

Modes of engagement

Alternating instrument combinations: solos, duos, trios, or quartet

Changing roles of players: solos with accompaniment, foreground-background (unconventional accompaniment); parallel play; use of silence

Each player pays keen attention to the support needs of a soloist; punctuating evocative moments, filling in spaces, allowing silence; providing material as "fodder"

Close listening and response to sound and gestural shapes: textures, melodic contours, rhythmic patterns, energy levels, phrase and pattern lengths, pace of movement of a phrase, dynamic levels

Spontaneously building musical materials, beginning with a melodic or rhythmic cell, which is examined and explored for its implications

Communally constructed tension and release, sometimes instigated by one individual

Musical materials

Use of modernist techniques: atonality and pointillism; attack and decay of notes; phrase lengths; rapid speed figures; angularity; rapid repetition of single notes

Ostinati as building blocks for musical material

Texture as a reference point for responding to the sounds played by others

Broad use of instrumental techniques and virtuosity

> Chick Corea: tone clusters, rapid string of notes, attention to register on the piano (high-low), glissandi on the strings, muted notes (stopped with a finger on the piano strings)
>
> Dave Holland: arco, pizzicato, repeated note figures (and in the early recordings, guitar), angular walks, sudden or gradual contrasts in tempo
>
> Barry Altschul: broad range of sounds and instruments, including conventional traps, plus whistles, vibraphone, temple blocks, bells, kalimba, conch shells
>
> Anthony Braxton: reed instruments ranging across many registers (contrabass to sopranino saxophones, contrabass to B♭ clarinets); use of extended techniques, from vocally screeching into the horns to overblown notes, sharply angular lines

Compositions used as a launching point for improvisation. Some were from the jazz repertoire. Band member compositions were at times based on rhythmic patterns: Holland's "Q&A," Corea's "Rhymes," Braxton's "Composition 6F" ("73 Degrees Kelvin").

Miles's Lost Quintet

A trumpet-fronted ensemble. While not a collective, the band increasingly comes to draw from an increasingly collective improvisatory process. There is a shift toward increasingly complex, abstract, and electronic sounds and, at times, a stronger pulse.

Modes of engagement

Subunits within the quintet: intense interplay first between Chick Corea and Jack DeJohnette, then between Corea and Holland, and often between all three. Corea and Holland increasingly enmeshed as an integral team

Soloists are supported in a foreground-background model of accompaniment, yet over time, there is an increasingly abstract collective improvisation within the rhythm section, particularly when Shorter or Corea is the soloist. In contrast, support for Davis's solos tends to be more linear, with a more clearly defined beat.

Use of imitation; "cat and mouse" model; call and response; one musician filling
   in the spaces left by another
Davis draws from new forms of composition: vamp based or structured as a
   series of musical events
Use of musical cues to signal shifts from one tune to the next

Musical materials

Broad use of instrumental techniques and virtuosity

Jack DeJohnette: mastery of the full drum kit; constantly altered
   patterns and subpatterns within the beat; virtuosic display of fills;
   variations in kinds of cymbal sounds
Chick Corea: chromaticism and tone clusters; phrases constructed
   using major and minor seconds; increasing electronic processing of Fender Rhodes electric piano to alter its volume,
   timbre, and sonic placement within the ensemble; playful
   alteration of core elements of compositions, particularly the
   figures within "Bitches Brew"; shifts between linear lines and
   dissonance
Dave Holland: sonic elements include arco, pizzicato, scraping the
   strings while playing arco; increasing use of electric bass, sometimes with wah-wah
   stylistic elements: shifting back and forth between walks and
   constantly shifting ostinato; increasing use of rapidly repeated
   notes; interlocking with Corea's ostinato patterns; gradually
   changing speed during passages; turning on a dime into double
   time and back; responding from moment to moment to each
   soloist, particularly Corea; assuming responsibility for holding
   the meter tight, allowing space for virtuosic displays by the
   percussionists
Later additions to the band:
         Airto Moreira: percussion instruments with both rhyth-
      mic and sonic characteristics
         Keith Jarrett: washes of electric/electronic sound,
      sometimes on two keyboards played simultaneously;
      wah-wah inflections; complex atonal juxtapositions to
      Corea

Use of ostinati

> Chick Corea: builds ostinati from single-note lines or from chords; fills in the spaces left by soloists in moments some-times as short as a breath
>
> Dave Holland: repeated fragments and variants of ostinati
>
> Jack DeJohnette: constant variation of related materials, inserted within and built around straight pulse and, some-times, abstraction

Economics and the Business of Jazz

It is in their relationship to the music business that comparisons between these three bands become more complex. Miles Davis remained under contract with Columbia Records from the mid-1950s through the 1970s, and was widely viewed as a cultural figure bordering on celebrity. When a Davis band was booked at clubs, concert halls, or festivals, it was actually Davis as bandleader who was hired, and who commanded attention. He could attract substantial pay, and his Columbia contract afforded him the ability to record essentially at will. Thus, he and his musicians were steadily on the road, and his varying projects (except for the Lost Quintet) continually recorded in the studio. His record-ings were produced by Teo Macero, an expert editor who could, sometimes on his own initiative, shape session recordings into marketable products. Those records, along with the public concert appearances, were strongly promoted with the resources that a major label could bring to bear. And a Davis recording or performance guaranteed critical attention.

One marvel of Miles Davis's work during this period was his successful navi-gation of the jazz, pop, and rock aesthetic and economic worlds while maintain-ing many musical values from open improvisation. Something similar has rarely been possible. Davis's 1960s quintet pianist, Herbie Hancock, gained and lost a contract with Warner Brothers Records while engaging in open improvisation on the jazz club circuit. In part thanks to the Davis pedigree, his Mwandishi band—like Circle—could access bookings, but was ultimately unable to re-main financially viable.[2]

During this period (the early 1970s), the Revolutionary Ensemble and An-thony Braxton maintained relationships with record companies, club owners, and festival promoters that ebbed and flowed. Often, there was little money to be made. Support was dependent on contributions at the door and—when available—grants and outside jobs.[3] Braxton's fortunes changed briefly while he was under contract on Arista's Freedom label from 1974 to 1980, and again much later in his career. The Art Ensemble of Chicago, whose members were, like those of the Revolutionary Ensemble, members of the Association for the Advancement of Creative Musicians, provides an interesting comparison with respect to record contracts; its great strength derived at least in part from its commitment as a group to self-sustenance as a collective enterprise.[4]

Circle, largely because it had two former Davis band members in its lineup, participated in the more mainstream jazz economy it shared with Miles Davis: clubs and concert halls. Yet *The Paris Concert* was, among its recordings released under the name Circle, the only one to garner attention;[5] the two trio recordings and two double-album studio compilations are attributed to Chick Corea.

After the demise of Circle, Anthony Braxton and Barry Altschul situated themselves squarely within a more experimental and thus economically contingent world of the jazz lofts. Their performances depended on the advocacy of visionary producers and promoters.[6] Corea, who had always played in the clubs, remained on that circuit. Free Life Communication members Dave Liebman—Corea's and Dave Holland's building mate—and Steve Grossman successfully made the transition from lofts to joining Miles Davis, in 1973 and 1970, respectively. While still with Free Life, Liebman had straddled at least two worlds: lofts plus rock halls with Ten Wheel Drive, and the jazz circuit with Elvin Jones. Holland's first recordings on ECM (beginning with *Conference of the Birds* in 1972) presaged his move away from the loft scene and his subsequent rise as a successful jazz musician on the club and festival circuits.

Musicians playing the lofts of the 1970s did not generally view themselves as inhabiting the same musical universe as Miles Davis. Bassist William Parker reflects a sense of frustration: "Before the late 1970s if you played with well known artists there was no guarantee, unless it was Miles Davis or that crowd, that you were going to step up."[7] What Parker means is that building a career with broader visibility and economic success in that decade relied on a musician's playing with a band of Davis's level of reputation, audience draw, and commercial backing.

Some hurled their strong frustration at Davis when he began playing electric instruments and playing rock venues. Val Wilmer quotes drummer Billy Higgins (at times a band member of Ornette Coleman's): "Take somebody slick as Miles Davis. They wired him up with all that electricity and shit only because that's what the media demanded."[8] The frustration is understandable yet ironic, given the aesthetic leanings of Davis's first electric band. The challenge facing musicians off the commercial grid was as much the success of Miles Davis as the failure of the jazz economy to make room for musicians playing more exploratory music. There are exceptions among those who had already built solid reputations, and thus could sell records and book venues that paid decent fees. The experience of Circle, aesthetically straddling the worlds of jazz and more experimental music, provides an interesting case study of the challenge faced by those who brought less conventional music into the broader marketplace.

Even while Davis began to address a potentially larger popular audience in 1972 with *On the Corner*, his work of the subsequent three years never left behind the freewheeling nature of the Lost Quintet. This spirit was rekindled within a new context in his 1974–75 band with guitarist Pete Cosey. While high-volume, sustained organ "haze" and a multiplicity of beats drawn from funk may seem more populist at least on the surface, the interplay of multiple voices can be heard as yet another "take" on open improvisation. Davis continued to balance major-label sponsorship with unconventional music-making throughout this period.

Is This "Jazz"? Circle in the Eyes of the Critics

Circle's presence in the clubs led to audiences and the jazz press viewing its music through the lens of mainstream commercial expectations of how "jazz" should sound. Audiences varied in their degree of openness, as Barry Altschul recalls: "The San Francisco clubs—the Keystone, the Both/And—and Shelly's [Manne Hole] was cool. I mean, it was okay. It was different for them [the audiences], but they were open to it. [The audience reactions] depended." He also remembers success stories: "[Saxophonist] Gary Bartz's father used to run a wonderful series of jazz concerts in Baltimore, at his theater. Circle played there for a real bebop audience. Let's just say they weren't hostile and malicious. Surprised, questioning, and 'what the fuck is this?' And that was where Braxton sawed a chair in half to a rhythm. [All the audience could tell was the] sound of the saw, so they didn't know what was happening. . . . We even played a state fair in Utah, in Mormon country." European audiences were generally more receptive.[9]

The support of surprised but tolerant audiences was not what the band found in some other venues. Recall *DownBeat*'s observation that a fall 1970 performance at the Lighthouse in San Francisco "reported a noticeable drop in business as the Chick Corea Quartet, known as Circle, followed Joe Henderson. The diet seemed to be too avant-garde for the Hermosa Beach crowd."[10] *Down-Beat* writer Leonard Feather summed up his response to the band in his review of one of its final, August 1971 performances, referring to it as virtuosic and communicative among its players, yet neither comprehensible nor emotionally connecting with its audience.[11]

The lightning rod for the critical attack on Circle was Anthony Braxton, player of the instrument bearing the heaviest weight of traditionalist expectations but least personally attached to the label "jazz." In 1970, Braxton had recently returned from a sojourn in Paris only three years after his recording debut. Just two years separated this time from the release of his celebrated solo recording, *For Alto*. Although *DownBeat* writer John Litweiler wrote glowingly about his early performances in Chicago,[12] Braxton's sonic approach became a point of critical attack, as Leonard Feather sarcastically asserted in the *Los Angeles Times*: "Undoubtedly the sounds that seemed ugly and freakish to me were quite meaningful to others, particularly his colleagues."[13]

It is telling that Circle's one African American member, Anthony Braxton, drew the most heat from the critics. Chick Corea and Dave Holland had established jazz "creds" from their association with Miles Davis, and Barry Altschul had built a reputation playing with Paul Bley. All three were white musicians who musically assimilated African American music. Corea holds that he tended to ignore the press's reactions to Circle.[14] Critic Denis Constant proposed that what listeners found compelling in the group had "more to do with the Occident—white America and Europe—than with the continents of color."[15] This statement coupled with Feather's questioning the legitimacy of Braxton's tone and articulation calls into question whether the criticisms were racially coded. If Braxton were not black, would his critics have challenged him as stringently? Why did they not accept him as eclectic or even in part informed by "white America and Europe"?[16] Graham Lock reminds us that black critics, among them Amiri Baraka, Stanley Crouch, and Ted Joans, subsequently attacked Braxton precisely for his European influences and interests, questioning the legitimacy of his blackness.[17]

Miles Davis's Lost Quintet and the Critics

The intensity and dynamism of the Lost Quintet were not lost on audiences and critics. Its fall 1969 European tour was much heralded. A critic from *Frankfurter Neue Press* lauded the band's November 7 concert in Berlin: "The electric piano provides the ideal for the wind instruments and determines the tonal colour. In this way Miles Davis and his saxophonist Wayne Shorter produced improvisations with a degree of maturity and melodic beauty which can have few parallels in the history of jazz."[18] A *DownBeat* critic enthused: "On this night he played like a god."[19] Equally stellar raves followed the expanded band's spring 1970 shows. The *New York Times*' John S. Wilson wrote: "Mr. Davis was a commanding figure as he blew typically crisp, sputtering phrases, mixed with sudden, keen leaps over a rumble of exotic rhythmic patterns, disappearing into the black murk of the Fillmore stage when his solo was finished and eventually emerging again to reassert his leadership."[20]

On those June evenings in 1970, the Davis Septet opened for singer-songwriter Laura Nyro, who greatly admired Davis. Her father, trumpeter Lou Nigro, recalls, however, that the Fillmore East was nearly empty for Miles's warmly received sets, in sharp contrast to the tremendous ovations for his daughter.[21] Not infrequently, rock audiences milled around outdoors or in the entrance hall of rock theaters during jazz sets, talking and smoking marijuana.[22] They attended shows to see the performances of their favorite rock bands, not to hear warm-up groups, particularly when they played unfamiliar music.[23] However, Michael Cuscuna recalls: "I was there and I don't remember that [most of the audience milling around] to be the case. The Fillmore East audience was always open and appreciative. Certainly some abandoned their seats when Miles took the stage, but others did so when Neil Young took the stage.[24] It was a revolving audience but always a respectful one."[25] Chris Albertson suggested to his *DownBeat* readers that the young rock audience at a July 25 concert at Madison Square Garden (where Davis's group was opening for Blood, Sweat and Tears) "showed signs of not fully appreciating Miles' music . . . but the 44-year old trumpet master continues to win over new followers from their ranks." Albertson pointed out: "The rhythm section and its driving force, Jack De Johnette [*sic*] can teach the rocksters more than a thing or two."[26] Miles Davis himself reports a substantial audience at the Fillmore West in April: "When we first started playing, people were walking around and talking. But after a while they all got quiet and really got into the music."[27] Regardless of whether the audiences were listening closely, the concert bookings available to Davis were rarely accessible to bands playing the lofts.

The recording *Bitches Brew* also had its champions. Writing in the *New York Times*, Carman Moore declared it "a landmark of recorded music."[28] But it also had its detractors. From Albert Goldman's review for the same newspaper:

> [In] "Bitches Brew" and at a recent appearance at the Fillmore, Davis sought to match the energy of the rock bands with an electric rhythm section that sounded as though it was playing the hectic holes on computer punch cards.

Shrilling into the trumpet's highest register with the bell of his horn plugged straight into the mike, Davis struck a musical ice pick into the kids' ears for the better part of an hour. Whatever one thought of the performance—which equated for this listener with the hot flashes of musical menopause—it was obvious the flamboyant jazz star was out to woo the youth audience with something they would not dismiss as merely "jazz."[29]

Echoing the "it's not jazz, it's rock music" chorus, Goldman presented what might be read as a scornful hope that young rock audiences might be led to jazz through their exposure to "pop jazz styles" (and it is not clear that he included Miles Davis): "Today, instead of resting secure on the basis of a mature public that has kept step with it, jazz must look for its survival to youth, which has been denied the opportunity to hear and enjoy the music in its most accessible forms. One can hope that the revival of pop jazz styles will provide the listening education needed to appreciate the more difficult but more rewarding hard-core styles."[30]

In addition to jazz purists, there were black cultural writers who felt that elements of rock music, particularly its electric instruments, diluted the authenticity of African American culture. At a time when engagement with black identity was viewed as an important response to a community under stress, Ron Welburn declared in 1971: "[Rock musicians emerged from] a technological lineage extending through John Cage, Stockhausen, Edgard Varese, all the way back to Marconi and the wireless. White rock is a technology, not a real music. . . . Black musicians should re-evaluate the technological intrusions now threatening our music; times may come when that technology will be useless. Our music is our key to survival."[31]

Seemingly absent from the talk of genre and technology was an acknowledgment of musical affinities between the Lost Quintet and other exploratory bands that had come out of the work of Ornette Coleman and the AACM. The world was afire with the pros and cons of "jazz rock." Yet the emerging hyphenated music called jazz-rock or jazz-fusion, building its audience within white youth culture, symbolizes a very real economic and cultural divide. What maintained the distance between Miles Davis and loft-oriented musicians such as the Revolutionary Ensemble and Anthony Braxton was differences that shared aesthetic sensibilities could not bridge. This is not to say that Davis "sold out," as some have claimed, but that his music, irrespective of its aesthetics, had become part of the Columbia Records brand. This surely explains why Columbia never recorded the Lost Quintet in the studio, and why Teo Macero crafted marketable structures from seemingly untamable material generated within the *Bitches Brew* sessions and the June 1970 Fillmore East concerts.

The new Miles Davis bands of 1971–73 and Circle can be viewed as contrasting visions of where the music of the 1969–70 Lost Quintet could theoretically have led. But without the corporate interest that followed Davis, the music of Circle—and the Revolutionary Ensemble—rarely if ever faced parallel marketing questions. Certainly, the high value that those bands placed on spontaneity allowed for limited consideration of postproduction work. But the bottom-line issue was economic: major-label record producers would only have considered how best to present this music if they considered it worthy of their investment. And therein lies a key distinction between the early 1970s work of Miles Davis and bands that I view as his aesthetic peers, fellow "children of Ornette Coleman."

Despite his position in the upper echelon of the jazz economy, Miles Davis always remained Miles Davis, a strong black man asserting his place as a creative musician. In this respect, he was no different from members of the Revolutionary Ensemble if not Anthony Braxton. Recall the metaphor offered by Greg Tate in chapter 1: "Miles' music makes you think of Nat Turner, proud without being loud because it was about plotting insurrection. In this sense Miles never changed. His agenda remained the same from day one: stay ahead."[32]

Timeline

1967

March: Chick Corea performs and records with the Stan Getz
    Quartet and with the Cal Tjader Septet
Spring: Barry Altschul tours and records with the Paul Bley Trio
May–July: Miles Davis Quintet records studio sessions
October: Keith Jarrett and Jack DeJohnette tour with the Charles
    Lloyd Quartet; Chick Corea records with the Donald Byrd
    Sextet (including Miroslav Vitous and others)
October–November: The Miles Davis Quintet tours Europe;
    Musica Elettronica Viva (MEV), formed in 1966, remains
    centered in Rome and performs throughout Europe

1968 Warren Smith's Studio WIS is in active operation at 151 West
Twenty-First Street, New York City; Steve Lacy performs with MEV
in its Rome constellation of personnel before returning to the States,
where MEV is to be reconstituted

February: Dave Holland records *Karyobin* in London with John Stevens's Spontaneous Music Ensemble

March: Chick Corea records *Now He Sings, Now He Sobs* with Miroslav Vitous and Roy Haynes

March–April: Anthony Braxton records *3 Compositions of New Jazz* with Leroy Jenkins, Leo Smith, and Muhal Richard Abrams

May: Kunle Mwanga moves from Paris to New York and opens Liberty House; income will help finance concerts at the "Peace Church"

May–June: Miles Davis Quintet plays studio sessions

July: Miroslav Vitous temporarily replaces bassist Ron Carter in the Miles Davis Quintet; Davis hears Dave Holland at Ronnie Scott's club in London, where Jack DeJohnette is also playing, with the Bill Evans trio

August: Dave Holland becomes Davis's bassist; Herbie Hancock plays final shows with the Miles Davis Quintet at Count Basie's in New York

September: Chick Corea replaces Hancock; Holland and Corea each play their first studio session with Davis (*Filles de Kilimanjaro*)

October: Holland plays with John McLaughlin, Jack DeJohnette, and an unidentified pianist; Keith Jarrett Trio records performances at Shelly's Manne-Hole

November: Miles Davis holds multiple electric keyboard studio sessions; Jarrett and DeJohnette go on tour with Charles Lloyd Quartet

December: Davis, with Holland, Corea, Wayne Shorter, and Tony Williams, perform in Boston and Montreal; this is Holland's and Corea's first live date together with Davis; Davis makes first attempts at live shows with two electric pianos (pairing Corea with, at separate shows, Wynton Kelly and Stanley Cowell); Jack DeJohnette records *The DeJohnette Complex* with Stanley Cowell, Bennie Maupin, Miroslav Vitous, and others

1969 Musica Elettronica Viva (MEV) releases its first recording; members Richard Teitelbaum and Frederic Rzewski return to the United States; Anthony Braxton records *For Alto* in Chicago; Anthony Braxton, Leroy Jenkins, and Leo Smith leave Chicago for Paris, where they have their premiere performance in a quartet with Steve McCall at the Theatre du Lucernaire

January: Dave Liebman moves into a loft at 138 West Nineteenth Street, which becomes the center of activity for what becomes Free Life Communication

February: Recording sessions for *In a Silent Way*, and Tony Williams makes his final appearances with the Miles Davis Quintet. By this time, he has formed Tony Williams Lifetime. Jack DeJohnette tours Europe with Stan Getz (with Miroslav Vitous and Stanley Cowell)

March: After periodically sitting in for Tony Williams, Jack DeJohnette becomes the quintet's drummer, joining Corea and Holland to form a completely new rhythm section; quintet has shows in Rochester, New York

April–May: Miles Davis Quintet has shows at the Village Gate in NYC; "Miles Runs the Voodoo Down" enters the band's repertoire

May: Jack DeJohnette records on Joe Henderson's *Power to the People*, with Herbie Hancock, Ron Carter, and others; Chick Corea records *Is* with Dave Holland, Jack DeJohnette, and others

June: Miles Davis Quintet performs at the Plugged Nickel (Chicago) and the Blue Coronet (Brooklyn, NY)

July: The quintet goes on US and European tour

August: Miles Davis's *Bitches Brew* recording sessions are under way with an expanded band

August–September: Wayne Shorter records *Super Nova* with Chick Corea, Jack DeJohnette, John McLaughlin, Airto Moreira, and others; Dave Holland moves into a loft in Dave Liebman's building at 138 West Nineteenth Street; Chick Corea follows soon after

September: Anthony Braxton records *B-X0 NO-47A* with Leo Smith, Leroy Jenkins, and Steve McCall

October: Braxton performs with Jenkins and Smith, and meets members of Musica Elettronica Viva at Festival Actuel in Amougies, Belgium

October–November: Miles Davis's Lost Quintet goes on European tour; plays studio sessions with expanded band (including percussionist Airto Moreira)

October: Jack DeJohnette, Herbie Hancock, John McLaughlin, and others record Miroslav Vitous's *Mountain in the Clouds*

November: Barry Altschul records with the Paul Bley Synthesizer Show

1970 Anthony Braxton, Leroy Jenkins, and Jerome Cooper each return to the United States from Europe and move to New York City; the Revolutionary Ensemble begins to rehearse at Ornette Coleman's Artists House and at Fred Brown's loft, both in New York City

January–February: Miles Davis records in the studio with an expanded band

February–March: MEV with Anthony Braxton performs at the Brooklyn
  Academy of Music and tours the Midwest

March: Wayne Shorter plays his final concerts in the Miles Davis Quintet at
  the Fillmore East, NYC; Airto Moreira joins the band

April: Miles Davis Quintet performs at the Fillmore West, San Francisco, with
  Steve Grossman on saxophone; Miles Davis holds *Tribute to Jack Johnson*
  recording sessions with Michael Henderson; Chick Corea's trio with
  Dave Holland and Barry Altschul holds first recording sessions (for *The
  Song of Singing*, and other material that is released later on *Circling In* and
  Circulus); Jack DeJohnette records *Have You Heard?* with Gary Peacock
  and Bennie Maupin

May: Miles Davis studio sessions include Keith Jarrett, Steve Grossman, Jack
  DeJohnette, and others; Anthony Braxton, Leroy Jenkins, Leo Smith, and
  others perform the "Peace Church" concert in New York; Braxton sits in
  with Chick Corea, Dave Holland, and Barry Altschul at the Village Vanguard

June: Miles Davis's band plays concerts at the Fillmore East with two electric
  keyboardists, Chick Corea and Keith Jarrett; holds first recording sessions
  of material to be released on *Live-Evil*

July–August: Miles Davis's Lost Septet plays its final concerts, with Gary
  Bartz on saxophone

August: Chick Corea and Anthony Braxton, among others, participate in the
  recording of Marion Brown's *Afternoon of a Georgia Faun*; Circle plays
  early recording sessions

September–October: Circle tours California; Chick Corea records *The Sun*
  with Jack DeJohnette, Dave Holland, and Steve Grossman. Miles Davis's
  band goes on tour, now including Michael Henderson (electric bass) and
  Keith Jarrett (electric keyboards) in place of Dave Holland and Chick
  Corea; Gary Bartz remains on saxophone and Airto Moreira on percussion; Jumma Santos is added as an additional percussionist

November: Circle tours Europe; Anthony Braxton plays in Gordon Mumma's
  "Communication in a Noisy Environment" at Automation House, New
  York City, with David Behrman and Leroy Jenkins

December: Miles Davis's new quintet plays four nights at the Cellar Door in
  Washington, DC, joined by John McLaughlin at the final show; Jack De-
  Johnette, Herbie Hancock, and others record Josef Zawinul's *Zawinul*

1971 The Revolutionary Ensemble rehearses at the Annex, connected to the
Public Theater in New York City. Likely dates are on the horizon for concerts at

the Public Theater and an extended engagement at Mercer Arts Center, New York City. Jack DeJohnette records *Compost (Take Off Your Body)* with Bob Moses and others

January: Chick Corea's trio with Dave Holland and Barry Altschul records *A.R.C.*

February: Circle's *The Paris Concert* is recorded live; Anthony Braxton makes recordings in the studio, to be released as *The Complete Braxton*. Dave Liebman records on Elvin Jones's *Genesis* and, with Steve Grossman and Chick Corea, Jones's *Merry-Go-Round*

March: Circle tours Europe; Miles Davis band launches East Coast tour

April: Corea makes his first solo piano recordings; Braxton performs in Paris; Davis band begins West Coast tour

May: Circle records *The Gathering* in New York City; Miles Davis West Coast tour continues

July: Circle has final performances, in California; Jack DeJohnette leaves the Miles Davis band and forms Compost

October–November: Miles Davis band returns to the road, touring Europe with Ndugu Leon Chancler on drums in place of DeJohnette. Keith Jarrett will depart in December

1972

February: Chick Corea records *Return to Forever*, with Joe Farrell, Stanley Clarke, Airto Moreira, and Flora Purim; Anthony Braxton records *Saxophone Improvisations Series F.*

March: Corea records on Stan Getz's *Captain Marvel*; the Revolutionary Ensemble records a live performance, released as *Vietnam*

May: Corea performs with Return to Forever at Carnegie Hall; Anthony Braxton performs at the Town Hall Concert, with Dave Holland, Philip Wilson, Barry Altschul, and others

June: Sam Rivers moves his studio downtown in New York City, naming it Studio Rivbea

June–July: Miles Davis records *On the Corner* with Chick Corea, Jack DeJohnette, Dave Liebman, Michael Henderson, and others; New York Musicians Jazz Festival is held at Studio Rivbea as an alternative to George Wein's Newport Jazz Festival

July: Liebman and Steve Grossman record on Elvin Jones's *Mr. Jones*; Barry Altschul plays in jam session with Sam Rivers in Central Park

Late 1972: Dave Holland and Barry Altschul join the Sam Rivers Quartet

September: Dave Liebman and Steve Grossman go on tour with Elvin Jones, documented on *Live at the Lighthouse*. Miles Davis band tours the United States with Al Foster on drums, joining bassist Michael Henderson, plus Carlos Garnett on saxophone, Cedric Lawson on electric keyboards, Reggie Lucas on guitar, Khalil Balakrishna on sitar, and two percussionists: James Mtume Forman and tabla player Badal Roy

October: Chick Corea records second Return to Forever album

October–November: Barry Altschul records on *Paul Bley and Scorpio*. Miles Davis records in the studio while recovering from an automobile accident; these sessions continue sporadically through January 1973

November: Dave Holland records *Conference with the Birds* with Sam Rivers, Anthony Braxton, and Barry Altschul

December: Dave Holland Quartet performs at Studio Rivbea; one of the performances includes Paul Bley. The Revolutionary Ensemble's recorded live performance is released in 1973 as *Manhattan Cycles*

1973

April: Jerome Cooper performs with the Sam Rivers Trio (including Cecil McBee). Miles Davis world tour begins, with Pete Cosey, Dave Liebman, Al Foster, and others; Davis remains on the road steadily through July 1, 1975

June: Sam Rivers Trio performs at Ornette Coleman's Artists House

July: Barry Altschul is one of two percussionists performing with Sam Rivers

Reconsidering *Miles Davis at Fillmore: Live at the Fillmore East* (1970) in Light of *Miles at the Fillmore* (2014)

The March 2014 release of *Miles at the Fillmore* (henceforth abbreviated MDF2014) allows a broad listening public to hear complete, unedited recordings of the June 17–20, 1970, shows given at the Fillmore East by Miles Davis's "Lost" Quintet. The contrast between these unedited recordings and the contemporaneously released *Miles Davis at Fillmore: Live at the Fillmore East* (henceforth LFE1970), heavily edited by producer Teo Macero, is eye opening.

Now we can easily and closely examine the extent of Macero's postproduction work in the music that we've come to identify as live performances. As we listen, we also can assess the nature of Macero's enterprise as editor and producer: his approach superimposes a kind of compositional process reflective of the structuring of the 1970 *Bitches Brew* studio recording. The unedited recordings offer clear evidence for the depth of musical affinity between the "Lost" Quintet and ensembles associated with experimental music. In contrast, Macero's edited versions deemphasize the band's leanings toward these musical values.

LFE1970 was released the same year that the June concerts were held, and packaged as a document encapsulating the four performance evenings. Macero pared the four sets down to what could fit on a marketable double album, twenty- to twenty-five minutes per side. If you listen to both discs, you will find a cross section of the set lists within the tracks simply labeled "Wednesday Miles," "Thursday Miles," "Friday Miles," and "Saturday Miles." The only constant across each evening's program on the recording is "It's About That Time" and, on three nights, "Bitches Brew." Macero focuses on producing shortened versions of two tunes per evening, freely drawing from segments—often very short slices—of other tunes to craft an organic whole. These brief segments are used to offer contrast or provide segues between the lengthier segments. Macero's editorial technique simulates Davis's own inclination to alternate freewheeling improvisations or up-tempo tunes with brief ballads ("The Mask" incorporates both types, in that it slows down midstream).

"Wednesday Miles" and "Thursday Miles" comprise the first half of the sets, starting with the usual set openers: the rapid-paced "Directions" and the slower-tempo "The Mask," followed by "It's About That Time," a vehicle for freely combining vamp-based playing and open improvisation. "Thursday Miles" includes just these first three tunes. "Friday Miles" and "Saturday Miles" focus on the second half of each evening's program, beginning with "It's About That Time."[1] Most of the sets conclude with "Bitches Brew" (which appears on three nights); the brief "The Theme" forms a coda to conclude every evening's set, as was Davis's general practice.

While the ensemble at the time of the Fillmore performances was a septet fronted by two horns, Miles Davis (trumpet) and Steve Grossman (saxophone), Grossman's role is substantially diminished on LFE1970 in favor of Davis's centrality as soloist. His saxophone solos are retained in "Directions," "The Mask," and "It's About That Time" ("Wednesday Miles" and "Friday Miles"), "The Mask" ("Friday Miles"), and "Willie Nelson ("Saturday Miles"), with just ten seconds of his solo retained in Thursday's "It's About That Time." They are removed entirely from "Bitches Brew" on Wednesday, Friday, and Saturday, and from "Directions" and "The Mask" on Thursday (with the trace of a solo noted earlier remaining in "It's About That Time"). Grossman's most extensive presence is his solo on "The Mask" on Friday and "Willie Nelson" on Saturday, both of which are unedited. He also appears on flute as part of a collective improvisation on "It's About That Time" on "Wednesday Miles" and "Thursday Miles."

The only complete tracks included on LFE1970 are "The Mask" on "Thursday Miles" and "Bitches Brew" and "Sanctuary" on "Friday Miles." In contrast,

"Directions" is shortened from its original 10-plus minutes to 2½ minutes on "Wednesday Miles" and 5½ minutes on "Thursday Miles." Thursday night's "Spanish Key," unusual in its presence on the road and as a rare encore, doesn't appear in Macero's edited version. Davis used the brief ballads "I Fall in Love Too Easily" and "Sanctuary," slightly compacted by Macero, as a change of pace between tunes that were improvisationally freewheeling and often faster (with the exception of "The Mask" and, when Miles slowed it down midstream, "Directions"). A recent addition to the set list, "Willie Nelson," closes out the unedited recording (plus "The Theme," forming a coda), with a shortened version ending "Saturday Miles."

Macero's focus is on beat-driven performances—although if this were his sole focal point, the inclusion of Friday's "Directions" would have pushed the balance further in this direction; the same would be true of Saturday's version, also not included, but the dual keyboard solos from 6:26 to 9:10 display parallel play as much as they do soloing within a strict meter. In place of the unpredictability and expansiveness of the originals, Macero hones in on Miles Davis's own solos and changes of pace between tunes, allowing only limited space for the open improvisation that increasingly dominated the band's live appearances.

These sonic excursions extended what had become a regular feature of the nightly Chick Corea, Dave Holland, and Jack DeJohnette free-for-alls, now with the addition of Keith Jarrett on electronically processed electric organ and Airto Moreira on percussion. Their improvisations often appeared in the midst of a tune, with Davis offstage, and signified the band's exploratory side, where the music is most often highly textural, moving in and out of tempo and intonation, speeding up and slowing down. We often hear in the unedited live performances rapid-fire cascading runs and intricate interconnectivity between the players. The band's inclination toward open improvisation and changing tempos, much of it lost on Macero's splicing block, remains, albeit abridged, within "It's About That Time" and "Bitches Brew." The removal of "The Mask" (included only on Friday's unedited recordings) eliminated some of the strongest evidence of the flexibility with which the band could move between open and more conventionally structured improvisation (the keyboard solos tend toward the former).

Macero's approach to the band's proclivity in live performances to suddenly change tempo or to substantially depart from strict tempo is paradoxical. While he limits what is retained of these features from the unedited performances, he recreates semblances of them in his most heavily edited—or perhaps we could say most compositionally shaped—versions of the shows, "Wednesday Miles" and "Thursday Miles."

One of the biggest surprises in comparing Macero's edits with the newly re-leased full sets is the similarity in content between the studio version of "Bitches Brew" and its appearance closing out "Friday Miles." "Bitches Brew" on the LP is substantially a collage constructed from musical segments recorded in the studio sessions. This model is repeated on LFE1970: an opening section is con-structed in postproduction by repeating a small unit of material, deleting short segments of the performance, and then repeating the entire constructed section. The result is a whole with a more clearly discernible form, yet one that no longer represents the ad hoc spontaneity of the band's live performances. Listeners have long come to expect the use of postproduction as a compositional device for studio recordings, yet there is much dissonance in the idea of its use in some-thing labeled a live performance.

Historically, a studio recording has been thought of as representing a live performance given within a controlled environment without an audience,[2] whereas a "live" recording recreated the audience experience. Like Macero's construction of "Bitches Brew" on the studio recording *Bitches Brew*, here, too, little semblance of the documentary function of jazz recordings remains. Atten-tive listeners could no more mistake either version of "Bitches Brew" as being a live performance document than they could Jimi Hendrix's multi-tracked and highly produced studio album *Are You Experienced*.

By 1970, the public had come to expect rock but not jazz recordings to be products of the studio. As Davis biographer John Szwed points out: "*Bitches Brew* was something of a Rosetta stone for a wide array of people, opening up the potential of the studio to everyone from Henry Mancini to ambient musi-cian and producer Brian Eno. . . . *Bitches Brew* perversely drew attention to itself as a technological artifact, forcing listeners to take an extra-musical position on what they were hearing."[3] Yet while LFE1970 was presented in its title and liner notes as a document of a distinctly "live" performance, it was no less a studio artifact than Macero's highly structured studio version. The result has an easily discernible form, yet one that no longer represents the ad hoc spontaneity of the band's live performances.

The single performance of the four nights that would best present Miles Davis as a beat-driven, funk-vamp-focused musician, or maybe even a jazz-rock pioneer—which appears to be Macero's goal—is "Spanish Key," played as a Friday night encore. Yet this rocking, buoyant performance is not included on LFE1970. If there were a single danceable work during these Fillmore East con-certs, this would have been it. In fact, "Spanish Key" would have exemplified the band's complexity, since meter and tonality break down at the end of Steve

Grossman's solo at 4:42, followed by a highly abstract improvisational trio by Corea, Jarrett, and Moreira, which is met with strong audience applause.

Comparing and Contrasting MDF2014 with LFE1970, Performance by Performance

Wednesday, June 17, 1970

The composition that Teo Macero sculpts from the Wednesday, June 17, set begins with a very brief version of the concert opener, "Directions." The bass vamp that had become a characteristic element of the band's performance of this Joe Zawinul tune becomes the ground on which Miles Davis plays his opening solo. A rapidly repeated note figure by Davis is followed by a descending melodic phrase, which on MDF2014 leads to the two repetitions of the "Directions" melodic theme. But on LFE1970, the music jumps instead to the 5:31 point in Davis's continuing solo from MDF2014; this twenty-five-second concluding segment begins with two upwardly sweeping gestures, then a rapid descending phrase, before heading into its final moments. The track ends with the vamp alone.

"Directions" cuts directly into a brief fifty-three-second segment from "Bitches Brew" that was drawn from the middle of a much slower-tempo Davis solo (at 11:01 on MDF2014). Here Macero imitates the kind of dramatic tempo change that occurs around the six-minute point in the uncut version. There, the pace slows to make a transition to Keith Jarrett's organ solo, which is removed by Macero. On LFE1970, after thirty seconds, the music again cuts abruptly, this time to a ripping fast twenty-two-second Miles solo (of unclear origin; it does not appear in the full Wednesday or even Thursday versions of "Bitches Brew").

On MDF2014, in "Directions," Joe Zawinul's melodic theme is used as a returning refrain, bracketing first a second one-minute Davis solo and then a minute-and-a-half Steve Grossman solo, which is followed by the brief Davis solo included on LFE1970. The vamp, on MDF2014, is used by Davis to slow the tempo as Chick Corea plays a downward portamento figure on his ring-modulated Fender Rhodes, bringing back the melodic refrain at the new slower speed. This is the tempo change that Macero emulates in his use of the "Bitches Brew" segment on LFE1970.

On MDF2014, the melodic refrain is followed by a particularly unruly two-and-a-half-minute Keith Jarrett organ solo (6:22–8:52). The tempo begins to become unsteady around 7:30, with the bass and drums growing increasingly out of sync and, by the eight-minute mark, relatively unmetered. Airto Moreira's *cuíca* squeaks,[4] and Corea's ring modulation renders this segment a sonic free-for-all, until a straight, yet continued slow meter returns at 8:43. Miles's reentry at 8:54 briefly introduces a more elegiac mood, which is broken by his rapidly careening runs, which are in turn interrupted by the return of the melodic refrain at 9:39. Miles's long tone at the top of his trumpet's register leads into a brief coda concluding the tune, which will be followed by an 11:04 version of "The Mask."

In Macero's highly edited version on LFE1970, a sustained organ sound concludes the brief "Bitches Brew" segment, segueing into the first minute and thirty-five seconds of "The Mask," which is here a loud and distorted organ, bass, and drum trio—essentially a bridge into "It's About That Time" that hints at the more open improvisational side of the band. The trio ends before the start of Dave Holland's slow walking bass that both defines "The Mask" and segues into the 2:38 point within a Miles Davis solo of "It's About That Time." After the concluding two-minutes-plus of his solo, Steve Grossman takes the lead.

On MDF2014, the opening Keith Jarrett–Jack DeJohnette duet is much quieter, continuing beyond the Macero edit. The walking bass line enters at 3:05 and undergirds a nearly four-minute Davis solo, followed at 7:01 by Grossman's solo. Jarrett's rising and falling sustained organ sounds lie beneath the surface of both until 9:01, when Jarrett begins his own solo. Corea's ring modulation and Moreira's squeaks form an eerie backdrop throughout these proceedings.

The MDF2014 version of "It's About That Time" segues from the slow pulse of "The Mask," with Moreira's shaking bells and whistles and Corea's ring modulation. Only fifteen seconds later, DeJohnette picks up the meter. Miles playfully considers motifs and variations of the A–Ab–Ab–F theme, shifting into a full-fledged solo around 2:30. Two minutes later, Grossman's solo follows. After its conclusion, both the edited and the unedited versions continue with a nine-minute, wah-wah-inflected, phrase-trading duet between Corea and Jarrett, which eventually shifts out of straight time; DeJohnette and the others play rapid runs, with Grossman soon joining in on flute. Corea, Jarrett, and Grossman all remain within the same timbral zone. Miles enters with thematic phrases from "It's About That Time."

On LFE1970, Macero moves the final six seconds that wind the section down to the beginning of "Bitches Brew," which opens with two minutes of its characteristic collection of motifs. Davis solos in both versions, followed by what in the unedited version is a two-minute Grossman solo, which is edited out by Macero; as a result, the music jumps to Chick Corea's solo, accompanied by bass, organ, and drums, each in free meter. Soon after the six-minute mark, Corea's solo begins to break apart, giving way to a flute-chime-organ trio that becomes an extended open improvisation. Macero shortens this section, removing 8:20–9:33, and quickly cuts to Davis's solo, which follows the collective improvisation. The accompaniment behind Davis begins out of time but quickly falls into the straight-metered vamp, leading back to the opening motifs and a screaming, feedback-filled conclusion.

Thursday, June 18, 1970

A Miles Davis solo, over the vamp at the core of "Directions," opens the set. Teo Macero substantially contracts the tune to half its length in LFE1970. As the solo prepares to segue into the tune's first melodic refrain at 1:36 (in MDF2014), Macero jump-starts Davis's playing by cutting directly to a particularly high-octane point (3:51) with rapidly repeated high pitches, to which the band responds with rhythmic intensity. But after just three seconds, Macero moves us suddenly ahead again, to 6:02 (on MDF2014), the final instant of Davis's solo and the start of a heavily wah-wah-inflected Chick Corea–Keith Jarrett keyboard duet, joined by Airto Moreira's *cuíca* sounds and propelled by Jack DeJohnette's constant beat. This segment provides the element of open improvisation and abstraction for the set.

Dave Holland reasserts the vamp around 3:50 (on "Thursday Miles"; 8:04 on MDF2014). Ten seconds later, Davis returns at a high energetic peak, assertively supported by Corea and the rhythm section; one minute in, Corea's ring-modulated Fender Rhodes injects a strong level of sonic complexity and rhythmic vitality. Again, at the peak of this solo, Macero removes the melodic refrain, seamlessly connecting the Davis solo at 8:48 to an even more rhythmically rocking point at 9:20 (LFE1970), where Holland's insistent electric bass tightly interlocks with Corea's syncopated, ring-modulated sounds and DeJohnette's razor-tight beat. Davis drops out at 9:30, with the rhythm section still pulsing ahead. The meter begins to collapse at 9:58 (5:25 in MDF2014), with Corea's and Moreira's angular phrases at the fore. Instead of fading out, Macero cuts the final seconds, and segues into "The Mask."

The device Macero repeatedly chooses in his edits of "Directions" is deletion of the tune's melodic refrains (at 1:36–1:52, 3:36–3:51, 5:42–6:02, and 9:01–9:20), thus removing any semblance of Joe Zawinul's original tune. Macero also cuts the second segment of Davis's solo (1:52–3:36), and the entirety of Steve Grossman's energetically charged solo. Gone is Grossman's entrance amid the intensity of Davis's rapidly repeated notes at the 3:51 edit, through his increasingly sonically abstract playing beginning around the five-minute mark; his multiphonics are met with equally formidable sound abstractions and a falling away of a metered beat in the rhythm section. Instead, the improvisational spotlight shines on Miles Davis and the heavily electronic-sounding troika of Corea, Jarrett, and Moreira, backed by the rhythmic force of Holland and DeJohnette. The jagged angularity of Grossman's saxophone lines is removed, and abstraction lies in the hands of the electric keyboards, supported by the rhythmic breakdown and buildup in the bass and drums.

"The Mask" on LFE1970 omits Grossman's minute-and-forty-second solo, jumping at 7:00 directly to the fast-paced duo-keyboard joint "solo" with bass and intricate drumming; otherwise, the performance of the tune is intact. Davis's solo (9:10 on MDF2014; 10:51 on LFE1970) moves at a slower clip over the bass line that defines this tune. It begins by picking up on a spare, staccato gesture developed by the keyboards. This leads into a brief development before segueing into "It's About That Time," which is shortened slightly. At 6:00 on LFE1970, Macero retains only ten seconds of Grossman's two-and-a-half-minute solo (8:13–8:24 on MDF2014), moving quickly into Corea's solo. Corea's rapid runs are echoed by Jarrett and, at 7:15 (LFE1970), also by Grossman's flute. Davis plays an elegiac line above the fray (at 8:14 on LFE1970; 10:30 on MDF2014), continuing until the conclusion of the track on MDF2014 (at 12:04). But "Thursday Miles" continues, closing with an explosive, electronically textured version of "The Theme." Macero draws Davis's oft-used concert coda from the ending of that evening's rendition of "Bitches Brew" (not included on "Thursday Miles," but ending every other LP side). The Saturday version of "The Mask" on MDF2014 (not included on LFE1970) parallels the version within "Thursday Miles."

Friday, June 19, 1970

"Friday Miles" opens with the final eighteen seconds of "The Mask," signaled by Davis's playing the A–A♭–A♭–F theme before segueing into "It's About That Time" (which immediately begins the track on MDF2014). Miles's extended solo gives way to Steve Grossman at 5:24 (on MDF2014; at 5:44 on LFE1970). Finally, Grossman's entire three-minute solo is presented intact on LFE1970. Davis then takes another brief solo (under one minute) in his upper register. This is followed by a two-keyboard duet, three minutes long in the unedited version, starting at 7:43 on MDF2014 but cut down to forty-five seconds on LFE1970,

where it provides a brief transition, a herald to Davis's return with a characteristic elegiac melodic line (at 10:47–11:27 on MDF2014). On LFE1970, the track
ends at 11:15, moving the balance to begin "I Fall in Love Too Easily," which,
along with "Sanctuary," remains otherwise the same in both versions.

The most heavily "constructed" track on LFE1970 is the third night's "performance" of "Bitches Brew," in which the edits and repeats of complete sections are reminiscent of the studio-recorded version. The opening of "Bitches
Brew" on LFE1970 begins with the concluding ten seconds of the unedited
"Sanctuary." Macero twice repeats a sixteen-second segment (0:46–1:02 on
MDF2014) and then allows the live performance recording to briefly continue,
from 1:02 to 1:23. Next, he repeats (at 1:49 on LFE1970) the entirety of the performance thus far (including the applause and the sixteen-second repeat). He
then continues (at 3:13 on LFE1970) with what appears at 1:23 on MDF2014.
At 2:12 the vamp begins, joined by Davis's solo, continuing through 3:10 (5:00
on LFE1970). Grossman's solo is cut entirely (3:11–5:40). In its place, Macero
continues with the ensuing sprawling quartet of two keyboards, bass, and drums
engaged in open improvisation, concluding at 7:57 (7:22 on LFE1970), and
then a relatively calm Davis solo. Davis's energy level rises, as does the register of
his playing, at 10:57 (on MDF2014; 10:35 on LFE1970), ending at 11:28 (11:17
on LFE1970). The vamp continues, first with both keyboards, then thinning to
mostly drums and bass. At 12:23 (MDF2014), the thematic gestures of "Bitches
Brew" are played until the conclusion of the tune (at 12:38 on MDF2014). The
set concludes with "The Theme," appended to "Bitches Brew" on LFE1970 and
appearing as a separate track on MDF2014.

Saturday, June 20, 1970

"Saturday Miles" opens with a substantially shortened version of "It's About
That Time." Gone are the first 7:58 minutes of the live performance (including the vamp, an extensive Davis solo, and at 6:00 Steve Grossman's saxophone
solo). Instead, a twenty-second drum solo (drawn from the opening of "The
Mask" [0:20–0:41], a tune otherwise not included on "Saturday Miles") provides a prologue to the balance included on MDF2014 (7:58–11:04). It consists
of a brief, abstract Keith Jarrett organ solo, which becomes a lengthy, pointillistic
collective duet with Airto Moreira's percussion. This is brought to a conclusion
by Jack DeJohnette's entrance with a drumroll, continuing briefly over some
applause, and the return of Davis at 10:43 (3:06 on LFE1970), accompanied
by Moreira. The seventeen-second transition between this tune and "I Fall in

Love Too Easily," which appears at the end of LFE1970 (3:26–3:43), is found at the beginning of MDF2014. LFE1970 includes only its first 1:07 minutes (deleting the final 0:14) before continuing with "Sanctuary" (deleting the opening twenty-seven seconds, the first statement of the theme). The final seconds are moved to the beginning of the next track, "Bitches Brew."

Both versions of "Bitches Brew" are otherwise the same, until Teo Macero's edit at 3:11 (on MDF2014; at 3:00 on LFE1970), where Grossman's saxophone solo is removed (3:11–5:31), and the music jumps to an open improvisation within the rhythm section with both electric pianists; Dave Holland's electric bass and Moreira's cowbells and other percussion are foregrounded. Around the six-minute mark, Jarrett's rapid, atonal organ phrases, and then around 7:30 Chick Corea's ring-modulated Fender Rhodes, come forward in the dense mix. The textures thin, with Moreira's whistle blaring, as the seven-minute mark approaches. At 8:06 (on MDF2014; 5:38 on LFE1970), there is another cut in LFE1970. This section is shortened, deleting the beginning of the Davis passage at 8:09 (5:41 on LFE1970), jumping to 8:21 and continuing to the end of the track (at 9:39 on MDF2014; 6:57 on LFE1970).

Macero begins "Willie Nelson" with the opening seven seconds of the Davis solo, but quickly cuts to 2:17 (on MDF2014), at the height of Davis's exposition. Grossman's solo picks up (at 3:07 on MDF2014; 0:58 on LFE1970) on a high-register wavering note from the end of Davis's solo, continuing to 5:30/3:21. Solos by Corea and then Jarrett follow. Davis returns (7:46/5:37), playing over Corea's Fender Rhodes. The volume decreases at 8:08/5:59, with the melodic and vamp returning at 8:17/6:08; Davis continues to solo to the end of the track, which on LFE1970 includes "The Theme" (placed on a separate track on MDF2014).

Concluding Observations

MDF2014 shows a highly exploratory band that was continuing its trend toward open improvisation heard in its March 1970 performances documented on *Live at the Fillmore East, March 7, 1970: It's About That Time* (Davis 1997). Drummer Jack DeJohnette's ability and growing inclination to shift on a dime back and forth between a metric and a non-metric beat helped the band freely mix and match a range of musical possibilities. Its inclinations toward open improvisation and changing tempos, regular features of its actual live performances, are given free rein on the unedited MDF2014. Yet on LFE1970 these are abridged, most notably where they typically found their broadest expression, on "It's

About That Time" and "Bitches Brew." Teo Macero's postproduction paring of the four evenings of performances generated a more commercially viable product that presents Miles Davis's band as a bridge to his subsequent more beat-oriented work. Yet the unedited performances provided on MDF2014 present a far more complex picture of a highly exploratory band, one that positions it squarely inside the more experimental camp with Circle and the Revolutionary Ensemble.

APPENDIX 3

Circle's Performance of Its Members' Compositions

Chick Corea and Dave Holland contributed several compositions to Circle's repertoire. Corea's composition "Rhymes," recorded on the second day of *The Song of Singing* sessions, appears on the set lists at the band's Hamburg Jazzhaus and the Amsterdam performances. Corea was constantly composing; some of his material from this period appears on *A.R.C.* Bits and pieces of new compositions found their way into Circle sets, sometimes popping up within other tunes. The Hamburg Jazzhaus performance (third piece on the program) includes an early version of Corea's composition "Return to Forever," which was, in 1972, to provide the title track on Corea's first recording with his band of the same name. Instead of the mannered, symmetrical phrasing of Corea's solos on that subsequent version, the pianist offers sprawling solo excursions captured on *Circle 1: Live in Germany*.[1] At three and a half minutes, we find a poignant example of Corea's translation of McCoy Tyner's quartal harmonic approach and four-note arpeggio patterns. In a tour de force solo, the pianist spins and turns melodic and rhythmic elements from the theme, refracting them through this quartal approach. During the Hamburg stand, Barry Altschul recalls Corea, with whom he was sharing a room, up late at night, composing the tune "Spain."

Dave Holland contributed two tunes to Circle's charts, "Toy Room" (first recorded on *The Song of Singing*) and "Q&A." Both appear on the Hamburg Jazzhaus, Amsterdam, and Paris concert set lists. In Paris, the two compositions were interwoven. "Q&A" became part of the repertoire of Holland's own band, with Circle members Anthony Braxton and Barry Altschul plus Sam Rivers, and was recorded in late 1972 on *Conference of the Birds*.

"Q&A" and Corea's "Rhymes" are both constructed on patterns that are primarily rhythmic (a characteristic of Braxton's "Composition 6F," also known as "73 Degrees Kelvin," to which we will soon turn). The composed section of "Q&A" includes a series of brief, contrasting rhythmic motifs (with pitches assigned for melody instruments). After several repetitions of the series, improvisation ensues, in which the musicians freely refer to, quote, vary, and toss around elements of those figures. Let me offer the Hamburg Jazzhaus performance as one example.

On that date, "Q & A" was preceded by Braxton's angular soprano saxophone solo and two very brief duets with Holland and then Corea. The duos lead into a speedy and sprawling full-band free improvisation, and segue into a whirlwind-paced "Q & A." The wide-ranging improvisation, in which each player draws freely from the opening series of phrases, progressively moves further and further away from the opening theme. A quieter, sparer section leads to pointillistic textures. At eight and a half minutes, imitative playing gradually points the way back to the thematic material, most decisively soon after ten minutes, in the collective voice of Braxton, Holland, and Altschul. Corea unleashes a barrage of tone clusters before joining his bandmates in unison.

Anthony Braxton was a prolific composer. He brought to Circle several recently composed works, the "Kelvin" series. Compositions from a series of works titled "Composition 6" (followed by a letter designation) previously appeared on Braxton's *3 Compositions of New Jazz* (1968, with Braxton, Leo Smith, and Leroy Jenkins), and on the *Creative Construction Company* recording from the "Peace Church" concert (adding Steve McCall). The piece from this latter series most often performed by Circle was "73 Degrees Kelvin," also titled "Composition 6F." Braxton described the form as "repetitive phrase generating structures . . . a phrase-based repetition structure that establishes a fixed rhythmic pattern—with open actual pitch possibilities based on suggested contour."[2] Braxton biographer Michael Heffley adds: "The material was repeated, altered, staggered by the four instruments, then the shape of the line improvised upon."[3] Barry Altschul observes: "That was a complicated rhythmic line. And the point was to just play that rhythm any way you thought of it. Using whatever notes you want, leaving out whatever notes you want, but letting the rhythm continue, even with the notes you left out. That was the concept of the tune."[4] In each performance of this work, the players would constantly change pitches, articulations, and instruments; Corea sometimes played tone clusters rather than individual notes. The rhythmic series cycles round and round in constant repetition. Performances of this composition were so greatly varied both sonically and in the group dynamics that I will detail four contrasting examples.

The studio version on *Circling In* begins with an introduction—multiple streams of rapid ensemble lines in rhythmic sync, followed by a pause. At around two minutes, the texture thins and the volume level decreases. By shifting from drum kit to mallet instruments and back, the changing timbral quality of Altschul's instrument choices adds great variety to the overall sound. Two minutes later, there are fifteen seconds of silence, from which a low-pitched, sustained cymbal roll emerges. It continues, subtly ebbing and flowing, and fades after a minute and a half. A brief pause gives way to a return of the Kelvin rhythmic series, this time articulated for the final minutes with a different instrumentation: clarinet, metallophone, cello, and wood blocks.

At the November 28, 1970, concert in Iserlohn, Germany (released in Japan as *Circle 1*), the set opened with this work, which receives an even freer reading than in the studio. The theme is repeated numerous times in rhythmic unison, with the instrumentation and note/cluster choices on each instrument constantly changing, and sometimes remaining silent for one of the pulses. Shortly before the two–minute mark, the bass moves out of sync with the other three musicians, and then Chick Corea takes off on an expansive, atonal solo, loosely playing with but not tied to the theme; Holland and Altschul back him, with only the drummer seeming to continue the rhythmic series. Dave Holland's solo, backed by free playing by Barry Altschul, refers to the theme, and Corea soon joins in, juxtaposing fragments of the theme, and playing out of metric sync with the bassist. Soon, the bass and piano call and respond, and then play soloistically in parallel.

At the three-and-a-half-minute mark, everyone lays out except Altschul. Anthony Braxton enters, playing recorder, and the two return to the theme. Corea soon joins in on the piano keys and then the strings, with Holland playing arco. Once Braxton returns on contrabass clarinet, Corea's piano becomes more pointillistic. Band members continually switch instruments and timbral qualities;

at least one of them is always repeating the theme. At six minutes, the texture thins; cymbals, arco bass, cello or violin, and piano are heard, joined at seven minutes by Braxton's clarinet. The overall ensemble sound builds a minute later. At eight minutes, Corea's playing builds upon atonal melodic fragments, which he scatters around the keyboard and begins to repeat patterns that spin around, before returning to the theme. Braxton seizes on the spinning gestures before the quartet returns to unison, breaks apart, and returns in the final minute. The crowd offers an enthusiastic response.

On *The Paris Concert*, Braxton's "73 Degrees Kelvin" is prefaced with "Lookout Farm," Altschul's virtuosic, seven-and-a-half-minute drum solo. After ten repetitions of the rhythmic series theme, Corea's solo initially stays relatively close to the rhythmic pattern until he brings back the theme, with variants. A busy collective-ensemble texture unfolds, from which individual voices poke out. Braxton briefly plays a folk anthem–like version of the theme (on slide whistle), around which the rest of the band toss clusters and crashing sounds, leading back to a collective texture constructed of angular gestures; Braxton's clarinet, followed by Altschul on woodblocks and then metallophone, return to the theme, joined by Holland's arco bass, before all gradually fade out.

At Jazzhaus Hamburg, after sixteen repetitions, the instrumentation and timbres remain relatively stable, except for Corea's increasing tone clusters and a sharp accelerando during the final repetitions. At the end of these, Holland begins to stagger his series and Corea embarks on a brief solo, the length of a few repetitions, and then alternates with Holland, both adhering relatively closely to the pattern. Corea, Holland, and Altschul all play the material in staggered rhythmic motion. The texture changes when Altschul plays on sticks, solo for a few seconds and then together with Braxton on recorder. Corea joins in unison, playing first on the keys and then, after laying out for a cycle, changing the texture by plucking the piano strings, with Holland on arco bass at the top of his register. The texture goes through yet another change with the entry of Braxton on contrabass clarinet. Altschul responds, broadening his timbral range by using a thunder sheet, cymbals, and sticks; the textural changes pick up speed with the increasing numbers of changes in instrumentation. Braxton is on recorder and Holland on arco bass, while Corea goes back and forth between keys, strings, and piano harmonics. The next major shift in texture comes at seven minutes, when Braxton plays clarinet, Altschul plays the *afuche* (a rotating cylinder wrapped in small metal beads that shake as the cylinder is turned), Holland plucks his bass at the top of the register, and Corea is at the piano. The percussion sounds change kaleidoscopically, with Corea out front, Holland in quick pursuit. At eight and a half minutes, Braxton, on clarinet, imitates and ex-tends Corea's repeating note pattern, moving up and down a half-octave scale, as Corea returns to the series, again joined by Braxton and the others, each leaving out random selections from the pattern.

The band's treatment of "Composition 6F" reflects a great diversity of ap-proaches. Each individual performance displays steadily changing instrumen-tation and tone colors. The pacing, densities, mood, and character of the solos (from abstraction to folk song), rates of change, and degree of references to the theme vary greatly. Clearly, "Composition 6F" provided rich material for im-provisation. That it did not originate stylistically from Circle's "jazz" repertoire removed any expectations regarding phrasing, metered pulse, or swing, making it an open forum where all four musicians' personal histories with jazz perfor-mance mattered little—they could stand fully on common ground.

Another Braxton work performed by Circle was "Composition 6A." Michael Heffley describes its formal structure as featuring "gradient logic in the accele-rando/ritard, diatonic formings in the 10-note scale, the rhythmic logics of the basic two feel and the 9/4 phrase."[5] The composition receives an intense and lengthy twenty-three-minute workout in the performance at Hamburg Jazzhaus. That show also included two other compositions from the "6" series: 6I and 6F ("73 Degrees Kelvin"). In this performance, the band goes through changes of mood that reflect the composition's structure: at the five-minute mark, it arrives at a slower and more lyrical and diatonic two-beat feel; at seven and a half min-utes, it accelerates into a 9/4 faster section, before a ritard leads into a repeat of the previous section and, a minute later, back again. Another accelerando occurs at ten minutes; another ritard restores the slower two-beat feel shortly after the ten-minute mark. This pattern periodically repeats during the balance of the twenty-three-minute-plus performance (which fades in, already at full speed, at the beginning of the recording). At twenty minutes, the 9/4 metric feel returns, in a martial mood, slowing before returning to the slower two-beat section, from which a drum-solo coda emerges and the recording fades out.

NOTES

Introduction

1. Keepnews 1997, 185.

2. A second "live" recording, *Black Beauty: Miles Davis at Fillmore West*, became available in 1973, but only in Japan.

3. Szantor 1970, 20–21; reprinted in Kirchner 1997, 254.

4. Crouch 1990, 35.

5. Tomlinson 1991, 249–50, reprinted in Kirchner 1997, 234–35, quotes Litweiler (1984) 1990, 227 and Crouch 1990.

6. Winner 1970.

7. Collective improvisation is a form of spontaneous musical invention by a group of musicians. It is first associated in jazz with the early twentieth-century music of New Orleans (Buddy Bolden, King Oliver, and Louis Armstrong) and, after World War II, the music of Ornette Coleman ("Free Jazz"), Sun Ra, Cecil Taylor, members of the Association for the Advancement of Creative Musicians (AACM; see chapter 1), the Jazz Composers Guild, John Coltrane ("Ascension"), and others. Collective improvisation, as practiced by the ensembles discussed within this book, generally unfolds organically. Miles Davis tended to impose a certain degree of structure in his role as bandleader, but at times he left the stage, allowing the music to freely progress in the hands of his musicians. Circle and the Revolutionary Ensemble

were guided more fully by a collective intuitive process, as was Herbie Hancock's Mwandishi band. I trace elements of collective improvisation within the Miles Davis Quintet of the
1960s and Herbie Hancock's band in Gluck 2012a, 142ff. Another approach to collective
improvisation is the range of processes by which a conductor directs an ensemble, exemplified in the work of Karl Berger, Butch Morris, and others; the conductor guides larger
structures and/or specifies kinds of textures, instrumentation, or musical gestures to be
improvised by the performers.

8. Nisenson 1996.

9. Ibid. A modal approach is sometimes narrowly defined as improvisation using a
defined series of notes (a form of scale) in place of chord changes, but the use of a pedal
point as a gravitational center is at least as important a factor in defining this musical
methodology.

10. Feather 1970b.

11. Gleason 1970.

12. Carr 1998, Chambers (1983) 1985, Freeman 2006, Szwed 2002, Tingen 2001a,
and Tingen 2001b.

Chapter One

1. Ornette Coleman, quoted in Litweiler 1994, 237.

2. For examples, see DeVeaux 1997, 312.

3. Rivers 1975.

4. Davis with Troupe 1990, 252.

5. Ibid., 249–52.

6. Kart 1986; quoted in Litweiler 1994, 82.

7. Davis with Troupe 1990, 249–52.

8. Kelley 2009, 166.

9. "Ornette's a jealous kind of dude, man. Jealous of other musicians' success. I don't
know what's wrong with him." The theme of jealousy on Davis's own part surfaces when he
adds: "A lot of the 'star' people who used to come and see me—like Dorothy Kilgallen and
Leonard Bernstein (who, they tell me, jumped up one night and said, 'This is the greatest
thing that has ever happened to jazz!')—were now going to see Ornette." Davis attributes
this to wannabe aspirations of white audiences: "They want to be hip, want always to be in
on the new thing so they don't look unhip. White people are especially like that, particularly
when a black person is doing something they don't understand. They don't want to have
to admit that a black person could be doing something that they don't know about." Davis
with Troupe 1990, 251.

Feather 1964 and 1968a, and Martin 2001 document Davis's hostile reaction to the
music of saxophonists Eric Dolphy and Archie Shepp, and pianist Cecil Taylor.

10. Kelley 2009, 405, reports that tensions were renewed between Davis and Monk
fifteen years later, when their bands played on the same bill in 1970. A backstage confronta-
tion at a Central Park concert in July had Monk calling Davis's music "bullshit," while Davis
responded that Monk simply didn't understand the music. Kelley notes that the audience
response was stronger to Davis's music at that gig and also performances at the Village Gate
(where the musicians reconciled) and the Holmdel (New Jersey) Jazz Festival. Reviewer
John S. Wilson wrote that the Holmdel audience "favored Davis's fusion experiments to

Monk's well-worn numbers." Although Monk was just eight years Davis's senior, the latter's new musical direction represented a perceived generational gap, this time with Davis viewing himself as the more forward-thinking musician.

11. Davis with Troupe 1990, 251. Italics added.

12. Coleman's term for his methodology is "harmolodic." Never decisively articulated, his concept addresses how a group can balance with equal weight freedom of the individual and the significance of the collective. One can be an individual within a group without diminishing either. For example, a melody played in unison by multiple instrumentalists might start on each musician's distinct pitch yet articulate the same intervals and shapes.

13. Chick Corea, interview by the author, December 11, 2011, by e-mail.

14. Corea 2013.

15. Among them were Bill Dixon, who served as organizer, Paul Bley, Carla Bley, Cecil Taylor, Roswell Rudd, Archie Shepp, Sun Ra, Alan Silva, and a number of others. Heller 2012, 39–40, 58–59. Young 1998. For contrasting concert reviews, see Morgenstern and Williams 1964.

16. The politically informed aspect of these groups, and the political association of John Coltrane's work with the emerging black nationalist movement drawn by Amiri Baraka, Archie Shepp, and others, are beyond the scope of this book. Miles Davis's ambivalent relationship to these questions is addressed in Martin 2001. E. Porter 2001 considers the views of Amiri Baraka, Greg Tate, Gerald Early, and Stanley Crouch regarding Davis's position in relation to black identity, nationalism, and social responsibility to the black community.

17. Lenny White, second drummer on *Bitches Brew*, points to the impact that Williams's new band had on Miles Davis: "To me Tony was the catalyst of Miles' band [the 1960s quintet]—he was the guy who turned Miles' head around. He's not given enough credit for that. I think that Miles was getting off hearing what Tony was hearing in the music, and was opening up their music for him to play. Tony was with Miles from the age of 17 to 23. In those few years, the records that he made changed drumming. Not just drumming, they changed musical styles." Undated interview, milesdavis.com.

18. "Music abstraction, like abstraction in visual art, can be understood as reducing forms to their basic elements: shape, color, and texture. . . . Melody supported by harmony could give way to tone color, non-melodic series of notes, musical textures, and densities of sounds, creating musical abstraction. Their goal was to capture sense impressions, to tap into the unconscious and offer not representation but reflection and imaginative refractions of external and internal reality." Gluck 2012a, 40.

19. The Boston Improvisational Ensemble was a chamber group led by a classical composer/art historian. Quote is from Panken 1997. Tony Williams adds: "They had cards and numbers and you're playing to time, watches, and big clocks; playing behind poetry, all kinds of stuff." Quoted in Ephland 1989. Also see Coryell and Friedman 1978, 87. Sam Rivers had a broad background in rhythm and blues, modern harmonic conceptions, the post–World War II European avant-garde, and jazz, among other musical forms.

20. This could include the representation of pitch on the vertical axis and time on the horizontal axis, and the density of lines as volume or number of sound events happening simultaneously.

21. Williams replaced Sunny Murray as Cecil Taylor's drummer before leaving to join Davis. Andrew Cyrille then joined Taylor's ensemble. Unfortunately, Williams's early stint

with Taylor was never recorded. A duet was recorded in the late 1970s for Williams's *Joy of Flying*.

22. The Coltrane gig lasted two weeks. In 1964, Rivers himself was hired by Miles Davis as a replacement for saxophonist George Coleman. Tony Williams had played Davis a recording of Rivers, and he was immediately hired. This brief period lasted only from spring through July 1964, when Rivers joined the Andrew Hill Quartet for a tour, and Davis found Wayne Shorter. Losin 2014.

23. Wallace Roney, e-mail correspondence with the author, July 9, 2012.

24. Ironically, after Miles replaced Sam Rivers, the band headed more distinctly in the freer direction championed by Rivers.

25. Although beginning in 1972, Davis's playing became far more rhythmic in character and, with his use of the wah-wah, electronic in sound.

26. Noted by Amiri Baraka and Greg Tate; see E. Porter 2001.

27. Sometimes separated by pauses.

28. Questions about whether and to what degree Davis was influenced or pressured by Clive Davis or other Columbia Record executives to play a more groove-based form of music have been addressed in Davis with Troupe 1990, 300, where Davis comments: "Some people have written that doing Bitches Brew was Clive Davis's or Teo Macero's idea. That's a lie, because they didn't have nothing to do with none of it. Again, it was white people trying to give some credit to other white people where it wasn't deserved because the record became a breakthrough concept, very innovative. They were going to rewrite history after the fact like they always do." The question is also considered in Szwed 2002, Tingen 2001a, Troupe 1998, Hall 1974, and elsewhere. Moreover, these sources have explored the musical and social influence of Miles Davis's wife at the time, Betty (Mabry) Davis, who introduced him to Jimi Hendrix and Hendrix's music.

29. Chick Corea, interview by the author, December 11, 2011, by e-mail.

30. "'Ostinato' is the term used in classical music for a repeating phrase; a 'riff,' its parallel in jazz, the blues, R&B, and rock music, is designed to establish a steady, repeating pattern, a rhythmic leitmotif above and around which musicians create interlocking or contrasting melodic and rhythmic phrases." Gluck 2012a, 91.

31. Chick Corea, interview by the author, December 11, 2011, by e-mail.

32. Ibid.

33. Tate 1992, 88–89.

34. The term is used as the title of Litweiler (1984) 1990. Also see Baraka 1968, Kofksy 1970, Wilmer (1977) 1992, Spellman (1966) 2004, Harris 2004, Monson (2007) 2010, Anderson 2007, G. Lewis 2008, and others.

35. Chick Corea, quoted in Nemeyer 2005, 32.

36. Chick Corea, quoted in Kart 1969a, 21.

37. Herbie Hancock, quoted in Johnson 1971, 14–15, 34.

38. Shorter's first recording session with Davis took place in the summer of 1962, when he was still with Art Blakey and the Jazz Messengers.

39. Coryell and Friedman 1978, 258; interview with Wayne Shorter.

40. Ibid., 259.

41. Shorter's time with Davis's Lost Quintet proved to be a fruitful one for his own creative work, which can be found on the recordings *Super Nova* (recorded September 2,

1969) and *Journey of Iska* (recorded August 26, 1970, during the final days of the Lost Quintet, by that time a septet). Additional recordings followed soon after.

42. Kart also observes: "The problem with such an approach lies in keeping inspiration open and fresh and maintaining a balance between spontaneity and control. Here, Shorter's recent adoption of the soprano saxophone is interesting. . . . Its newness seems to have opened areas of emotion for him on both horns [soprano as well as his prior mainstay, tenor]." Kart 1969b, 28.

43. Holland was backing singer Elaine Delmar.

44. DeJohnette had been spending time at Ronnie Scott's. He recalls: "So Dave Holland, Jon McLaughlin [*sic*], Pat Smythe. Another drummer, too, who actually plays with Cecil Taylor, was Tony Oxley [and he] played drums because I was playing piano. I'd sit in and play piano. Then I'd play some drums, melodica. So we would be there jamming everyday." Quoted in Brown 2011, 46.

45. Dave Holland, quoted in Chénard 2011. In another interview, Holland describes DeJohnette as the one who first passed along the message, repeated later that evening by Jones. Detheridge quotes Holland as expressing reservations about coming to the United States on a work visa that year, fearing that he could get drafted to serve in Vietnam. He notes that he was being encouraged by musical colleagues to go, but hadn't yet made up his mind. By the time the interview was published, he was nearly two months into the new gig. Detheridge 1968a.

46. Davis relates: "My interest was in finding an electronic bass player because of the sound it added to my band. I was still on the lockout for someone who would eventually play that instrument all the time in my band, because I didn't know then if Dave would want to switch to playing that instrument. But for the time being he could replace Ron on gigs I had lined up, and we could cross the other bridge when we came to it." Davis with Troupe 1990, 294.

47. This is how Davis describes it in ibid., 295, confirmed by Kart 1969a.

48. Herbie Hancock, quoted in J. Wilson 1968.

49. "Mademoiselle Mabry" (Miss Mabry) and "Frelon Brun" (Brown Hornet); the balance of the record had been made back in May by the Miles Davis Quintet with Herbie Hancock and Ron Carter. Wayne Shorter, Tony Williams, and Davis bridged the personnel between the two groupings.

50. Shortly before, guitarist George Benson had participated in Davis sessions.

51. "The roots of the local university are in vocational and general education for the workingman." http://www.wlv.ac.uk/default.aspx?page=21422. Accessed March 11, 2015. Other sources referenced about Wolverhampton include http://blackcountryhistory.org /places and http://www.wolverhamptonhistory.org.uk. Accessed March 15, 2015.

52. Dave Holland, quoted in Chénard 2011.

53. With Steve Brett and the Mavericks in Midland ATV's *For Teenagers Only*. Dave Holland, quoted in Detheridge 1968b.

54. Dave Holland, quoted in Gourse 1989.

55. Dave Holland, quoted in Chénard 2011.

56. Allen 2003.

57. Gourse 1989.

58. Dave Holland, quoted in Feather 1968a.

59. Although Dave Holland doesn't appear on McLaughlin's *Extrapolation*, having recently departed for the United States.

60. Recorded February 18, 1968. http://www.discogs.com/Spontaneous-Music -Ensemble-Karyobin/release/1022101.

61. Dave Holland, quoted in Feather 1968a.

62. Atterton 1968. Atterton cites the location of the club, Seventh Avenue and 132nd Street, and a stand length of nine days; the set list was largely from the most recent recordings by the Miles Davis Quintet: *Miles Smiles, Nefertiti,* and *Miles in the Sky*.

63. Dave Holland, quoted in Chénard 2011.

64. Chick Corea, quoted in Coryell and Friedman 1978, 147–48.

65. Chick Corea, interview by the author, December 11, 2011, by e-mail.

66. Coryell and Friedman 1978, 148.

67. Jack DeJohnette recalls a time in the Davis band when Corea picked up Davis's trumpet and played some lines from Dizzy Gillespie. Brown 2011, 51.

68. Chick Corea, quoted in Nemeyer 2005, 30.

69. For example, a quintessential Powell solo, from a 1949 performance of his tune "Celia," opens with a steadily moving double-time (sixteenth notes) passage, two bars in length. In the first bar, four notes travel upward and four back down; a four-note chromatic spiral between the two—that appears throughout the solo—prepares the change in direction. The spiral leads double-time passage into a flowery restatement of two bars of the melody to "Celia." The next motif is a descending phrase that provides another building block for the solo, from which Powell creates endless rhythmic melodic variations. Overall, the variation of fast and slower passages gives the solo rhythmic vitality, which in tandem with symmetrical movement of the various motifs upward and downward offers coherence and simplicity. Powell (1956) 1988.

70. These features predominate in Corea's premier recording, *Tones for Joan's Bones* (Corea [1966] 2004). While the harmonic language of the title track to Corea's second recording, *Now He Sings, Now He Sobs* ([1968] 2002), is closer to McCoy Tyner's pentatonic and quartal vocabulary, we find traces of Powell's influence. Six- or seven-bar phrases are followed by pauses, allowing time for the listener to digest the proceedings. Segments of upward movement conclude with downward motion to suggest a sense of completion and symmetry. Straight quarter notes alternate with triplets to further the rhythmic variation. The insistent exploration of a single motif sequentially with slight differences calls to mind John Coltrane, a feature found periodically in "Litha" from *Tones for Joan's Bones,* yet with a simplicity and directness that suggest Powell's model.

71. Chick Corea, quoted in Nemeyer 2005, 30.

72. Chick Corea, quoted in Myers 2011. The date must have been 1957–58.

73. Ibid.

74. Chick Corea, quoted in Coryell and Freedman 1978, 148.

75. See, for example, Corea's solo in "Bitches Brew" in concert at Salle Pleyel, November 3, 1969, and his broad use of percussive two-note spikes during the comping throughout "Directions" on *Live at the Fillmore East,* March 7, 1970 (although it is often difficult to distinguish between these gestures and conventional chords due to the ring modulation, which heightens the listener's perception of atonality; Corea's solo is an unfolding of single-note lines). For Circle examples, see "Quartet Piece I" and "Quartet Piece II" from *Circulus,* and the thick clusters within "Danse I" from *Circling In.*

76. Tone clusters are "groupings of harmonically unrelated notes played as if they are a chord. . . . Unlike even the most complex chord, a cluster is built from contiguous notes, major and minor seconds. It is inherently dissonant. A cluster may be described by its lower and uppermost notes and by its relative note density." Gluck 2012a, 42–43. The harmonic ambiguity characteristic of tone clusters allows Corea greater leeway to play the piano as a percussive instrument, unencumbered by chordal implications.

77. For example, tone clusters of major and minor seconds juxtaposed to melodic lines moving stepwise in similar intervals ("Major Seconds Broken and Together"), alternating two-note chord fragments alternating between major and minor thirds, perfect fourths, and major seconds ("Studies in Double Notes"), similar fragments alternating between major thirds and major seconds ("Perpetuum Mobile"). Bartok (1940) 2004. Composed 1926–39.

78. For a brief discussion, see Gluck 2012a, 42–43. The example discussed is "Well, You Needn't" from *Monk's Music* (1957).

79. Which continued periodically through 1968, and again in 1972, while Corea was putting together the first *Return to Forever*. In March 1967, he recorded Getz's *Sweet Rain* with Ron Carter and Grady Tate.

80. As did his appearance on Bobby Hutcherson's *Total Eclipse*.

81. Feather 1968c.

82. This time playing music largely from the Miles Davis Quintet of the 1950s, plus "Agitation" from the Miles Davis Quintet of the 1960s, and a new tune by Joe Zawinul, "Directions."

83. Stanley Cowell played acoustic piano and Hohner clavinet; he also confirms that Tony Williams was the drummer; e-mail correspondence with Cowell, March 7 and 13, 2013; source for Kelly: Losin 2014, confirmed by Dave Holland.

84. Nemeyer 2012, 32.

85. Chick Corea, quoted in Nemeyer 2005, 37.

86. With Wayne Shorter, Dave Holland, Tony Williams, and John McLaughlin, who had just arrived in the States to join Tony Williams Lifetime.

87. Including on a scheduled but canceled January 1969 tour of Japan. Although a January 6 date had already sold out, Japan refused to grant visas for the band due to its policy of refusing entry to anyone with an arrest record. In this case, Tony Williams had "an old arrest record (including one for traffic tickets)" but no convictions. *DownBeat* 1969, 10.

88. Jack DeJohnette, quoted in Panken 2009.

89. Stern 1978, 23–26, 51–52, 54.

90. Brown 2011, 22–23.

91. Jack DeJohnette, quoted in Robson 2012.

92. Billy Hart, interview by the author, June 17, 2008.

93. G. Lewis 2008, x–xi.

94. G. Lewis 2001/2002, 100; G. Lewis 2008, ix. Lewis continues: "intermedia, the relationship of improvisation to composition, scores, computer music technologies."

95. DeJohnette played on two mid-1960s Blue Note recordings by alto saxophonist Jackie McLean: *Jacknife* (1965, with pianist Larry Willis, bassist Larry Ridley, and trumpeters Lee Morgan and Charles Tolliver [separately, except for one tune when they play together]) and *Demon's Dance* (1967, with pianist Lamont Johnson, bassist Scott Holt, and Woody Shaw on trumpet). The latter was the final of McLean's twenty Blue Note recordings

until *One Night with Blue Note Preserved* (1985), documenting an all-star live performance that marked the relaunching of the label, reuniting McLean, DeJohnette, and Shaw, and adding pianist McCoy Tyner and bassist Cecil McBee.

96. Jack DeJohnette, quoted in Panken 2009.

97. A performance of the band, which also included Stanley Cowell (piano) and Miroslav Vitous (bass), is documented on Getz 1969. http://www.allmusic.com/album /the-song-is-you-mw0000101272. Accessed March 11, 2015.

98. Evans (1969) 1998.

99. Jack DeJohnette, quoted in Panken 2009. Wallace Roney also hears Roy Haynes's influence on Jack DeJohnette. July 9, 2012, e-mail correspondence with the author.

100. Dave Goodman ascribes Tony Williams's approach to the drums to incorporating elements of Art Blakey's sense of "feel," Max Roach's concept of "technique," and Philly Joe Jones's understanding of "creativity." The "technique" that enhanced Williams's skill at playing in an integral ensemble balanced "extremes of and dynamic gradations between various combinations of the elements of: volume (loud and soft); tempo (fast and slow); harmonic density (simple and complex); melodic motion (stasis and motility); rhythmic density (continuous and broken); pitch (high and low); timbre (conventional and extended); and duration (long and short)." Jack DeJohnette engaged with a similar blend of qualities in his work with Davis. Goodman 2011, 363–65.

101. An excellent example is found during a recorded concert version of "Bitches Brew" performed in Berlin on November 7, 1969. In the midst of Miles's solo, while Corea comps but sparely and rhythmically (particularly with slowly rising and/or descending figures and then more rapid, pointillistic lines), DeJohnette's flexible drumming comes to the fore. His emphasis is twofold: constantly varied patterns on the cymbals, his accents ever changing—which hint at the vamp undergirding this section of the tune (while bassist Holland's lines at this point are in rapid motion); and periodically moving around the tom toms, creating fills that provide glue for the ensemble. His playing is in dialogue with Corea (who is filling the spaces within Davis's solo lines), and fans the music toward Davis's back, pressing him onward. The cymbal play changes dramatically, becoming much sparer and in freer time during the early stages of the solo that Shorter next constructs from a single phrase.

102. Dave Holland, quoted in Carr 1998, 256.

103. Jack DeJohnette, quoted in Panken 2009.

104. Gigs from March through August included dates at the Cellar Door, Washington, DC; Duffy's Backstage, Rochester, New York; the Spectrum, Philadelphia; the Plugged Nickel, Chicago; the Blue Coronet Club, Brooklyn; Morgan State Jazz Festival, Baltimore; Newport Festival, Central Park, New York City; Juan-les-Pins Festival, Antibes, France; Rutgers University Stadium, New Brunswick, New Jersey; Sheraton Park Hotel, French Lick, Indiana (French Lick Jazz Festival); and Grant Park, Chicago.

105. "Attack" and "sustain," along with "decay" and "release" (ASDR), are aspects of what might be considered the "life cycle" of a sound or more technically its amplitude envelope shape. "Attack" refers to the initiation of the sound, how suddenly or gradually it begins. "Sustain" describes the sound's behavior following its attack, specifically how long it remains at its peak volume level before it begins to "decay," or decrease in volume until it ceases to sound (its "release").

106. Stanley Cowell, who played briefly with the band as a second keyboardist during

this period, confirms this dynamic, including in the band's appearances in Montreal. E-mail correspondence with Cowell, March 7, 2013.

107. Corea found Tony Williams to be a major influence on his thinking about electric instruments: "When Tony left along with guitarist John McLaughlin, the first time I saw them after that was with Tony's Lifetime trio—with John and Larry Young on organ. I saw them perform down at the Vanguard, and they blew me away. That group did a lot to change the sound of jazz. . . . It's the first time the rock sound was fully integrated into jazz. There were no horns, just Tony's driving drums, John's rock guitar and Larry's hot organ. In fact, the first time I saw Lifetime I had to put plugs in my ears. It was the loudest thing I had ever heard, but I loved it. What they were doing was kind of early for jazz-rock fusion." Quoted in Myers 2011. On December 19–20, 1969, Tony Williams Lifetime appeared on a bill together with the Miles Davis Lost Quintet, plus Indian and African musicians, back at the Village Gate in New York. The concerts were announced in notices in the *New York Times* December 18–20.

In another recorded fragment from the show, the band plays a speedy version of "So What." Like "'Round Midnight" and "Walkin'," also on the set list, the tune is from the repertoire of the Miles Davis Quintet of the 1950s and early 1960s. At the core of "So What" is a strong solo by Shorter, again powered by Williams, showing the drummer to be the consummate accompanist as he presses the soloist ever forward, periodically offering drumrolls of varying velocities. In "Walkin'," Williams drives hardest behind Shorter. "Agitation" is the sole tune played that night originating in the repertoire of the Miles Davis Quintet of the 1960s.

108. Stanley Cowell makes a similar observation about the Montreal shows. E-mail correspondence with the author, March 7, 2013.

109. The technique used by pianists and guitarists to accompany soloists, conventionally consisting of chords, melodic interpolations, and rhythmic figures.

110. E-mail correspondence with Wallace Roney, July 9, 2012.

111. Chick Corea, quoted in Kart 1969a. Corea adds: "Also there was the shadow of Herbie [Hancock] and what he had done hanging over the band. I couldn't do what Herbie had done, not that I particularly wanted to, and I didn't have anything else either."

112. Interestingly, Dave Holland played a session with Jimi Hendrix on March 25 at the Record Plant in New York City, joining John McLaughlin and Buddy Miles. In it, Holland plays a conventional role as a rock bassist, anchoring the simple chord changes (I have the recording, but it is mentioned in Nicholson 1998, 136–37). Holland and McLaughlin were reunited several times soon after, including on McLaughlin's *Where Fortune Smiles* (May 1970), with John Surman, saxophone; Stu Martin, drums; and Karl Berger, vibes.

113. At times, DeJohnette traces the general rhythmic pattern of a tune with heavy drum strokes, emphasizing nearly every pulse. This occurs in "Nefertiti" (first set), which opens as a ballad, but soon increases in tempo and swing. Even on the moderate-tempo "On Green Dolphin Street," the first-set opener, DeJohnette spices the soloists' work with unusual accents, cymbal filigree, and fills. In the up-tempo tune "No Blues," his intense vitality energizes the group, as it does again in the second-set opener, Jimmy Heath's "Gingerbread Boy."

114. Chick Corea, quoted in Kart 1969a.

115. In April and May.

116. Many famous shows by Latin and other jazz musicians, some recorded, took place at the Village Gate. John Coltrane appeared there, as did Jimi Hendrix, as did the musical

"Jacques Brel Is Alive and Well and Living in Paris." For more about the Davis Quintet's Village Gate residence, see Szwed 2002; according to Losin 2014, shows took place on April 25–26 and May 23–24. Later shows during Davis's summer tour, July 29–August 10, may have been canceled.

That year, in addition to his own recordings, *Is* and *Sundance* (with Dave Holland and Jack DeJohnette), Chick Corea played on Wayne Shorter's *Super Nova*; the first of Corea's record dates with Eric Kloss, *To Hear Is to See*, was followed the next year by Kloss's *Consciousness*. The latter is reviewed in *DownBeat*, February 4, 1971, 42.

117. Williams 1970, 21.

118. Wayne Shorter, quoted in Mercer 2004, 127–28.

119. Szwed 2002, 288.

120. Corea recorded the tune on May 11–13 with Holland and DeJohnette plus trumpeter Woody Shaw, flutist Hubert Laws, and saxophonist Bennie Maupin.

121. It was following that show that Miles Davis was shot while sitting in a car with girlfriend Marguerite Eskridge outside her Brooklyn apartment. Davis writes: "I later found out that the reason I had been shot was because some black promoters in Brooklyn hadn't liked the fact that white promoters were getting all the bookings. When I played the Blue Coronet that night, they thought I was being an asshole by not letting the black promoters do the booking." Davis with Troupe 1990, 305–7. Club owner Dickie Habersham-Bey, interviewed years later, gave his interpretation of the event: "There's always been guys that want to take over the business when they see you doing good business. The week I had Miles . . . he was working for me regularly; anytime he had a week off he would call and say 'hey Dick, I'll bring [the band] in.' This guy who was monopolizing the business—he's dead now, he got shot on Flatbush Avenue . . . the name is not important. I booked Miles that week [the week Davis was shot], the Village Gate had Gloria Lynne. Now he made a deal with me to have Gloria Lynne at my place, I told him I couldn't, so he told Miles 'don't show up' [at the Blue Coronet]; certain people tried to bulldoze musicians at that time." Quotations from W. Jenkins 2011.

122. Kart 1969b, 28.

123. Festival producer George Wein points to Davis's interest in James Brown, while Miles Marshall Lewis holds that it was Sly and the Family Stone. Wein, Chinen, and Cosby 2004, 463–64; M. Lewis (2006) 2010, 64. Lewis writes: "Miles Davis watched all this from the sidelines and began to wonder what it's like to matter to a young audience hyped enough to riot in the rain over your music."

124. It is not clear whether anything preceded this tune at the Central Park concert, but when compared with other set lists from the period, it seems plausible that "Directions" was the opening tune.

125. Corea also periodically played the cadential figure of the tune to maintain a semblance of the basic form, giving Shorter extensive leeway to explore.

126. Pointillism is a term drawn from late nineteenth-century French art, particularly the work of Georges Seurat, who painted using small dots of color in place of sustained gestures of brushwork. It is our perception that the colors blend. In twentieth-century European musical composition, the term was used to refer to frequently brief individual notes, at times distant in pitch from one to the next. While our ears hear individual notes, we perceive larger textures that emerge from the sum of those pitch points.

Pantonality refers to a range of approaches, from atonality to twelve-tone compositional techniques, in contrast to Western harmony. *Polytonality* refers to the juxtaposition of more than one tonality at the same time. The term *gesture* borrows the idea of a series of physical motions, as in dance, to describe a series of sounds or notes. It is a synonym for *phrase* or *sequence*. A melody is the most familiar kind of sound gesture. An "angular" gesture is characterized by constant changes in direction (up or down, sometimes in leaps), in contrast to the more linear (and often stepwise) qualities of conventional melodies.

Chapter Two

1. Jack DeJohnette, quoted in Mercer 2004, 128.

2. The recorded versions of only the closing composition, "Sanctuary," and maybe the penultimate, "Miles Runs the Voodoo Down," actually suggest a live performance. Miles Davis's solo on "Spanish Key" also points us in this direction; at one point the solo references "Sanctuary," hinting at the trumpeter's often used mode of calling a change of tune. But here it proves to be no more than a hint rather than functioning as a segue.

3. Also known as Khalid Yasin.

4. Davis's reference is to Stravinsky's neoclassic works of the 1920s and '30s, among them *Pulcinella*, *Concerto for Piano and Wind Instruments*, and *Duo Concertante*.

5. Davis with Troupe 1990, 298–300.

6. Jack DeJohnette, quoted in Brown 2011, 50.

7. Jack DeJohnette, quoted in Tingen 2001b. An essay/review of the *Complete Bitches Brew Sessions* boxed set.

8. Ibid.

9. Joe Zawinul, quoted in Ouellette 1999, 34. I believe that Davis's "sketches" refers to a collection of rhythmic or melodic phrases or vamps extracted from Zawinul's scores that could be utilized as building blocks within the recording sessions.

10. Lenny White, quoted in Tingen 2001b.

11. The set includes recordings from sessions spanning August 1969–February 1970.

12. Belden 1998, 121–32; Belden and Cuscuna 1998, 142–43.

13. Included in Tingen 2001a. For explication of the August 1969 *Bitches Brew* sessions, see 310–13.

14. One of the differences between the studio version of "Miles Runs the Voodoo Down" and its previous live performance incarnations is Dave Holland's bass line. The studio presentation of the bass is simpler and more understated than the boogie-woogie-inflected bass line that shaped the character of its predecessors. "Miles Runs Voodoo Down" on record displays some of the dynamic tension found in the live band in the rising and falling of complexity and tension in Jack DeJohnette's drumming during Chick Corea's electric piano solo. Following that, DeJohnette tracks Miles Davis's playing quite closely during Davis's closing solo, further subdividing the beat.

15. Belden 1998, 125.

16. Dave Holland relates: "The process was being recorded. . . . That's what Miles was onto. He was onto recording the process of discovering this music and developing it. And that's why it has this sort of searching quality. Because everybody is trying to figure it out, where are we going with this. How do we make these three keyboards work together." Dibb 2001, DVD at 1:21:59–1:22:22.

17. Detailed in Belden 1998, 129–30, and in Tingen 2001a, 67–69, 312–13.

18. Stockhausen 1991. For more information about this work, see "Masterpieces of 20th-Century Electronic Music: A Multimedia Perspective," documentation of an exhibition at Columbia University's Low Library. http://music.columbia.edu/masterpieces /notes/stockhausen/index.html. Accessed March 15, 2015.

19. Emmerson 1998, 136. Schaeffer's concept was to use the sonic qualities of each sound as a guide and reference point to organize his recorded materials. Simon Emmerson observes: "One of Pierre Schaeffer's ideals was to strip down the sound to its intrinsic components and to appreciate its musical potential independent of its origin or cause." Conventions like rhythm, melody, and harmony were replaced by the attributes of sounds. This could include spectral qualities (timbre), how a sound unfolded over time (envelope shape), and other factors unrelated to conventional musical implications. Sounds could be reversed, looped, and shifted in pitch (and thus speed), and echo could be applied, all disguising references to the original source. Schaeffer's first important work was "Etude aux Chemins de Fer" (Train Study) from Cinq Études de Bruits (1948). Schaeffer (1990) 2010.

20. Chadabe 1997; Holmes (1985) 2012. Schaeffer spoke of the sound-based compositional process as revealing a dynamic, unfolding relationship from within and between the materials: "At each moment of the work of expression, as recording unfolds, sound reacts, proposes its own solutions, incites, elicits ideas, helps the formation of the piece. . . . When I admit a sound at the output, when I let a sound come out, I must immediately treat it, not as an element whatever, a piece of wood, a fragment of puzzle, but as a pawn or a figure, a person with three dimensions, etc. and I cannot play with it exactly as I please." Quoted in Palombini 1993, 4. Whether Teo Macero applied this Schaefferian principle to his editing of Bitches Brew or imposed his own ideas external to how the recorded materials "propose its own solutions" is an important question, discussed below.

21. Zak 2010, 153. For a history of recorded sound, see Sterne 2003 and Chanan 1995. Zak places the first such studio editing a year earlier than Pierre Schaeffer's initial work, looking to singer Patti Page's 1947 hit "Confess." This song features two overdubbed voices (of the same singer, spatially separated, one with added reverberation), "creat[ing] a narrative structure and dramatic conceit unique to the record." Zak 2010, 159. Guitarist Les Paul used overdubbing techniques to create multiple layers of guitar, all played by the same performer in subsequent takes.

22. See Brennan (undated) and Lewisohn (1988) 2013.

23. Davis with Troupe 1990, 251–52.

24. Teo Macero, quoted in J. Lewis 1994, 21, and cited in Tingen 1991, 67; Tingen 2001a; and Gluck 2012a, 118. Also see Hall 1974, 13–15.

25. David Rubinson, quoted in Gluck 2012a, 119.

26. Davis with Troupe 1990, 294. Previously, Davis and Macero had a conflict over the recording Quiet Nights, which Davis thought never should have been released: "After that thing Teo Macero did on Quiet Nights, I wanted to control whatever music I put on record. I was moving more and more to using electronic instruments to make up the sound that I wanted, and I felt that saying 'Directions in Music by Miles Davis' [on the album covers] would indicate that." Ibid.

27. Svorinich 2015, 106. The document is archived in the Teo Macero Collection at the New York Public Library.

28. Ibid., 104–8. Svorinich also observes that customary practice would have given the

artist little voice in the postproduction process, an issue confirmed and addressed above by Davis Rubinson.

29. A topic discussed at length in appendix 2.

30. The term *vamp* is often used interchangeably with *riff* or *ostinato*, Here, it is a repeating bass line.

31. During the Lost Quintet (and in 1970, Sextet and Septet) performances and the studio version of "Bitches Brew," the opening is most often played for 2½–3 minutes, occasionally shorter, and once as long as 4 minutes (the Fillmore East, New York City, June 19, 1970). On the recording, both repetitions of the opening (the last being the coda) are approximately the same length. During live performances, the coda was generally 45 seconds to 1½ minutes long, and immediately segued into the next tune. At the August 2 and 16 concerts, the coda was much shorter. At the Fillmore West in San Francisco, the opening was preceded by a 2-minute introduction played by Chick Corea, joined toward the end by Dave Holland.

32. The term *pedal point* was used in the introduction, where in the modal music of Coltrane and Davis it refers to what I called a *gravitational center*. This is a more general term than *key*, since the conventions of diatonic (major and minor) harmonies are not present. In this case, the note C grounds all other musical activity, since it forms a point of reference due to its repetition and low pitch.

33. Throughout the life of the band, Chick Corea offered playful variations on the descending "staircase" motif; at Salle Pleyel, he rapidly arpeggiated the motif and at another point he changed speeds, repeating the phrase more slowly and then more quickly, followed by the "crashing chord." In Berlin, Davis played the staircase motif, and Corea hinted at the coming vamp during the opening. During the coda, the rhythm section periodically played rapid lines as an undercurrent of the various motifs played by Davis.

34. Monk 2006; performed in Oslo, Norway. The song was composed by Harry Warren and Al Dubin for the film *Broadway Gondolier* (1935), and pianist Fats Waller recorded it in 1935.

35. Davis had played on the same bill as Blood, Sweat and Tears very shortly before the *Bitches Brew* recording sessions: at venues in Texas, July 19–20; at Madison Square Garden in New York City, July 25; and at Rutgers University in New Brunswick, New Jersey, July 27. Was the quotation a casual passing reference, or was it an acknowledgment of reciprocity (affirmative or negative) between the two bands and their cross-fertilization (Blood, Sweat and Tears trumpeter was jazz musician Lou Soloff)? Might it have been intended as critical commentary about his rock venue bookings, where he was granted second or third billing to rock groups?

36. The Stockholm and Berlin shows are included on the *Miles Davis Quintet: Live in Europe 1969*, the Bootleg Series, vol. 2. Davis 2013. March Fillmore East and April Fillmore West shows were each released on CD: Davis 2001 and Davis 1997. The complete Isle of Wight Festival performance in England is included on the 2004 DVD *Miles Electric: A Different Kind of Blue*. Lerner 2004. Recordings of the shows at Freeport, Grand Bahama Island, and Tanglewood in Lenox, Massachusetts, are available at Wolfgang's Vault Concert Vault, http://www.concertvault.com/ (accessed March 15, 2015), and Davis 2010.

37. For discussion within this book, I compared ten versions of "Bitches Brew." These included, from 1969, performances of the tune at three concerts from the fall European tour: Salle Pleyel in Paris, November 3 (first of two sets); Folkets Hus in Stockholm,

November 5; and Berliner Jazztage at the Berlin Philharmonic, November 7. (Audiences had not yet heard the studio recording; its release was several months away, in April 1970.) These shows were also the first opportunity the public had to hear the quintet perform "It's About That Time" after listening to it at home, since *In a Silent Way*, which features the tune, had only been released in late July 1969.

Versions from 1970 compared include one spring concert at the Fillmore West on April 10 (immediately following Corea and Holland's recording *The Song of Singing*), with Steve Grossman replacing Wayne Shorter on saxophone; two shows during the June stand at the Fillmore East with the sextet (adding percussionist Airto Moreira), on June 17 and 19; and three performances with the septet (adding second keyboardist Keith Jarrett) at the CBS Records Convention in Freeport, Grand Bahama Island, on August 2; at Tanglewood in Lenox, Massachusetts, on August 18; and the band's final performance, at the Isle of Wight Festival in England on August 29. The addition of Jarrett at the Fillmore East and his eventual replacement of Chick Corea are mentioned in *DownBeat* magazine, January 20, 1972, p. 36.

38. The result is in part a pitch shift. Thom Holmes defines ring modulation as "a form of amplitude modulation in which special circuitry suppresses the carrier signal and reproduces only the sidebands. Two additional frequencies are created in place of the original carrier signal. One is equal to the sum of the two input frequencies, and the other is equal to the difference between them. If the input signal has many harmonics, such as a guitar or the human voice, the resulting output signal is complex and rich—a kind of ghost of the original sound." Holmes (1985) 2012, 230; illustration on 211. Documentation on the synthesizer company Moog Music's website adds: "At lower to medium levels, the MF Ring can be used to accompany and accentuate notes. As Mix is increased, you will notice more synthesized and bell-type sounds. At maximum, the input signal is completely gone and only the sum and difference frequencies are heard." MF refers to Minifoogers, a model developed by Moog Music. http://www.moogmusic.com/products/minifoogers/. Accessed March 15, 2015.

39. The tour spanned October 26–November 9, 1969, with shows at the Teatro Lirico, Milan; Teatro Sistina, Rome; Stadthalle, Vienna; Hammersmith Odeon, London; Ronnie Scott's Club, London; Salle Pleyel, Paris; Tivoli Konsertsal, Copenhagen; Fokets Hus, Stockholm; Philharmonie, Berlin; and De Doelen, Rotterdam. The repertoire now incorporated "Bitches Brew," "Spanish Key," and Joe Zawinul's "Directions."

40. In the second set, Corea's "Bitches Brew" solo is accompanied by rapid bass lines racing up and down Holland's fingerboard, a duo with light additions from DeJohnette. This pattern develops further when Corea's solo takes a more atonal turn. At one point, Holland offers variants of a phrase Shorter constructed in the saxophonist's preceding solo. There is much breathing space within Holland's flurry of figures, just as Corea does the same within his own complex constructions. When Corea's notes and collections of notes become sparser and spread apart, Holland contributes pairs of notes that are also spaced apart. At the close of the solo, the Fender Rhodes tremolo figure adds an eerie quality to the instrument's sound. Davis then plays a high-register, muted, elegiac section, followed by a return to the opening themes.

41. For this listener, it is impossible for a horn-and-drums combination of this intensity, particularly just two years after John Coltrane's death, not to call to mind Coltrane and Rashied Ali's duets on *Interstellar Space* (1967).

42. If considered harmonically, this could be heard as a C-minor chord, first inversion.

43. Holland plays material related to the vamp, but does not state it directly; and he speeds up and slows down as he follows Corea.

44. Merlin 1996. Merlin's extensive Miles Davis "Sessionography" is available on the Web and included in part in Tingen 2001a.

45. Merlin 1996.

46. The November 19 and 28, 1969, sessions included Chick Corea and Steve Grossman (Grossman would join the Davis touring band five months later), Herbie Hancock on second keyboard, Ron Carter on bass, Billy Cobham on drums, John McLaughlin on guitar, Airto Moreira on percussion, and for the first time, sitarist Khalil Balakrishna and tabla player Bihari Sharma. Bass clarinetist Bennie Maupin and electric bassist Harvey Brooks joined from the *Bitches Brew* sessions. In the January 27–29 and February 6, 1970, sessions, the touring band was supplemented by Maupin, Josef Zawinul, McLaughlin, Cobham, Moreira, and on the twenty-seventh, Balakrishna. Some of the tunes were released on *Big Fun*.

47. Starting on February 18, 1970, Davis recorded material that would be released on *A Tribute to Jack Johnson*. This was a guitar- rather than keyboard-centered studio band, supplemented by Herbie Hancock on Farfisa organ. By the April 7 session, groove-oriented bassist Michael Henderson had replaced Dave Holland in the studio, hinting at the change that would come in the touring band in early fall 1970. On May 19, 21, and 27, the sessions began to include keyboardist Keith Jarrett as well as guitarist John McLaughlin, collecting material that would be released as *Live-Evil*. Chick Corea returned to the sessions, doubling with Jarrett, for the June 3 and 21 sessions.

48. For instance, Charles Sherrell's bass line on James Brown's "Say It Loud, I'm Black and I'm Proud," and Larry Graham's on Sly Stone's "Sing a Simple Song"; both are quoted in *A Tribute to Jack Johnson*.

49. Lenny White, quoted in milesdavis.com.

50. Chick Corea, quoted in Toner 1974, 15.

51. Goddet 1979, 363–64. Translation by Mark Dermer, 2010; quoted in Gluck 2012a, 145.

52. Herbie Hancock, quoted in Gluck 2012a, 145. Keith Waters offers theoretical analysis that demonstrates points within the 1965–68 Miles Davis Quintet recordings where some rhythmic and harmonic structures retain conventional functions, while others do not. Waters 2011, 76–81.

53. Jack DeJohnette, quoted in Mercer 2004, 128.

54. Winner 1970.

55. The increasing use of rhythmic ostinati characterizes Chick Corea's playing during the second show. In "Directions," Corea bridges the end of Shorter's solo and his own by playing heavily accented ostinati.

56. Dave Holland, interviewed in Lerner 2004, at 35:33–35:52.

57. John Mars, interview by the author, November 19, 2014.

58. Wayne Shorter, quoted in Mercer 2004, 130.

59. Miles Davis, quoted in Szwed 2002, 289–90.

60. Chick Corea, quoted in Nemeyer 2005, 37.

61. Dave Holland, quoted in Mercer 2004, 130.

62. Dave Holland, quoted in Nemeyer 2012, 32.

63. Chick Corea, quoted in Mercer 2004, 130, 129.

64. This is around the fifty-two-minute mark. Earlier, approaching four and a half minutes, the camera focuses in on Corea at the drums and soon after on DeJohnette on the Fender Rhodes.

Chapter Three

1. Radano 1993, 140ff; G. Lewis 2008, 215ff.

2. Ness 1976.

3. G. Lewis 2007, 8.

4. Ratliff 2007.

5. L. Jenkins 2006; Other Minds Festival, Jenkins bio; *Guardian* 2007.

6. Leroy Jenkins, quoted in Panken 1993.

7. For more on the story of Jenkins's time with the AACM in Chicago, see G. Lewis 2008, 1–3, 10, 13, 23, 135. See also G. Lewis 2007.

8. Leroy Jenkins, quoted in Panken 1993.

9. Kunle Mwanga, quoted in Panken 1994.

10. Radano 1993, 29–47, presents a portrait of the musical and cultural environment of Anthony Braxton's youth.

11. Anthony Braxton, quoted in ibid., 73.

12. Braxton subsequently studied at the Chicago School of Music, and then Roosevelt University, also in Chicago.

13. Braxton enlisted in 1964.

14. Cage (1961) 2011. "Experimental Music," 8.

15. Billy Hart, interview by the author, June 17, 2008.

16. Braxton (1970) 2000.

17. Anthony Braxton, quoted in Lock 1988, 151.

18. Braxton 1968 (1993).

19. Heffley 1996, 309.

20. Richard Teitelbaum, interview by the author, April 12, 2008.

21. Anthony Braxton, quoted in Panken 1995.

22. I wonder whether the omission of Miles Davis's band from the Festival Actuel lineup was caused by a scheduling conflict or by a programming decision from either Miles's management or the festival's organizers. After a fall 1969 European tour, it would be two years before Davis's next appearance on the continent. His band that followed the Lost Quintet returned to the Fillmore West in San Francisco in October 1970 and then the Cellar Door, a Washington, DC, jazz club, in December. His appearances at rock festivals seem to have become a thing of the past.

23. Davis began his 1970 summer season with a show in July at a venue that mixed rock, jazz, and pop acts, the Schaefer Music Festival in New York City's Central Park.

24. Welch 1970, 16.

Revolutionary Ensemble bassist Sirone (Norris Jones) felt that the Festival Actuel exploited the musicians. He later recalled: "First of all they were supposed to have the BYG festival in Paris itself but with what was going down [the student protests] they moved it out, into Belgium. O.K. that was a whole new deal and the promoter, Mr. Karakos had all the artists; lined them up in a circle in a field where they were going to be putting up a tent and all that shit; all the guys lined up in a circle except Sirone. His interpreter stood in the middle of that circle and gave out the most insulting remarks and speech about the change of the festival and here are the new contracts and all the times had changed and everything else and the last word was you can take it or leave it and he just walked away. I had a talk with him, a *serious* talk with him because it was painful to see a lot of these guys I admired being treated like this. You'd go down to the office at BYG and you'd see the guys hanging out daily, for what? A damn recording. Not me, man, I left. . . . He [Karakos] recorded everyone but it was totally degrading." Quoted in Spann 2006, 86.

25. The festival was originally slated to take place in Paris. However, the previous spring was a time of student protests there. In May 1968, students and workers demonstrated in the streets of the city, occupied the Sorbonne, factories, and other institutions, and clashed with police. Now, in 1969, the police refused to allow the festival to take place in Paris. Thus, the promoters moved the event to Belgium.

26. Richard Teitelbaum, interview by the author, April 12, 2008.

27. Ibid.

28. Curran 1995, and expanded in Curran 2006. Also see Curran and Teitelbaum 1989, Curran 2000.

29. MEV existed in parallel with fellow spontaneous improvisation group AMM, a British ensemble founded in 1965 by guitarist Keith Rowe, saxophonist Lou Gare, and drummer Eddie Prévost, soon joined by Cornelius Cardew and others.

30. Curran 2006, 485.

31. Rzewski 2006, 491–95.

David Bernstein describes some of the instrumentation used by MEV members. Frederic Rzewski "performed with a thick piece of plate glass cut in the shape of a piano to which he also attached a contact microphone. Using plastic scrapers, he created shrieking high-frequency sounds, and with his fingers played his glass plate as if it were a percussion instrument. He also had a collection of amplified springs of various kinds, which he plucked, bowed, scraped, and struck, producing an array of thunderous and shrill sounds. Rzewski designed what he called a 'photoresistor mixer' with which performers using penlights could control the movement of sound in space." Alvin Curran "performed on a five-liter tin can made by AGIP, one of the principal producers of motor oil in Italy. It had the three bands of Italian colors, white, red, and green, a contact microphone, an African thumb piano taped on the top, and could produce extremely loud drum-like sounds. Curran also played a twisted old trumpet with a contact microphone in the bell with which he would use breathing, vocal sounds, and trumpet tones to distort the diaphragm of the microphone." On Richard Teitelbaum: "In 1967, after a trip back to the United States to explore 'biofeedback music' utilizing electronic interfaces with human neurological and physiological systems, Teitelbaum returned to Rome with a Moog synthesizer along with a brainwave amplifier also designed by Moog that made it possible for him to use alpha wave signals produced by the brain as control voltages for his synthesizer." Additional instruments were played by fellow MEV members Jon Phetteplace, Ivan Vandor, and Allan Bryant; Carol Plantamura used her voice. Bernstein 2006, 535–50.

32. In Curran 1995 and Curran 2006, 483. Curran continues: "It is the art of stepping outside of time, disappearing in it, becoming it. It is both the fine art of listening and responding and the more refined art of silence. It is the only musical art where the entire

'score' is merely the self and the others, and the space and moment where and when this happens. Improvisation is the only musical art which is predicated entirely on human trust."

33. Anthony Braxton explains *restructuralism*: "At a certain point in any information continuum, for evolution to occur, the structural properties or the whole mentality surrounding that information undergoes a change. Restructuralism is my word for that phenomenon.... For instance, after Charlie Parker played his music, the language dynamics of that music would create a whole reality that could help human beings. That's what we see when we talk of the post-bop continuum; they're the people who have been able to make a reality out of Charlie Parker's solutions." Braxton contrasts innovators of fundamental principles with "stylism"—"people usually take that information and use for whatever . . . [and if they dominate] there will be no forward motion"—and "traditionalism": "forward motion with respect to having better understanding of the fundamentals and of the route a given lineage has travelled. Evolution in this context would mean a better understanding of what has gone before; and the use of that information to help people comprehend their time and their place." He regards a balance between the three as the mark of "a healthy culture." Quoted in Lock 1988, 163–65.

34. Anthony Braxton, quoted in Panken 1995.

35. Curran expands on his theme: "These were times of life-and-death issues that people questioned. And you questioned everything. And even at the far edges or imaginary far edges of radical movements, as we imagined we were, but didn't have that concept, we acted almost, in a way, like a band of brigands. Almost as if we were acting lawlessly in a land where [it was] possible there would no longer be any laws in the near future. Where law would be rendered useless, because people would understand how to spontaneously organize themselves and act accordingly. [Yet] we had a moral obligation to see that no one killed themselves or injured themselves. We did act as the police, but in a gentle way. Clearly, one had an instinctive moral obligation to see that in a case where you confer such freedom so suddenly on a mass of people and you don't even know who they are, their names, where they come from, or what, that good God, this is a social emergency. Anything could happen" (Alvin Curran and Richard Teitelbaum, interview by the author, June 13, 2012).

36. Anthony Braxton, quoted in John Litweiler's liner notes to Braxton's *3 Compositions of New Jazz* (Braxton [1968] 1993).

37. And three years after the demise of Circle.

38. From an author interview with drummer John Mars, November 19, 2014, speaking about his conversations with Braxton in Toronto. Mars's reflections place the latter musician's observations in context: "The first time that I was privileged to be in Anthony Braxton's company was on Bill and Chloe [Onari] Smith's enclosed back porch, in December 1974. During that visit, Anthony Braxton, Barry Altschul, and Dave Holland were all staying in the home of my friends, the promoters the Smith family. We were such a group of very different personalities and ethnic backgrounds there. My friend Bill Smith is a jazz history expert-publisher-producer and artist. His ex-wife Chloe, a woman artist, is a relentless promoter of the music. Those two made it possible to hear Roscoe Mitchell and Cecil Taylor concerts in Toronto back then. Anthony was avidly promoted by Bill, who as a reed player himself was greatly influenced [in his own music] by Braxton and Mitchell. I appreciated [that] when listening to Anthony extrapolate on the work of some musical hero of his, the talk was not all-technical *musician*-type talk. . . . He was such a genuine fan of so many

musicians from so many disparate styles. . . . He had a humble way of carrying himself, and that stuck with me, too."

Mars adds: "I remember thinking to myself that I was surprised to find that many of Braxton's heroes were white guys: 'Father' Charles Ives, Henry Cowell, and Paul Desmond, for example, were all stressed to me on that first day and during Anthony's other visits to Toronto."

See the discussion of Braxton's meeting with Free Life Communications in chapter 4, as well as Lock 1999, 159–62, which addresses criticisms of Braxton's racial perspective.

39. Before Braxton's arrival, John Stubblefield and Philip Wilson were the only AACM members in the city.

40. Mwanga had for a time served as booking agent for the Art Ensemble of Chicago.

41. At the end of that time, he relocated to his own apartment in the Village, where he stayed for the duration of his time in New York City before returning to Paris. Radano 1993, 155.

42. Dialogue from Kemper 2002.

Drummer Warren Smith, an Artists House regular visitor and performer, appreciates the difficulty of keeping an artist's space open despite a lack of revenue to cover expenses: "Ornette was fortunate in that he was able to hold out until he actually got some money. And of course James Jordan [Coleman's cousin, manager, and later an administrator with the New York State Council on the Arts] was able to assist him in that. And he was able to control a whole building space in which he had both private living quarters and a studio" (interview by the author, October 18, 2011).

43. Riggins 1972, 34.

44. Cherry was trumpeter in Coleman's classic quartet during the late 1950s and early 1960s.

45. Karl Berger, interview by the author, September 25, 2011.

46. Jerome Cooper, interview by the author, September 24, 2011.

47. Leroy Jenkins, quoted in Primack 1978, 24, 50. Jenkins views the period when he lived at Artists House as the time "when I went to the University of Ornette. He put the finishing touches on me. I spent three months up there, staying at his house, doing everything. Answering the door, helping him copy music, arguing about his harmolodic theory." Ibid.

Karl Berger similarly relates: "I really sort of studied with Ornette. Not officially." He adds this affectionate anecdote: "He has a way of talking that is like harmolodic talk. He does exactly what he does in music. He'll say a sentence, then he'll use a word in the middle of the sentence to start another sentence. And do that two or three times in one sentence. So nobody understands what's going on. He says everything he wants to say, but it's sort of shortened. And that's how he plays. He plays the same way" (interview by the author, September 25, 2011).

48. Karl Berger, quoted in Panken 2008.

49. Litweiler 1994, 138.

50. See *DownBeat* 1972, 36. Ted Daniels's *Tapestry*, with Jerome Cooper on drums, was recorded at Artists House in 1974. See Sharpe (undated). Prior to that, Ornette Coleman's *Friends and Neighbors* was recorded there in 1967.

51. Rockwell 1974.

52. CMS cofounder Karl Berger also remembers a later date, when "there was a festival where I played there with the group with Dave Holland, and also with David Izenzon's

group. David Izenzon, Ingrid, and myself, we had a trio called Mind's Eye or some title like that. That's when I had started to work with David Izenzon. Basically, he was the leader. He was looking at it more like a collective. J. C. Moses was the drummer" (interview by the author, September 25, 2011).

Another Artists House concert series during that later period included bands led by pianist Dollar Brand, bassist Jimmy Garrison, and others.

53. Karl Berger believes that "Ornette got pushed out of that building. It was racial. They didn't want him in the building. He was the first one in SoHo living there. Then other people began moving in. And it became fashionable. And four or five years later, they pushed him out. They found a reason. They found a way. It was warfare in this building. People wanted him out of there. It was racial, but it was also probably sound [level] related. He was really harassed. From there he went to Rivington Street, and he rented a schoolhouse. And there he got really robbed and beaten up. It was terrible. It [the neighborhood] was a drug scene. He was alone on the last floor of an empty schoolhouse" (interview by the author, September 25, 2011).

Jerome Cooper adds: "There was a painter who lived above the Artists House—we would be rehearsing—and this cat would start mopping his floor and water would be coming down" (interview by the author, September 25, 2011).

54. A shorter, purely instrumental version of the tune follows. The calypso-inflected "Long Time No See" is equally upbeat, with Coleman playing short, tuneful phrases and following them with variations and responses, closely in tune with Ed Blackwell's snare-drum-centered beat. Coleman appears on trumpet, interlocking with Dewey Redman's saxophone on "Let's Play." "Forgotten Songs" is one of Coleman's simplest, most singable and folklike melodies, around which the two saxophonists interweave a garland of melodic lines. The set closes with the rapid-fire stop-start "Tomorrow." Redman offers a focused and intense solo, integrating multi-phonics and wails over Charlie Haden's rapidly bowed, sustained-note arco bass. After this virtuosic display, Coleman follows with a comparatively calm, well-organized solo.

Altogether, the entire recording is a celebration of good feeling and friendly music-making, as Coleman, surrounded by invited "friends and neighbors" (Jean Delmas reports that a photograph shows Gil Evans, Pharoah Sanders, and Don Cherry in the audience), is reunited with a rhythm section from his early days in New York City. As Karl Berger observes: "That 'Friends and Neighbors' feeling was exactly what happened in that period." Source: liner notes translated by Don Waterhouse, RCA edition, Paris. A second session from Artists House, *Ornette Coleman Broadcasts*, recorded on September 22, 1972, was released on the J For Jazz label: JFJ 803; Ornette Coleman Discography, Jazz Discography Project. Nobuaki Togashi, Kohji "Shaolin" Matsubayashi, and Masayuki Hatta. http://www .jazzdisco.org/ornette-coleman/discography/. Accessed March 15, 2015.

John Litweiler reports a Lee Konitz–Chet Baker session there, listing Coleman as producer. Litweiler 1994, 137.

55. Kunle Mwanga, quoted in Panken 1994.

56. Maryanne Amacher (1938–2009) was a composer of sound art and an installation artist.

57. Except where otherwise noted in the rest of this chapter, quotations by Alvin Curran and Richard Teitelbaum are from a June 13, 2012, conversation with them conducted by the author at Teitelbaum's home in Bearsville, New York.

58. Morton Feldman (1926–1987) was an American composer connected with John Cage's circle of musicians and artists.

59. Gendron 2010, 557–74.

60. The location was 8 West Eighth Street. http://www.nyss.org/exhibition/give-my-regards-to-eighth-street/. Accessed March 15, 2015.

61. Richard Teitelbaum: "I had visited Wesleyan, and I had this idea about doing a kind of MEV-type world music thing. Putting together a band, coming out of MEV [and] moving toward combining different kinds of cultural diversity. We had mostly European and American people in the band. Although we were doing 'Sound Pool' [audience-participation improvisation], which was pretty open, so a lot of people were playing but it was still pretty much Western music. On the other hand, we were starting to hear Ali Akbar Khan and Ravi Shankar, recordings of Buddhist chant, gamelan, and stuff like that. So I had the idea to put together a group of musicians, actually having musicians from as many different cultures as possible—play together, improvise together. Since Wesleyan was a situation when they had captive musicians, I thought that would be a good situation for that. I applied to the PhD program and was accepted. I guess they gave me some money. My real interest was to put together a group of world musicians."

What Teitelbaum means by "captive musicians" is that Wesleyan College had a world music program that was being taught by musicians from many different cultures. Teitelbaum's experiences in starting the World Band, upon his arrival at Wesleyan in September 1969, were highly positive: "People were receptive. We started rehearsing every week. I don't know if *rehearse* is the right word. I had a nice house that [artist] Barbara Mayfield and I were sharing with two other graduate students. It was a big house, so we'd just invite everybody to come once a week and jam, basically. First, it was mostly students, I guess. It was kind of very open. It was still under the influence of the 'Sound Pool' kind of thing. Anybody could play. Or 'Zuppa,' it was very open. It was pretty free at that point. And so it kind of grew. At first it was two, then four, six, and then eight. Then we did a concert, that I still have tapes of. It was like thirty to sixty people were playing, a lot of people. And what was sort of happening was that it was from very different cultures. There'd be the Javanese gamelan people, so it was soft and all that. And Indian and whatever, and also this guy Doogie Mitchell, who was Navaho Indian.

"I think a lot came from MEV. The MEV history, the earlier MEV, was like five or six people basically. It was pretty much really the same people most of the time; it did develop a chemistry. What kept happening is, as Alvin said, we kept opening it up more and more, which for one thing that accomplished was breaking up a lot of preconceived habits. So we had Franco Cataldi, who had never played a note on the trombone. All of a sudden, he was the trombone player. You never knew what the hell he was going to do. From there it moved down to the 'Sound Pool,' where it could be fifty or one hundred people playing. It was a kind of constant renewal. It kept changing."

62. Also participating in one of MEV's shows, at Haverford College, was Serge Tcherepnin, a composer and electronic instrument builder.

63. Alvin Curran, quoted in Friendly 1970.

64. This exchange is from an interview conducted by the author, May 13, 2012.

65. Gottlieb did similar planning for a Living Theater tour. Cofounded in New York City by Judith Malina and Julian Beck in the late 1940s, Living Theater is an influential experimental theater company that, in Beck's words, sought "to move from the theater to the

street and from the street to the theater." Lacking a physical building during the late 1960s, the group temporarily reinvented itself as a touring company. For more about Saul Gottlieb and the Radical Theatre Repertory, see Munk 1969. For more about the Living Theater, see http://www.livingtheatre.org. Accessed March 15, 2015.

66. Among those who responded was John Richard Ronsheim at Antioch; he was Cecil Taylor's roommate at the New England Conservatory in the 1950s.

67. Curran describes this elsewhere as "followed uninterrupted by free improvisation with audience participation." Curran 2010, 628.

68. Bill Curran, interview by the author, May 13, 2012.

69. Teitelbaum adds: "I think that was the general feeling."

70. Bill Curran, interview by the author, May 13, 2012.

71. P. Davis 1970, 21; an advance announcement of the show appears in the *New York Times*, "Concert by Film Musicians," February 15, 1970. The film reference in the headline was to *Zabriskie Point*, for which MEV had composed the sound track. The concert was also reviewed in *High Fidelity*, May 1970, 20–21.

72. Curran: "I think we were over our heads in enthusiasm. Suddenly we were in the beginnings of BAM [Brooklyn Academy of Music] . . . as a new center of contemporary artists. So it was itself a kind of an experimental breeding ground, and I remember at that time, the Living Theater, which we were very close to, with Judith Malina, were actually living in Brooklyn, right [near BAM]. So there was a kind of a crucible of groups and events and scenes and people, but somehow the dimensions of the Brooklyn Academy. . . . [If there] were something like that happening at the Kitchen or in its [BAM's] former venue [it would have been different] . . . but somehow the architectural dimension and specificity of this three-thousand- or two-thousand-seat theater was overwhelming. And MEV seemed, I remember this very clearly, the MEV attempt to create a 'Sound Pool,' which we did success-fully actually, seemed insignificant on this stage. It was a huge theater. It wasn't full. There were people walking in and walking out. It was clearly a scene. I specifically remember at one point a kid shows up carrying the inside [the harp] of a piano. He's dragging, schlep-ping this thing onstage. He says: 'Give me a contact mic.' I don't know. It was so utterly real if you were a participant, but the reality was we were in this classical proscenium theater."

73. Curran 2010, 628.

74. Courtesy of Richard Teitelbaum. The recording was originally made for the Antioch College radio station by Tuscarola Sound Recorders. Additional tracks on the recording are from a July 28, 1975, return concert, without Anthony Braxton.

75. As documented on the anthology *Musica Elettronica Viva: MEV 40* (2008), which spans performances from 1967, 1972, 1982, 1989, 1990, 2002, and 2007.

76. It is not presently clear who was playing bass and drums, quite possibly Antioch students.

77. A fifth ensemble piece on the recording is likely from a subsequent MEV concert at Antioch, on July 28, 1975.

78. As discussed and referenced in appendix 3.

79. Visible in the MEV photograph included in this book.

80. "The score presents performers—any number of trained as well as untrained musicians—with a sixty-five-note numbered melodic line, which they are instructed to execute in a simple increasing algorithm (1, 1–2, 1–2–3, 1–2–3–4, and so on) at an accelerating piece. These strict parameters might lend the piece the character of an etude

or exercise, but as the music unfolds, more voices enter, and the boundaries of the original phrase become frayed and inscrutable, any technical sterility or dryness evaporates. What emerges instead is a Philip Glass-esque quality of hypnosis and fascination, a listening experience akin to being immersed in a river: it's impossible to take stock of everything, but small glimpses and discrete perceptions rise to the surface as you're swept along." From the Icky Music blog: https://www.tumblr.com/search/les+moutons+de+panurge. Accessed March 15, 2015.

81. Kunle Mwanga, quoted in Bey 2007.

82. Kunle Mwanga, quoted in Panken 1994.

83. Mwanga produced a second Creative Construction Company concert at the New England Conservatory, with saxophonist Henry Threadgill replacing Braxton, and then three more concerts at the Peace Church. These included the "Five 'Terrible' Musicians" with saxophonist Dewey Redman, drummer Eddie Moore, pianist Muhal Richard Abrams, and saxophonist Edwin Dougherty, and a concert featuring Leo Smith, drummer Thurman Barker, and Henry Threadgill. When Braxton returned to Paris (1971–74), Mwanga became his manager and booking agent. In that capacity, he produced Braxton's 1972 concert at Town Hall in New York City, with singer Jeanne Lee, saxophonist John Stubblefield, Dave Holland, and Barry Altschul (with financial support from Ornette Coleman). Later, he produced a 1975 show by the Art Ensemble of Chicago and Braxton at UC Berkeley, a two-week stand at the Five Spot in New York City by the Art Ensemble, and starting in 1976, concerts by saxophonist David Murray.

84. Litweiler 1994, 138.

85. The first motif has two parts; a dissonant tone cluster is repeated twice (A–B♭), played by trumpet and flute, juxtaposed to a four-note bass motif: D [up to] G [down an octave to] G [up to E]; on the second repetition, the bass ends the phrase by jumping down an octave, emphatically repeating the E).

86. The main theme is a variant of the bass line (D [up to] G [down to] F [up to] A).

87. Violin: G–A and trumpet/flute: A–B♭, with the bass repeating a G, possibly joined by Abrams on clarinet. Fn4: C–(up to) G—pause—repeated D–(up) G–(down) D–(up) G up and down toggle.

88. Part 2 continues with the harmonica, and then travels through a similarly broad range of solo and ensemble sections, textural qualities, and levels of intensity. As the three-minute mark approaches, the level of energy spikes with rapid drumming, piano clusters, and free playing on trumpet. Around six minutes, Braxton offers his most energetic and angular solo of the performance, highlighted by squeals, honks, and repeated figures. McCall builds tension with cymbal thrashes and then movement all around his kit, joined by Jenkins and the others. The full-ensemble open improvisation winds down with a chromatic solo line on violin by Jenkins, followed by a relatively quiet section around ten minutes: Abrams plays shimmering runs as Jenkins continues, with Braxton adding a long, slow melody; the others join in this more somber mood; at 11:45 the group returns to echoes of the opening motifs. A minute later, Davis plays solo; behind him are hints of Abrams's piano, delicate percussion, and Jenkins's pizzicato, through the conclusion of this section, at 14:33.

"Life Spiral" is a repetition of the thematic material that opened part 1. The second set, not described here, appears on a second recording, *Creative Construction Company, Volume II*, which consists of a Jenkins composition of similar length, "No More White Gloves (with Sand under Your Shoes Doing a Dance)."

89. L. Smith 1973. The passage continues: "this is the fundamental principle underlining my music, in that it extends into all the source-areas of music-making, i.e. each single rhythm-sound, or a series of sound-rhythm is a complete improvisation. in other words, each element is autonomous in its relationship in the improvisation. therefore, there is no intent towards time as a period of development. rather, time is employed as an element of space: space that is determined between the distance of two sound-rhythms (here the reference to rhythm is in reference to its absoluteness: the sum of the elements and the placement of them) and space/silence that is the absence of audible sound-rhythm (just as each sound-rhythm is considered an autonomous element in an improvisation, so, too, must space and space/silence be considered; and when space and space/silence are really-realized, then we will know so well how to perceive and appreciate their uniqueness each time they appear, as easily as we perceive and appreciate the uniqueness of each sound-rhythm): i seek another dimension in music."

90. Potter and Smith 1976, 26, cited in Radano 1993, 161n.

91. Anthony Braxton, quoted in Radano 1993, 162.

Chapter Four

1. Chick Corea, interview by the author, December 11, 2011.

2. Chick Corea, quoted in Nemeyer 2005, 32.

3. Brooklyn-born Dave Liebman "began playing saxophone at twelve years old after a few years of classical piano, a good musical move that my parents insisted upon. The beginning of my interest in jazz was at first from hearing guys play at jam sessions up in the Catskill Mountain resort area where I began playing [saxophone] summers when I was thirteen years old. These were all heavy New York musicians who would jam after the show/dance bands were finished." He spent time as a teenager attending shows at the major jazz clubs in the city. Seeing Coltrane's quartet with Eric Dolphy at Birdland when he was fifteen became the "raison d'etre for my whole life, why I did this jazz thing at all. It affected me that much!" (Interview by the author, September 28, 2011.)

Liebman studied for a year with pianist Lennie Tristano, but developed his playing through experimentation and listening.

4. Dave Liebman, interview by the author, September 28, 2011.

5. Ibid.

6. Dave Liebman, interview by the author, April 9, 2013.

7. Ibid.

8. Chick Corea, quoted in Nemeyer 2005, 32.

9. Particularly on Fifty-Second Street.

10. The original landowner was a British military officer who had fought in the French and Indian War. He bequeathed the land of his "Chelsea" estate to his grandson, Clement Clarke Moore, an urban planner better known for crafting the poem "A Visit from St. Nicholas." After donating a portion of the land for an Episcopal seminary, Moore carved out plots to be used for housing that was to comprise apartment buildings fronted by green gardens.

In the intervening years, Chelsea became home to abolitionist James Gibbons, whose safe house was an Underground Railroad stop. The laying of train tracks ushered in an era of commerce, and Chelsea became the site of the first Macy's and B. Altman department stores.

During the early twentieth century, Chelsea's Twenty-Third Street served for a time as the center of New York's theater district, and its Hudson River piers docked luxury cruise ships. The most anticipated ship, which of course never arrived, was the *Titanic*. In the 1930s, the world's largest apartment complex was built in the neighborhood; one year, New York Yankee baseball stars donned Santa Claus suits and distributed gifts to the tenants' children.

In the 1950s and '60s, beat writers and poets, along with folk musicians, lived in the Chelsea Hotel. Among them was Bob Dylan. In the 1970s and '80s, punk-rock musicians moved to the building as well.

11. Stephenson 2009.

12. Warren Smith is a Chicago native who relocated to New York City. He was raised as a musician and educated at the University of Illinois, Urbana, where he expanded his musical experience, meeting John Cage and Gunther Schuller, and playing the music of Harry Partch.

13. Warren Smith and his associates started out in a space in midtown, at 509 West 59th Street (off Tenth Avenue). They moved to 151 Twenty-First Street, between Sixth and Seventh Avenues, when percussionist Peter Berry decided to give up his loft. "I gave him $300 in cash and the rent was something like $97 a month" (interview by the author, October 18, 2011). Smith supported the studio, and his family, by playing club dates, Broadway shows [with *West Side Story*, he became the first black musician to work in a Broadway pit orchestra], television shows, and studio sessions at Atlantic and Columbia Records, where he did sessions with Aretha Franklin and many others. At Atlantic Records he became part of a "rhythm section team that included Eric Gale and Cornell Dupree and either Chuck Rainey or Jerry Jermott on the bass, and either Bernard Purdie usually, or Herbie Lovelle as the drummer" (ibid.). In 1969, he began teaching college, and in 1971 joined the American Music, Dance and Theatre Program faculty at SUNY–Old Westbury at the invitation of the program founder, saxophonist and composer Makanda Ken McIntyre.

14. Warren Smith, interview by the author, October 18, 2011. At various points, Hammiet Bluiett and Jabo Ware's Baritone Saxophone Retinue, Marion Brown's tuba ensemble, Max Roach's quartet with Billy Harper, Cecil Bridgewater, and Reggie Workman (or Calvin Hill), and Roach's M'BOOM percussion ensemble were among those in residence or rehearsing at the studio. Smith observes: "[Newport Jazz Festival producer] George Wein wasn't giving up much; he had most of the established people. These were people who had no money and no name. They were looking for an outlet, so they'd come to us. . . . It became the place for musicians to rehearse and present. So it was kind of organic" (ibid.). While music presented at Studio WIS was eclectic, there was substantial room for innovation and experimentation.

15. Smith's own path had recently crossed with an expanded version of the previous Miles Davis Quintet, arranged and conducted by Gil Evans, recording multiple takes of "Falling Water." Recorded on February 16, 1968, four takes were released on disk 4 of Davis (1996) 2004. http://www.jazzdisco.org/miles-davis/discography. http://www.plosin.com/MilesAhead/Sessions.aspx?s=680216. Accessed March 11, 2015. Smith subsequently became a member of Tony Williams Lifetime. Tony Williams Lifetime (1971) 1999.

16. Dave Liebman, interview by the author, September 28, 2011.

17. Ibid., October 28, 2011.

18. Bob Moses had previous experience hosting sessions in his own loft in the late 1960s, farther downtown on Eldridge Street.

19. Dave Liebman, interview by the author, September 28, 2011.

20. Barry Altshul, interview by the author, September 19, 2011.

21. Thelonious Monk (1917–1982) was a noted pianist and composer of the bebop era and later, known for his distinct minimal, angular style of playing. Charles Ives (1874–1954) was a modernist American composer known for his juxtaposition of complex rhythms, polytonalities, and popular and art musical sources. Pianist Bud Powell (1924–1966) parallels Charlie Parker as a prime developer of bebop.

22. Dave Liebman, interview by the author, April 9, 2013.

23. Dave Liebman, quoted in Radano 1981, 105.

24. Dave Liebman, interview by the author, April 9, 2013. What Liebman terms "completely free in the language of *Ascension*" refers to the spirit of the original rather than a literal reworking of its thematic material or structure.

25. Lewis Porter describes the ten-musician work as "a forty-minute piece that linked passages of hollering group improvisation with intense solos. *Ascension* has a distinct form, which includes composed ensemble passages, and group improvisational sections based upon various scales, in between which are placed Individual solos, supported by the rhythm section." L. Porter 2006 (1999), 263. While *Ascension* built on the collective concept behind Ornette Coleman's *Free Jazz* (1960) for double quartet, the focus on Coltrane may reflect the greater influence of the latter among these young players, who had followed Coltrane's career closely as he rose through and beyond the world of bebop. They were listening closely as he very publicly explored, in clubs and recordings, pathways around and through perceived limitations of harmony and metric rhythm. Each approach Coltrane attempted drew deeply and widely from various musical cultures, and his commitment to the craft of the saxophone was a model to the young.

Also, *Free Jazz* was more a study in dialogue between players, each one commenting on another's phrase, than about the sheer collective energy sought on Nineteenth Street. In *Free Jazz*, individual soloists briefly dip in and out of the mix, riding above a steady rhythmic pulse. The music suggests a more angular version of the conversational qualities of New Orleans jazz. Like jazz of the 1930s and 1940s, it swung. In contrast, *Ascension* is emotionally and technically relentless in comparison, part and parcel to the growing intensity in Coltrane's aesthetic arc through his final two years. The saxophonist explained: "Of course this is the late '60s. Coltrane had just died in '67. I think at least for me and my immediate group of friends we were most immediately affected by the last years of Coltrane, what is called the late Coltrane period. Just being young guys, as it always is, you want to emulate what you hear around your environment. We were most affected by that and of course the whole free jazz thing. *Ascension* is the record that sort of stands out like 'let's do that, play group . . . many horns at the same time; a couple drummers,' it turns out to be like that; no basic heads, no melodies, no chords, just completely free association. And a lot of energy, which of course is a big component of it" (Dave Liebman, recorded on Mahaffay 2009).

While Coltrane's strivings were vested with a black nationalist interpretation by poet Amiri Baraka, saxophonist Archie Shepp, and others—factors adding heft to Coltrane's cultural importance—this interpretation held less significance for the largely white cohort of Dave Liebman.

26. Dave Liebman, interview by the author, April 9, 2013.

27. Ibid., September 28, 2011.

28. Radano 1981, 109.

29. Dave Liebman, interview by the author, September 28, 2011. Moses's father did public relations for Charles Mingus, Billie Holiday, Stan Kenton, Dizzy Gillespie, and Thelonious Monk. When he was a teenager, his drum teachers were his father's clients: Art Blakey, Elvin Jones, and Max Roach. As a young adult, Bob Moses's own loft, on the Lower East Side at 19 Eldridge Street, hosted musicians, all of them white, interested in combining aspects of rock and jazz. Among them were Larry Coryell, Bob Moses, Jim Pepper, Billy Elgart, Arthur Harper, Charles and JoAnne Brackeen, Chris Hills, and Mike Nock. During this period, 1966–68, Nock, Hills, Coryell, and Moses jammed regularly with saxophonist Steve Marcus, and with Art Pepper formed an early jazz-rock band, the Free Spirits. Nicholson 1998, 34; Radano 1981, 98.

30. Dave Liebman, interview by the author, September 28, 2011.

31. Richie Beirach, quoted in Radano 1981, 115.

32. Ironically, Free Life musicians would later seek and often find acceptance in the clubs by playing more mainstream music.

33. G. Lewis 2001/2002, 100.

34. The best known of its groups, the Art Ensemble of Chicago, embedded its diversity of musical values within a cultural symbiosis of black pride and Africanisms, including dress, musical traditions, and instruments. The Art Ensemble's slogan was "Great Black Music: Ancient to the Future." The AACM also saw itself as a collective of composers playing original music. In contrast, a few years after its founding, Free Life Communication moved away from an overt rootedness in Coltrane and other black music in favor of the aesthetics of Euro-American avant-gardists, among them John Cage.

35. "WBAI is listener-supported radio. As a member of the Pacifica chain of radio stations, it provides a vast array of original programming to listeners in the Metropolitan New York City region and worldwide on this site." http://wbai.org/about.html. Accessed March 11, 2015. The station's "Free Music Store," founded by producer and composer Eric Saltzman in 1968, presented live-broadcast concerts before an audience. The music spanned a wide array of forms and cultures. A web-based archive of programming may be found at http://www.pacificaarchives.net/recording/bc0709. Accessed March 11, 2015.

36. Liebman recalls: "We were a fledgling organization with official 501c nonprofit status. I was the president, we had a secretary, we took minutes, et cetera. We tried to do it according to *Robert's Rules of Order*, a book on parliamentary procedure that my mother had given me, since she had run organizations throughout her life" (interview by the author, September 28, 2011). Free Life Communication grew, attracting new members. At its height, Liebman believes, sixty people were affiliated.

Michael Moss, who became the group's secretary and later co-president, recalls a membership of twenty to thirty at the time. Moss, interviewed by the author on October 6, 2011, recalled that he "was born into a musical family. . . . I started playing music at a very early age. My father taught me piano, something I continue to play and use as a compositional tool. However, when I was nine, I started playing clarinet, and added saxophone, flute, and bass clarinet later on. It was on those instruments that I played as much music as I could, playing in the band in high school and college." Moss's father taught him to play jazz standards when he was nine years old, and he "listened to a lot of Eric Dolphy and Trane in the '60s. Every time he [John Coltrane] would come out with a new album, I would listen to it and see where they were going." After completing graduate school at the University of Wisconsin at Madison, Moss returned to New York in 1970, enrolled at the New School for Social Research to complete a master's degree in clinical psychology, and "was playing [saxophone] constantly. I don't think it was anything organized. It was more in people's apartments." He attended a Free Life Communication meeting and began to play music with various members of that collective.

37. Rubin subsequently opened the Rubin Museum on Sixteenth Street. The mission of the Space, directed by Maurice McClelland, was "to provide low-cost practice space for fledgling theater, music, dance and television groups in Manhattan." Fellow resident organizations included Eric Salzman's Quog Music Theater, the Alwin Nikolais/Murray Louis Dance Company, Robert Wilson's first theater company, and Joseph Chaikan and the Open Theater. Teltsch 1993.

38. At 334 West Thirty-Sixth Street, between Eighth and Ninth Avenues.

39. A subsequent leader of the collective, Michael Moss, describes it as "a wide-open space . . . the acoustics were great. They had given us a Steinway grand. The building was four flights, but there were two flights for every floor. For people to make concerts, they had to walk up to the fourth floor. Of course, all the drummers had to bring all their stuff up. We attracted a young, healthy audience, ones who could climb the stairs. We had no seating besides pillows" (interview by the author, October 6, 2011).

40. Dave Liebman, interview by the author, September 28, 2011. Moss adds: "Anybody who had experimental music that didn't really fit into a club would perform" (interview by the author, October 6, 2011).

These groups engaged in collaborative work. Liebman remembers that "one of the premises was to combine modern dance with painting with jazz, free jazz especially" (interview by the author, September 28, 2011). See Kisselgoff 1972, 51, and Kisselgoff 1974.

41. Dave Liebman, interview by the author, September 28, 2011.

42. Ronald Radano observes: "On the whole, the audience was usually a small group of middle-class youths who believed the music and the musicians of Free Life Communication represented the attitudes and beliefs of the counter-culture." Radano 1981, 119.

43. Among the additional musicians on the band's 1973 recording are guitarist John Abercrombie, tabla player Badal Roy, and percussionist Don Alias. Alias had performed on *Bitches Brew*, and Roy on several Miles Davis recordings from 1969 through 1974. Alias toured with Davis in 1971, and Roy in 1972–73.

44. Its new home was drummer Mike Mahaffay's Sunrise Studio at 22 Second Avenue. Free Life participated for three years in an annual festival that included Michael Morgenstern's Jazzmania at 14 East Twenty-Third Street (Madison Avenue), Joe Lee Wilson's Lady's Fort at 2 Bond Street, and John Fischer's Environ, 476 Broadway (between Broome and Grand Streets). Michael Moss recalls that the four lofts ran "a weekend of music. We'd charge ten dollars for everything that was going on in all four places. It was pretty lively. . . . We were quite successful. We were all together. We all collaborated, used each other's mailing lists to get the word out. We played in each other's places. We put ourselves on the map" (interview by the author, October 6, 2011).

It was during this period that the era of jazz performed in lofts began to take off. In SoHo, the best known was Sam Rivers's Studio Rivbea on Bond Street, where Anthony Braxton, Leroy Jenkins, and other AACM members who had moved to New York City found a musical home.

45. And unlike Free Life Communication participants, trio members were known figures in the jazz world, not in need of the kind of performance opportunities the collective upstairs provided.

46. Among the few (and only occasional) black collective jam session participants, Lennie White played on *Bitches Brew*, and Al Foster became Miles Davis's regular drummer during Davis's final decade following his postretirement return to the stage.

47. Dave Holland, quoted in Williams 1970, 21.

Barry Altschul recalls that "[Chick] had already given notice around the end of '69 [although he continued through August 1970]. And we did a gig, we played together, and actually, Miles talked to me about Dave and Chick leaving the band. At the time, he wanted Chick and Dave to stay in the band longer, because *Bitches Brew* had just broken, and he wanted to keep that band. Chick and Dave wanted to leave Miles to continue on the freer path that they started with Miles" (interview by the author, September 19, 2011).

48. Dave Holland, quoted in B. Smith 1973.

49. Dave Holland, quoted in Williams 1970, 21.

50. Billy Childs, quoted in Gluck 2012a, 142.

51. Chick Corea, quoted in Tingen 2001a, 118.

52. Dave Holland, quoted in Williams 1970, 21.

53. Ibid.

54. Dave Holland, quoted in Nemeyer 2012, 32.

55. Chick Corea, quoted in Nemeyer 2012, 32.

56. The full quotation: "No matter what kind of music or musical form, I was always intrigued by the viewpoint of the drummer in a music group. An intimate connection with what the drummer was doing was always essential to making the music rich, tight, and whole. Drums has always been my second love, after the piano. In fact, as the years rolled on, the two instruments seemed synonymous—seeming to provide the same function. There is always some drums next to my piano in my music rooms." Chick Corea, interview by the author, December 11, 2011.

Corea noted, in an interview with Eric Nemeyer: "He [Barry] was willing to work with the tunings and timbres of his kit to accommodate what we were going for. I gave him the Paiste flat ride cymbal to play that Roy Haynes handed down to me. It was (and is still) my choice for a cymbal ride sound for a piano trio." Nemeyer 2012, 32.

57. Quotations in this and the next six paragraphs: Barry Altshul, interview by the author, September 19, 2011.

58. Ibid.

59. Mars's personal odyssey as a drummer helps place Altschul's approach in historical and musical perspective: "In the 1960s, from a very young age, I was studying bebop drummers, mostly all those that had been with Monk, plus Joe Morello with Brubeck, and trying to learn how they managed to sometimes actually play melodically and did amazing turnarounds. Then I discovered Milford Graves, and I learned how to be completely free floating and how to leave time signatures completely out of the picture. Then there was Sunny Murray, who was really propulsive. I also liked Beaver Harris, who followed Milford and Sunny in Albert Ayler's group. Next I heard Tony Oxley on John McLaughlin's *Extrapolation* LP, which came out in 1969. I liked the precision of Oxley and the crisp sound of his ride cymbal. He wasn't playing as free as those guys did with Ayler, because the music was completely different. But still there was this sense of freedom there. . . . Albert [had]

miraculously invented a new music where he and all his exceptional colleagues could forget about trying to find 'the one' or a 'beat' or whatever. Time signatures, among many other things, completely disappeared at times. . . . Barry Altschul came next for me. I certainly knew the stuff he did with Paul Bley, but I really got into Barry with Circle and the Dave Holland record *Conference of the Birds*, with Braxton, Sam Rivers, and Barry. . . . Right away I knew that this is how I wanted to sound as a drummer." (This and the following quotation are from an interview by the author, November 19, 2014.)

Mars spoke at length with Altschul during a 1974 Toronto visit by the Anthony Braxton Trio (Braxton, Altschul, and Dave Holland). While conversing at the home of Bill and Chloe Smith, Mars "got to ask Barry questions about his influences. Pharoah Sanders came up in a conversation about the sound effects. When it came to my wondering about the flood of detail coming from that right hand of his, I asked Barry where do all these ideas of his come from? We had the same favorite drummers, but especially, it was Frankie Dunlop, who had played with Thelonious Monk. . . . Barry and I talked about the melodic solos of Monk's other drummers, like Ben Riley and Shadow Wilson, but mostly we talked about Frankie, who we determined was our absolute, mutual favorite amongst all of Monk's drummers."

60. John Mars, interview by the author, November 19, 2014.

61. Sam Rivers, quoted in Minsker 2005. Rivers recalled that "Alan Douglas [a producer for Arista Records] was from Boston, and I knew him from there. I called him up when I moved to New York, and he set up a few jam sessions for me. Like one with Jimi Hendrix. Alan set that up, for me to play with Jimi down at his place in Woodstock, New York. Jimi had a studio in the city as well, but we went out to Woodstock for a few days and played some creative music." Ibid.; also see Rivers's obituary in the *Orlando Sentinel*: http://articles.orlandosentinel.com/2011-12-27/entertainment/os-sam-rivers-dead-122711-20111227_1_monique-rivers-williams-rivbea-orchestra-jazz-icon. Accessed March 11, 2015.

62. Barry Altschul, interview by the author, September 19, 2011.

63. On the first day of Chick Corea's trio session, April 7, Davis was in the studio with John McLaughlin and, unexpectedly, Herbie Hancock, recording *A Tribute to Jack Johnson*. Hancock had stopped by the studio to give him a copy of his new recording, *Fat Albert Rotunda*, but was pressed by Davis to sit in on Farfisa electric organ—an instrument Hancock had never before played. His solo on "Yesternow" is quite remarkable.

64. Dave Holland, quoted in Williams 1970, 21.

Chapter Five

1. Barry Altschul, interview by the author, September 19, 2011. Altschul, who would soon join Chick Corea and Dave Holland's upcoming trio, recalls even more instrument swapping and trading at a June 1970 two-keyboard show he attended at the Fillmore East in New York's East Village.

2. Goodwin 2012.

3. Herbie Hancock, interview by the author, December 19, 2008; quoted in Gluck 2012, 62.

4. Corea 2013.

5. Chick Corea, quoted in Myers 2011.

Fragments from an audience recording of a performance at Rutgers University provide an unusual glimpse at the band with Corea on acoustic piano. Apparently, his Fender

Rhodes broke. The crispness of the piano compared with the Fender Rhodes leads Corea to play rhythmically pointed yet more McCoy Tyner-esque modal material, spiked with periodic ostinato. Jack DeJohnette adjusts his volume levels to suit the situation. The ostinati remain a dominant feature within Corea's accompaniment during Wayne Shorter's solo on "Miles Runs the Voodoo Down."

Corea's solo is worthy of attention because of its mix of modal qualities and angularity found later in his playing with Circle. In the middle section, Corea and Dave Holland engage in a tightly woven duet. Despite Corea's steady stream of freshly generated musical material, Holland remains close at hand. Corea remains rooted in the more abstract material as Miles plays his own solo, returning to more conventional comping (again harmonically drawing from Tyner) during "Masqualero."

6. And others: of particular note as an early adapter is Sun Ra.

7. In Davis with Troupe 1990, 295, Miles Davis explains his motivation: "I'm crazy about the way Gil Evans voices his music, so I wanted to get me a Gil Evans sound in a small band.... It didn't have nothing to do with me just wanting to go electric, like a lot of people have said, just to be having some electrical shit up in my band. I just wanted that kind of voicing a Fender Rhodes could give me that a regular piano couldn't." Davis's text seems to confuse his later use of the synthesizer with this earlier use of the Fender Rhodes, which seems to be his intended reference in the passage.

8. Herb Deutsch, e-mail communication, May 1, 2013. The September 25 concert included drummer Jim Pirone, reedist Bob Stein, and Steve Elmer playing percussion and piano.

9. Stanleigh 1969.

10. Hughes 1969. See also Moog Archives 2004, and the Museum of Modern Art Archive, MOMA 1969.

11. For more about Hyman, see Wilson 1970b.

12. Grossman was a participant in the Free Life Communication jam sessions in Dave Liebman's Nineteenth Street loft, as discussed in chapter 4. He subsequently joined Liebman in Elvin Jones's band.

13. Shorter recorded in the studio with Davis in late January and again on February 6, 1970. He and Gary Bartz played tenor and alto saxophones, respectively, a few days later (February 9) on McCoy Tyner's *Extensions* (Tyner [1972] 1996). This was followed by a February 17 Davis studio date and then Shorter's final live performances with Davis, on February 21 in Ann Arbor, Michigan, and on March 6–7 at the Fillmore East.

After his departure from the Davis band, Shorter's musical interests pointed in a direction that was simultaneously textural and lyrical, as exemplified on *Moto Grosso Feio* (Shorter [1970] 2013), recorded on April 3, a month after the Fillmore date (with Dave Holland and John McLaughlin playing twelve-string guitar; two bassists, Miroslav Vitous and Ron Carter; and two percussionists, Chick Corea and Michelin Prell). *Moto Grosso Feio* and the recordings made during this period by the three future founders of Weather Report (Shorter, Vitous, and keyboardist Josef Zawinul) provide an interesting study in the musical trajectory leading to that new band, which would add driving percussion to Shorter's lyricism and textural approach. Shorter and Zawinul had known each other since 1959, and collaborated on both 1969 Miles Davis recordings.

Late August was a busy time for this cluster of musicians. Vitous's *Purple*, recorded August 25, paired the bassist with Joe Zawinul (plus John McLaughlin and drummer Billy

Cobham, who had played on Davis's *A Tribute to Jack Johnson* [Davis (1971) 2000]). A day later, Shorter recorded the Brazilian-inflected *Odyssey of Iska* (Shorter [1970] 2008) with future Weather Report drummer Alphonse Mouzon. The initial recordings for Josef Zawinul's *Zawinul* (Zawinul [1970] 2007) were recorded on August 10 (completed in October), joining the keyboardist with Vitous plus Herbie Hancock, providing Zawinul with dueling Echoplex-processed electric pianos, Hancock drummer Billy Hart, and others, but not Shorter.

A little-known, unreleased Shorter recording from October 1970, *The Creation*, assembles a fascinating version of Weather Report that was not to be, combining Shorter with Vitous, Mouzon, percussionist Barbara Burton, and pianist McCoy Tyner. The choice of Tyner may have reflected Shorter's fascination with the music of John Coltrane, in whose classic quartet Tyner played. This was also just eight months following Shorter's appearance on Tyner's recording. Six years earlier, Shorter recorded *JuJu* (1964) with Tyner and Elvin Jones, two-thirds of the Coltrane Quartet rhythm section at its height. This was the second of Shorter's eleven Blue Note albums,

Weather Report's eponymous first album was recorded throughout February 1971, just four months after *The Creation*. The two recordings share personnel, yet on *Weather Report* Zawinul (and not Tyner) is playing keyboards. Miles Davis percussionist Airto Moreira is also added as percussionist. The new band embarked on its first tour in June 1971, traveling across Europe, with Dom Um Romao replacing Moreira (who remained on the road with Davis). Studio sessions for the second Weather Report recording, *I Sing the Body Electric*, took place soon after that tour, in November 1971. Other album segments were recorded live in Japan in January 1972, a few months before the release of the recording. By the time of the group's third recording, *Sweetnighter*, in 1973, the textural elements were joined by more elements of a groove, leading to the departure of Vitous and the emergence of a more populist band, as it came to be known through the early 1980s.

14. Jack DeJohnette, interviewed in the Lerner 2004 DVD, at 36:48–37:24.

15. Late in Steve Grossman's solo and into Corea's, he returns to the rear of the sound field.

16. J. Wilson 1970b.

17. Neil Rolnick, interview by the author, March 7, 2015.

18. The third was bassist Cecil McBee.

19. A negative *DownBeat* critic writing about the April 23 concert in Berkeley, California, comments: "What the other instruments laid down was a kind of crazy quilt of silly electronic effects. . . . Without Miles, though, I suspect it would all amount to just very intense and rhythmic novelty music, laced with pure shuck." Hadlock 1970, 28.

20. The June Fillmore shows are discussed in great detail in appendix 2; comparisons are drawn between the highly edited *Miles Davis Live at the Fillmore East* (1970) and the unedited versions of the same concerts, *Miles at the Fillmore* (2014).

21. The player could select one of three settings: electric piano, harpsichord, or organ.

22. Quieter for Chick Corea, and after a diminuendo, quieter yet for Wayne Shorter's soprano saxophone, louder for John McLaughlin's guitar, changing during Miles Davis's playing, varying during Joe Zawinul's electric piano, and then barely perceivable for Bennie Maupin's bass clarinet solo (more conga, electric guitar, and electric piano than drums). Some of the dynamic terracing of the drums and the thickening and thinning of ensemble layers were surely effected in the postproduction mixdown.

23. One example is a wildly spiraling Keith Jarrett organ solo on June 17 that leads into a collective loss of stable meter and a free-for-all improvisation.

24. Bartz had previously recorded with Art Blakey and the Jazz Messengers (1965–66) and with McCoy Tyner (1968); he steadily continued to record with Tyner into the early 1980s. Two additional records followed in subsequent decades.

25. Recordings exist of two July shows in New York City (Wollman Skating Rink on July 6 and Madison Square Garden on the twenty-fifth), and one show on August 2 at a CBS Records Convention on the island of Nassau in the Bahamas. Losin 2014 documents additional summer concerts on July 3 at Hampton Roads Coliseum in Hampton, Virginia, July 8 at Harvard Stadium, July 10 at the Hollywood Bowl, July 15 at the Spectrum in Philadelphia, July 19 at Randall's Island in New York City, and August 16 at the State University of New York at Stony Brook. The shows August 18 at Tanglewood and August 29 at the Isle of Wight Festival mark the final moments of the band before the departure of Corea and Holland. Afterward, Keith Jarrett remained on keyboard, and Miroslav Vitous briefly filled in for early September shows until Michael Henderson joined on September 13.

The new lineup, with Gary Bartz (who had played at the Tanglewood and Isle of Wight engagements), Jarrett, Henderson, and DeJohnette, remained stable, with Ndugu Leon Chancler assuming the drum chair for the October and November 1971 shows. After that, Davis created a new band, retaining only Henderson and a group of percussionists from the previous lineup.

26. *The Cellar Door Sessions*. Davis 2005. Previously, only heavily edited clips included on *Live-Evil* were known to the listening public.

27. Jack DeJohnette, quoted in Panken 2009. DeJohnette adds: "I think Miles was at the pinnacle when he did those Cellar Door sessions, and I'm glad that they released the different nights. . . . You can hear the development. Each night it was different."

28. Ratliff 2005.

29. Electric guitarist John McLaughlin joins the band for material familiar from the 1971 release of *Live-Evil*. His phrasing in "Directions" and "What I Say" (Saturday night's second set) is in keeping with early Mahavishnu Orchestra recordings. By the third set (only his second during the stand), he has begun to fit within the rhythm section, where he provides another layer of sonic and rhythmic interest. His solo in "Directions" is set against a rhythmically off-kilter pulse (and ONE [two] AND THREE-AND four . . . / and ONE . . .). This leads into a free scramble, reminiscent of the Lost Quintet, in which McLaughlin's lengthy phrases dance around Henderson's serpentine yet arrhythmic lines, DeJohnette's thrashing cymbals, and Jarrett's organ sounds until setting into a cat-and-mouse chase between Jarrett, Henderson, and DeJohnette along with Moreira's bells and whistle—all racing at once, but not in tandem.

30. Jack DeJohnette, quoted in Brown 2011, 57.

31. Veal writes: "Specifically, in these Stockhausen works, compositions were no longer organized by clear-cut beginnings and endings. Instead, various parameters of a musical performance—which could include electronic manipulations—were typically subjected to slow moving processes of gradual change and transformation. On *On the Corner*, this type of transformation is most apparent in the continuous reconfiguration of the instrumentation, which featured individual parts dropping in and out of the mix while being subjected to a variety of electronic treatments. This 'process' approach was also reflected in the solos, which seem to unfold according to an episodic, rather than linear logic." Veal 2009, 267.

32. Davis credits British cellist Paul Buckmaster with introducing him to Stockhausen's music and ideas. Davis with Troupe 1990, 298, 322.

33. A process the composer termed "intermodulation," in which sounds are transformed sonically by applying characteristics of other sounds. Ironically, Stockhausen's goal in these works was to eliminate differentiation between cultures with new musical forms characterized by hybridization. See Stockhausen 1978, 468–76; Maconie 1976, 206–26.

34. See Maconie 1976, 177–81.

Davis describes Stockhausen's influence in *Miles: The Autobiography*: "Through Stockhausen I understood music as a process of elimination and addition. Like 'yes' only means something after you have said 'no.' I was experimenting a lot, for example, telling a band to play rhythm and hold it and not react to what was going on; let me do the reacting. In a way I was becoming the lead singer in my band." Davis with Troupe 1990, 329.

35. Davis with Troupe 1990, 330.

36. Ratliff 2012.

37. Jon Pareles described the 1975 *Pangaea* as "two sets of volatile music . . . edgy extremes . . . a nearly atonal sonic cross fire of horn cries, guitar wah-wahs and roiling percussion. The 41-minute 'Zimbabwe' is a galloping funk workout, savagely frenetic, with unison lines like abstract shrieks; the 47-minute 'Gondwana' drifts from a leisurely riff to a screaming guitar solo to jazzy ruminations." Pareles 1990.

38. Ratliff 2006.

Ratliff's *Times* predecessor John Pareles observed that "his groups moved toward funk, dissonance and raw aggression; a full set might use a single drone harmony as instruments screamed and snarled . . . [yet] they still sound shocking and revelatory." Pareles 1988.

39. Tate 1992, 79–81.

Robin Kelley asks: "But how could anyone listen to tracks like 'Billy Preston,' 'What I Say,' 'Maiysha' or 'Sivad' and not hear a compelling soundtrack for a blaxploitation movie? Any number of Miles's songs from that era could have backed Melvin Van Peebles's 1971 classic, 'Sweet Sweetback's Baadasssss Song,' whose own theme bore a likeness to Miles's 'Shhh,' only louder." Kelley 2001.

40. Jack DeJohnette, quoted in Panken 2009. DeJohnette adds: "But that's what Keith and I brought to that. Keith, like myself, can lay down and get in a groove and just sit with it, and that's what Miles loved, was the ability to sit with that. Keith and I both had played at the Fillmore with Bill Graham. We had done that circuit with Charles Lloyd before. So we'd already experienced that. Miles came after that, and he went out to the Fillmore."

41. As Chick Corea observes, the band—which played quite freely when Davis left the stage—was nevertheless unquestionably under his leadership: "The only organization was Miles' spearheading. He'd go out and play, and you'd follow; whenever he'd stop playing, he never told the group what to do, so we all went and did *whatever*." Quoted in Toner 1974, 15; emphasis added.

42. Davis with Troupe 1990, 320–21.

Chapter Six

1. Chick Corea, quoted in Nemeyer 2005, 30.

2. *Village Voice*, May 14 and 21, 1970, announcements; *DownBeat*, September 17, 1970, Strictly Ad Lib column.

Although the two bands represented a study in contrast (Haynes's representing a more straight-ahead tradition), a common strand could be found in Chick Corea's 1968 trio recording *Now He Sings, Now He Sobs*, which included Haynes and bassist Miroslav Vitous.

3. Panken 1994.

4. This and subsequent Barry Altschul quotations in the chapter are taken from an interview by the author, September 19, 2011.

5. Anthony Braxton, quoted in Panken 1995.

6. Williams 1970, 21.

7. Dave Holland, quoted in B. Smith 1973.

8. Unless otherwise indicated, this and subsequent Chick Corea quotations through the end of the chapter are taken from an interview by the author, December 11, 2011.

9. Chick Corea and Dave Holland, quoted in ibid.

John Mars hears in Holland's playing "some great loping/looping Scott LaFaro thing . . . certainly a different way of walking the bass. The interplay between Barry and Dave on various records was sometimes quite reminiscent of Ornette's various 1950s, early 1960s bass-drums combinations. . . . Holland got the freedom from playing with Miles, and he knew how to respond to each twist and turn, and he contributed really astonishing compositions to Circle" (interview by the author, November 19, 2014).

10. John Mars observes that Anthony Braxton's role impacted Chick Corea's approach to playing with Circle: "What Braxton does is bring Chick Corea into the right place," in contrast with the trio recording that Corea, Holland, and Altschul made without Braxton, *A.R.C.*: "Anthony kind of reigned in Chick Corea in that Circle band and made him respond to his signals. The other guys did that too" (interview by the author, November 19, 2014).

11. Dave Holland, quoted in B. Smith 1973.

12. *DownBeat* magazine reported that an initial informal session took place on August 2, but this may be incorrect, since Corea and Holland played with Miles Davis at a CBS convention in Freeport, Grand Bahama Island, that same day. *DownBeat*, September 17, 1970, 39.

13. Chick Corea recalls: "I remember Upsurge Studio well. The Circle quartet did a film there once. The film was projected on a wall, which we faced, and we improvised to what we were looking at. Never heard anything about that project since" (interview by the author, December 11, 2011).

14. Ibid.

15. Both sets of duets were released on the recording *Circling In*.

16. Corea and Braxton's duets are relatively atonal. For the first minute of "Danse I," both instruments play a steady stream of notes, which become far sparser in the next half minute; silences punctuate the sounds. Braxton's clarinet line then becomes more lyrical, and Corea responds with late Romantic chromatic chordal accompaniment, which grows more atonal and then fades.

The second "Danse" begins quietly. Corea plays chromatic gestures, joined first by Braxton blowing into the bore of his clarinet. Then Braxton reinserts the mouthpiece and plays sustained notes that stretch the limit of the clarinet's upper range. Corea actuates the strings of his piano by dropping keys and maybe a cymbal onto them (with the sustain pedal held so that the sounds ring). After a pause, Braxton's melodic line becomes more lyrical and then agitated as Corea's playing gets busier, dense with thick chords and clusters, growing frantic and then quieting to silence.

17. There is a perception of increasing speed around the four-minute mark, when Corea plays four notes for each of Holland's.

18. The piano notes and tone clusters are often muted by placing a hand on the piano strings. The timbre of the bass matches the muted piano's quick attack and decay.

19. The work opens with glissando piano strings, joined by spare guitar notes. A rhythmic gesture on guitar and tapping inside the piano provide a brief contrast before a return to the open textures, this time played by guitar, bass marimba, and celeste. A serene clarinet melody played by Braxton is supported by Corea's lush piano, with the guitar continuing a steady stream of angular lines. At five minutes, the tone changes when Corea plays lengthening phrases beginning with rapidly repeated Bs. Holland's walking bass is joined by rapid speed straight time on the drums. After laying out, Corea returns in full force, his solo coming to a close when Holland takes over, first alone and then accompanied by wood blocks and gritty, fragmented electric guitar. The repeated note figures periodically reappear. The latter portion of the improvisation contrasts musical registers, high and low: Braxton on contrabass clarinet, growling and snarling low in the instrument's range and Holland on arco bass—he begins in its highest register, suggesting a country fiddler, but then growling like Braxton in the low register.

A new section pairs Holland's arco bass and Braxton's contrabass clarinet at the bottom of their registers, soon joined by Corea, also on his lowest bass notes and piano strings. The piano sounds ring out. Heading toward the finish, Braxton plays an angular solo on alto saxophone, backed by Corea's sweeping glissandi on the piano strings and plucked chords, with Altschul on vibraphone, matching the angularity of Braxton's lines. A clarinet line, played by Holland, cries out behind Braxton's saxophone, orchestra bells chiming. From a period of silence emerge vocal sounds, whistles, and animal calls. A spoken voice repeats the words "we exist" and other phrases, accompanied by coughing, yelling, and kalimba, as the performance concludes.

20. "Quartet Piece #3" begins with an Anthony Braxton's alto saxophone solo backed by Dave Holland's angular walking bass. Next, loud percussion sounds, springs and thunder sheet, are interjected around and behind the duet. Toward the end of this section, Braxton screeches into his saxophone. The percussive sounds grow louder, from which emerge Holland's angular arco lines. After a brief pause, scratchy electric guitar and bells are heard for a minute around 3:30. An overblown conch or other wind instrument plays a melody suggestive of taps, joined by percussion strikes on cymbals and vocal sounds. Following a cymbal roll and a brief period of silence, a quiet celeste, temple bell, metallophone, and piano ensemble improvisation emerges. A vibraphone, piano, and metallophone texture begins sparsely and grows into a circling fury.

At nine minutes, quiet section begins; piano and bass marimba play minimally. Two horns in harmony cry out, juxtaposed to repeated staccato piano phrases. From this relatively static texture, a wild, energetic collective improvisation emerges; the two horn lines intertwine, juxtaposed to pounding piano clusters and soloistic drumming on the full kit. A dense, ascending piano phrase in the upper register ends the performance.

21. Liner notes from Brown 1970.

22. I have always thought of the music through this representational lens, ever since I first heard it played in a college class. Listening again, I find myself wondering whether the

performers were aware of this program before playing (at least one with whom I spoke has no such recollection). It seems equally plausible that the composer kept the programmatic ideas to himself and achieved his goals by addressing strictly musical considerations during the session—or maybe the program followed rather than preceded the music-making.

23. Possibly less influential on Circle was side 2, "Djinji's Corner," a busy, kaleido-scopic, open improvisation. It begins with a rapid angular line, played in harmolodic unison (while not every musician is playing the same pitch, they are in sync rhythmically and in gestural shape). The instrumentation features saxophones, drum kit, and bass, possibly building on the open blowing Marion Brown experienced with Coltrane. Despite the nearly continuous level of multilayered activity, each artist retains his or her distinct voice. Jeanne Lee's vocalizing at 15:15 leads to a quieter, sparer and more textural section. Very dry elec-tric guitar, sustained individual piano notes, Lee's intoned syllables, and active percussion help build a steadily moving stream of sound, followed by a sudden return to the opening figure.

24. Corea continues: "*Return to Forever* [in contrast] was an experiment in lyricism with a groove and a particular South American rhythm flavor. It was also an outreach to audiences."

25. The reference is to Dave Holland's recording *Conference of the Birds*, with Anthony Braxton, Sam Rivers, and Barry Altschul. Holland 1972 (2013).

26. John Mars, interview by the author, November 19, 2014.

27. Neil Rolnick, interview by the author, March 17, 2015.

28. An extensive discussion of Circle's treatment of works composed by its members can be found in appendix 3. The focus is on prolific composer Anthony Braxton's "Compo-sition 6" series of works, with brief comments regarding performances of Dave Holland's "Toy Room" and "Q & A," and Chick Corea's "Rhymes."

29. "Nefertiti" was included on the set lists of at least three recorded performances, including the show in Iserlohn, Germany, on November 28, 1970; the "Paris Concert" at the French national radio station's Maison De L'ORTF on February 21, 1971, recorded and released on ECM Records; and at the Third International Jazz Parade in Bergamo, Italy, March 19, 1971.

30. It was the third tune recorded at the first session, April 7, 1970; Circle recorded it again on *A.R.C.* January 11–13, 1971.

31. Formally, the piece is organized as a lengthy ostinato, repeatedly played in unison by Davis and Shorter, supported by Herbie Hancock's ever-changing chord fragments. The melody remains static while the dynamic, ever shifting action is placed in the hands of drummer Tony Williams.

Corea and Holland first played "Nefertiti" with Miles Davis when it became part of the touring repertoire of Davis's Lost Quintet. There, the theme would be repeated several times and then left behind, giving way to solos. The trio's and subsequently Circle's treat-ment follows an even more conventional theme-solo mode than the Lost Quintet approach. The solos have become further-ranging collective and solo improvisations than in the Davis performances.

32. The tune also appears during the December 3, 1970, show in Amsterdam, the Netherlands.

33. The performance opens with an introduction by Corea, who delivers a brief abstracted version of the theme, followed by the band's entry. Corea's solo begins in the angular bebop mode for which he had been known on his prior acoustic recordings. His

phrases lengthen, leading into more chromatic variants, and returning to phrases in closer relationship to the chord changes. Two minutes in, Corea's phrases become much lengthier and turn to playing and repeating imitations of melodic patterns, some picked up and repeated by Holland. Corea's harmonic material by the third minute of his solo is decidedly quartal, but quickly becomes more chromatic. Around four minutes in, Corea builds and releases tension, using different phrase lengths; pauses; and then references the theme, moving into a holding pattern. As the six-minute mark approaches, he repeats a single note with his right hand while playing ascending series of fourth chords with his left. The solo closes out with lines back within the chord changes, and he gives way to Braxton's solo at seven and a half minutes.

Braxton's solo begins melodically, with long, sustained opening notes, then quickly shifts to jagged edged lines, soon winding, angular, and arpeggiated in downward motion. What follows are rapid many-note gestures that create a sense of circularity, spinning gradually upward, until Braxton arrives at a melodic phrase, which he repeats and varies, returning to angularity. What varies mostly are the pace and register; a characteristic gesture is a downward quintuplet resolved with a final melodic upward leap. Just before nine minutes, longer sustained notes briefly call out like a clarion before a return to angularity. Corea's comping often references the chord changes, albeit with often chromatically complex voicings. Holland generally holds tight to the changes until soon after the ten-and-a-half-minute mark, when all but Braxton and Altschul lay out.

The saxophone-drums duo engages in an intense, flowing presentation of the sort pioneered by John Coltrane and Rashied Ali. Braxton presents a fast-moving phrase and then repeatedly asserts it before moving to a variant. Honks and screeches provide contrast between segments, particularly when approaching twelve minutes, where Braxton's tone becomes purer, his phrases fractured, moving upward, returning to a series of growls at twelve and a half minutes, followed by staccato articulations and then faster-moving repeated patterns. Around fourteen minutes, Braxton is at the top of his range, screeching as he tries to reach higher, into the altissimo range, pressing the limits of his horn. Lower growls lead him back to the theme, on which the band joins in.

Corea then solos close to the chord changes at just after fifteen minutes. Holland plays a solo equally within the chord changes at the sixteen-minute mark, with Corea rhythmically punctuating behind him. As the seventeen-and–a-half-minute mark approaches, Corea and Holland briefly engage in imitation, back and forth. A minute in, Holland plays freely with the meter of his playing, slowing it and then speeding it up, while Altschul maintains a regular pulse. A minute later, his playing speed increases to a rapid, steady flow as he explores variations on a series of arpeggiated patterns. Around twenty-one minutes, the recording fades out as a radio announcer does a voice-over.

34. Anthony Braxton, interview by Ted Panken for the liner notes of *Anthony Braxton—Andrew Cyrille*, Duo Plindrom 2001. Intakt CD 089 (2004). http://www .intaktrec.ch/interbraxton-a.htm. Accessed March 11, 2015.

35. With percussionist Steve Jackson. The set list includes "Moon Dance" (Grossman), "Slumber" (Dave Liebman), "The Sun" (part 1 and part 2, Corea), and "The Moon" (Corea). It was recorded at Upsurge Studio on September 14, 1970, and released only in Japan (1970 and 1978). See http://www.discogs.com/Chick-Corea-The-Sun/release /3922172, and http://inconstantsol.blogspot.com/2014/07/chick-corea-sun-far-east -express-1970.html. Accessed March 11, 2015.

36. *DownBeat*, November 26, 1970, 37.

37. Ibid.

38. "Communication in a Noisy Environment" was described in the *New York Times* as "an ensemble of happenings on three floors, with television screens and loudspeakers to relay what was taking place on the different levels." Instrumental music and projected images unfolded amid a Citroen automobile, a leaf- and log-strewn floor, rifle targets, and images of wild animals. "The planned chaos of image and sound was gradually raised to a level at which communication was impossible." Ericson 1970.

Allan Kaprow invented the term *happening* in the late 1950s to refer to a form of performance art that engaged both artist and audience. This was part of a broader exploration of multimedia, conceptual, and participatory art from the 1950s to the early '70s undertaken by Fluxus; Andy Warhol and the Exploding Plastic Inevitable with the Velvet Underground; John Cage and others associated with the Merce Cunningham Dance Company; Experiments in Art and Technology; San Francisco Tape Music Center; and others, some noted below. See Kirby 1965, Cotter 2006, and Gluck 2012b.

Braxton's involvement in the event reflected his continued affinity with John Cage's aesthetic, in this case the juxtaposition of music and other media, as in Cage's Variations series.

Electronic composer Gordon Mumma was the organizer of "Communication in a Noisy Environment." It featured Mumma, Braxton's colleague violinist Leroy Jenkins, composer David Behrman, and visual artist Robert Watts, and was part of the 1970–71 premiere season of the series Intermedia at Automation House. Located on East Sixty-Eighth Street, Intermedia was a successor to the Electric Ear series, which had been housed at the Electric Circus discotheque on St. Marks Place in Greenwich Village. Electric Ear was a contemporary music series inspired by the work of Morton Subotnick, founding artistic director of the discotheque; Intermedia at Automation House was produced by Thais Lathem (who had codirected Electric Ear) and Lucy Mann, with Mumma serving as artistic and technical coordinator.

Automation House was also the new home of the American Foundation on Automation and Employment, the Institute of Collective Bargaining, and the recently established Board of Mediation for Community Disputes. Its founder, labor-management mediator Theodore Keel, sought to project an image of progress, and thus desired electronic art to abound within the building's design and programming. New Yorker 1970, Gluck 2012b.

39. *DownBeat*, February 4, 1971, 42. Belgium is specifically discussed in this report.

40. Corea recalls: "Along with the inspiration and encouragement I got from my music mentors and heroes was a simple philosophy of life that inspired me from the writings of L. Ron Hubbard—whose books I came across in 1968. Encouraged by his books and courses along with my lifelong immersion in the musical universes of Bird, Miles, Monk, Bud, Horace, Trane, Bartok, Stravinsky, and many other masters—my desire [was] to be free to express myself, as I wanted to grow stronger."

During the life of Circle, all four band members were involved in Scientology training at various points. Corea understood this connection as rooted in a creative impulse: "I always wanted to be free enough to just be myself and have the courage to manifest what I really believed and envisioned and what I really wanted to create musically. This is not the easiest thing to accomplish given the usual pressures that life presents. My musical heroes all manifested this freedom of expression. To me, it was always the most striking of all their qualities: this freedom to create in a personal direction no matter what the status quo was trying to dictate."

41. Several of the works on Braxton's album are guided open improvisations in which the composer specifies types of sound events that could occur: rhythmic elements, combinations of instruments (including solo sections), tempo (ballad, for instance), velocities of musical lines, and other criteria. Other compositions created a bridge between improvisational forms with through-composed writing. The titles on the album jacket are schematic drawings, like those often found on Braxton's Arista Freedom releases.

The music of *The Complete Braxton* is stylistically eclectic, a reflection of Braxton's inquiring, open approach to aesthetics and his lack of interest in conventional lines of stylistic demarcation. For example, while Braxton at times draws from the jazz tradition of a "head" followed by improvisation, we can hear in his angularity and pointillism the modernist tendencies found in Stockhausen, Boulez, Schoenberg, and Webern, interwoven with hints of ragtime and other forms rooted in black musics. Radano 1993, 174–79, offers a thoughtful treatment of this recording in the context of Braxton's work with his fellow Circle members.

Michael Heffley offers structural detail about some of the compositions that appear on the recording. He describes "Composition 6L," one of the soprano saxophone and piano duets and the opening track on side 4, in this way: "a traditional ballad, Braxton style. A stately, regular procession of chords leads to an atonal statement of 'two melodic phrases structured in a canon response pattern as a basis for extended improvisation' [quoting from Braxton's *Composition Notes A* (Hanover, NH: Frog Tree Press, 1988), 184–92]. Braxton's *Notes* extort improvisers to play within the context of what he wrote: 'a dirge-like music that breathes very slowly with linear melodic-like musical phrases.... Too often the extended continuum of restructuralism seems overly preoccupied with abstraction and pandemonium at the expense of real creativity.' His own solo moves around lyrically in groups of thirds; the piano moments begin to manifest less regularly, and he plays a bit more out, though still with restraint and a dynamic flux, coming to rest in his initial intensity level, after bubbling out of it." Heffley 1996, 366.

42. See *Jazz Journal,* June 1971, 8–9.

43. *Piano Improvisations,* volumes 1 and 2.

44. May 17, 1971, released in Japan as *Circle 2.*

45. *Oakland Tribune,* July 4, 1971.

46. Preview in *Los Angeles Times,* July 30, 1971.

47. *Los Angeles Times,* July 30, 1971.

48. Also see Corea's comments in a 1974 interview: Toner 1974, 14–16.

49. Chick Corea, interview by the author, December 11, 2011.

50. Altschul adds: "I mean, I was at Coltrane's Birdland gig, *Live at Birdland*, there's twenty or twenty-five people in the audience. And six of us were kids from high school checking out Coltrane."

51. Anthony Braxton, quoted in Wilmer 1971. Braxton pointed out that in general, he could live without performing and, one would presume, the interpersonal and professional costs involved: "I'm completely happy with the group only in the sense that I really enjoy playing with them. It's one of the few groups I actually can play with because if something were to happen and we couldn't play, I'm pretty sure that I'd go back and this time I'd get me a day-job. It sounds kind of strange to say that but what I'm really saying is that like I'm not impressed with performing music to the extent where if I can't make it with this group I'd

run and form another group so that I can tour and perform with it. I don't care about that shit." Ibid.

52. Documented on a recording from May 1975: Stan Getz, *My Foolish Heart: Live at the Left Bank*, Label M Records, 2000.

53. Dave Holland, quoted in B. Smith 1973.

54. Dave Holland's *Conference of the Birds* was recorded November 30, 1972, at Allegro Studio in New York City: Dave Holland (bass), Sam Rivers (alto sax, tenor sax, soprano sax, and flute), Anthony Braxton (soprano sax, bass sax, contrabass sax, flute, clarinet, bass clarinet), Barry Altschul (drums, percussion).

Holland: "Anthony [Braxton] had gone to Paris for a while, and worked over there, but he'd been making trips back to New York, and it was during one of these trips that we did *Conference of the Birds*. Three-quarters of the band was Circle, and we had already achieved an identity as a collection of people. Barry and I also started playing with Sam Rivers after we got back to New York. We were going over to Sam's loft, and playing two or three hours a day with him." Quoted in Panken 1994.

55. Sam Rivers's trio originally included Warren Smith on drums and Richard Davis on bass, as Smith notes: "Now Sam also had a trio, which I first entered into with Richard Davis playing the bass, and then various other bass players, Cecil McBee, Hakim Jami, and Dave Holland. And I stayed with them for a long time and then eventually Dave Holland came in and Barry Altschul took my place. We did some recordings when Barry and I both played. I played the vibes and there are some things he used two drummers on. Joe Daley filled the chair on the 'Tuba Trio' recordings and performances" (interview by the author, October 18, 2011). Jerome Cooper adds that Cooper and then Norman Connors also preceded Altschul. Interview by the author, September 24, 2011.

56. After coming to the States with Don Cherry, Berger had formed his own band, with Holland on bass (after Henry Grimes left); at this point, Holland was playing with Miles Davis. Berger became interested in musical education while "working with a group led by drummer Horacee Arnold, with Reggie Workman, Sam Rivers [and Mike Lawrence]. We played a program called Young Audiences for the schools. That was at the time the only real steady gig in New York. Playing for the kids. So we'd go out twice, three times a week, play two, three concerts a day, one hour long educational concerts. We'd ask: 'what's improvisation.' They'd come up with some melodies." In 1967, Berger heard that John Cage was leaving his teaching position at the New School and got the job, where he began to develop the pedagogical techniques that would serve as the core of the Creative Music Studio curriculum. "From there came the idea that maybe we should have workshops because the minds of people are really open. I realized that there was not these stylistic barriers that people artificially have up all the time. Let's have workshops where there's no talk about style at all. You don't use any words that relate to style. You just work with what is the common basis of what is any kind of music. That was my main question" (interview by the author, September 25, 2011). In 1971, the organization had opened an office at Carla Bley's Creative Jazz Composer's Orchestra Association, 500 Broadway, in New York City. The first CMS workshop was organized in Woodstock, New York, in 1972, followed by a festival in 1974. Also in 1974, CMS ran a concert series at the Peace Church in New York City.

57. Along with Sam Rivers, Bob Moses, Frederick Rzewski, Ingrid Sertso, Richard Teitelbaum, Garret List, and others.

58. Dave Holland, quoted in B. Smith 1973.

Chapter Seven

1. The AACM is introduced in the introduction.

2. Jerome Cooper, interview by the author, September 24, 2011.

3. A term Cooper uses to describe his approach. From the description of Cooper's 2010 recording *A Magical Approach* (Mutable Music): "What is multi-dimensional drumming? Imagine a drummer who plays this flute with one hand, bass drum and high-hat with his feet, and triggers drum loops, chord sequences and bass patterns with his other hand. . . . An instrument's name and structure doesn't stop him from playing them like a drum." http://www.mutablemusic.com/magicalinfo.html. Accessed March 11, 2015.

4. Jerome Cooper, interview by the author, September 24, 2011.

5. Sirone, quoted in Spann 2006, 78.

6. Jerome Cooper, interview by the author, September 24, 2011.

7. Sirone, quoted in Spann 2006, 78.

8. Jerome Cooper, interview by the author, September 24, 2011. Cooper adds: "Fred did the cover for my latest record, and for the Revolutionary Ensemble record. He's a really nice cat." Artists House is introduced in chapter 3.

9. Felipe Luciano, quoted from Kemper 2002.

10. A precursor of the lofts as settings for rehearsals and performances was the Jazz Composers Guild, an unsuccessful attempt to organize a racially integrated group of musicians in New York City during the mid-1960s. The guild produced concerts for its members; in turn, they all agreed to not seek opportunities outside that structure. Guild organizers, including Bill Dixon, Cecil Taylor, Archie Shepp, Sun Ra, and Michael Mantler, built on October Revolution in Jazz, a four-evening festival organized by trumpeter Dixon and Peter Sabino at the Cellar Café on West Ninety-First Street. Their goal was to provide a forum for the emerging new music that lacked support from commercial venues. October Revolution performers included seventy-five then-lesser-known musicians, among them Milford Graves, Giuseppi Logan, Don Pullen, Alan Silva, Roswell Rudd, John Tchicai, and Joe Maneri. Sun Ra, Paul Bley, and Jimmy Giuffre also performed. Shows were followed by panel discussions addressing themes connected to race and the economics of jazz and, more broadly, the differential opportunities available to black and white musicians. Cultural critic A. B. Spellman wrote in the *Nation* magazine: "Almost everybody who's doing anything at all in the way of avant-garde jazz in New York passed through the Cellar during these programs, if not to play, then to participate in the panels or to listen." Spellman 1965, 149.

This audacious project depended heavily on mutual trust and responsibility, but soon collapsed due to conflicts regarding power and control and individual career decisions that undermined that trust. The racially charged environment that intensified in the mid-1960s was also the backdrop for differences of opinion concerning whether musical organizations should be black separatist or integrated. See Piekut 2009, 193 (full article: 191–231); Morgenstern and Williams 1964, 32–33; Wilmer 1977, 213–15; and Anderson 2006, 138–41.

11. William Parker, quoted in Carpenter 2002.

12. Another anomaly may be found in John Coltrane's contract with Impulse Records during the 1960s. Since he had developed a strong commercial following during the early 1960s, Impulse continued to record and release a steady stream of Coltrane sessions despite his steady movement in the direction of open improvisation.

13. Brief discussion on this point can be found in chapter 8.

14. One might describe this as a counterculture, albeit one quite different from the more widely known and predominantly white youth counterculture of the 1960s and early 1970s, which was served by rock venues like the Fillmore East in New York City and the Fillmore West in San Francisco.

15. The festival arose from a meeting of black musicians, a grassroots response to George Wein's Newport Jazz Festival, which was about to debut in New York. Two of those people had opened performance lofts (Sam Rivers and James DuBoise), and three had previous organizing experience (Juma Sultan, Ali Abuwi, and Noah Howard). A handful of other musicians participated in the meeting, notably drummer Rashied Ali, who later opened his own club. The group formulated a series of demands for black community involvement in the planning and venue choices of Wein's festival, a better appreciation of the African American rootedness of the music, and stronger involvement by musicians over performance decisions. Not receiving a response, they created an alternative festival, the New York Musicians Jazz Festival. Juma Sultan was quoted in the *New York Times*: "We tried to bring to the attention of Newport producers that they weren't doing anything for Harlem and other black communities in the city. . . . We tried to point out that George Wein, the producer, wasn't hiring black musicians who are part of and represent this city in jazz today." *New York Times* 1972.

It was at this point that more members of the various black music collectives nation-wide began to coalesce in New York; among them were Oliver Lake and Julius Hemphill in 1973, Arthur Blythe in 1974, David Murray in 1975, and within the two years following, AACM cofounder Muhal Richard Abrams, Henry Threadgill, George Lewis, Lester Bowie, Amina Claudine Myers, Kalaparusha Maurice McIntyre, and Chico Freeman. Lake, Hemphill, Hamiett Bluett, and Murray subsequently founded the influential World Saxophone Quartet.

16. Including nightly events at Studio Rivbea and Studio We, plus two other venues: Ornette Coleman's Artists House and the Free Life Communication loft on West Nineteenth Street, both discussed elsewhere in this book. See Looker 2004, 224–26; Wilmer (1977) 1992; Heller 2012; and Hermes 2012, 22–23.

Studio We, run by James Duboise (and Juma Sultan) at 193 Eldridge Street, had already opened its doors in 1970, with a full schedule of concerts beginning during the 1972 NYJMF. Ornette Coleman's Artists House, at 131 Prince Street, a less formal setting, had also been in operation since the 1960s. In 1973, Joe Lee Wilson opened Lady's Fort in his own loft at 2 Bond Street; the following year, Rashied Ali opened the club Studio 77 (renamed Ali's Alley) at 77 Greene Street (between Spring and Broome Streets), and Michael Morgenstern opened the Jazzmania Society at 14 E. Twenty-Third Street (at Madison Avenue). Soon, John Fischer's Environ would appear at 476 Broadway (between Broome and Grand Streets), joined by the Brook on West Seventeenth Street (owned by actor Susan Sarandon's brother) and Stanley Crouch's Tin Palace, at Bowery and Second Streets.

Free Life Communication, relocated at Mike Mahaffay's Sunrise Studio, was part of this scene. James Duboise recalls: "When I first went to this building there was a musician living there named Burton Greene, a piano player. He went to Copenhagen and he left me there to take care of the apartment [which was known as an early jazz loft]. He said he was going to go away for a month; he stayed away for a year and a half. You know in New York City a year and a half is a long time. Between the time he left [through the summer],

I started doing concerts there, right on that spot. I started doing these concerts in 1970. We had hundreds of musicians. I can't even think of the names. Richard Youngstein, Mark Whitecage, Jo Lee Wilson. . . . At the very beginning, I had no idea of what I was doing. All I knew was there wasn't [anyone] doing anything. It come to me that since the musicians were out there, the good musicians that they were, that we try to do concerts there, and it caught on. They loved it. They was the ones it made it a success because there was no place else really to go. They couldn't get no gig at say the Five Spot or Bottom of the Gate because the big musicians, the famous musicians were playing there. Commercially it was good business. When we opened the place at Studio We there were musicians there day and night. Off and on, hit or miss.

"Then in 1972, we had a jazz festival. That was the real beginning. That's when we did a thing, we had maybe over two hundred groups. We had something like sixteen big bands. Frank Foster. Loads of big bands. Some were done at Studio We and we did concerts at the Apollo Theater, Folklore Center, Harlem Music Center, Free Life Communication, New Federal Theater. . . . I think we did maybe twenty locations." Young 1993. Thanks to Michael Heller for providing a recording from the WKCR archive. The Folklore Center was generally a setting for folk music, but began to occasionally program free-jazz performances that year. Wilson 1972, 63.

17. During the NYJMF, Rivers fronted a different band nightly. Among the musicians appearing with him were Clifford Jordan, Dewey Redman, Cedar Walton, Jimmy Garrison, Roswell Rudd, Anthony Braxton, Paul Bley, Rashied Ali, Andrew Hill, Noah Howard, Milford Graves, and Joe Lee Wilson.

18. Once Rivers began to successfully access grant funding, he began to produce and host concerts by other musicians, and Rivbea became a highly influential performance loft. William Parker remembers: "About '73 was when he had his full schedule going, he had music seven nights a week." Carpenter 2002. Unfortunately, the loft closed soon after an extensive 1976 festival.

19. Jerome Cooper, interview by the author, January 16, 2012. Warren Smith adds: "We were like family. We all had children of the same age. Our children would go to the concerts and form a second generation of an audience for us" (interview by the author, October 18, 2011).

20. Jerome Cooper, interview by the author, January 16, 2012.

21. McCormack 1973, 16; also see "Mercer Stages Are a Supermarket," *New York Times,* November 1, 1971; "Historic Hotel New Home for Theatre Dream," *Sunday Record* (Bergen County, New Jersey), March 12, 1972; "Rags to Riches," *New York Post,* August 4, 1973; "A Pinch of Moog, a Dash of Light," *Village Voice,* March 30, 1972.

22. Cooper points out that later that year, the building next door to the Mercer Arts Center, the Grand Central Hotel, fell down and hit the Mercer Arts Center, which itself collapsed. Interview by the author, July 19, 2012.

23. Riggins 1972, 34. Cooper attributes the success of that concert to the increase in the number of concerts held in lofts, which emulated Ornette Coleman's idea.

24. Jerome Cooper, interview by the author, November 16, 2012. Cooper adds that regarding the club's demise, "the nail in the coffin was when [trumpeter] Lee Morgan got shot. And Jerry the owner, I don't know what happened, but he opened a restaurant on Spring Street and—I'll never forget—Jerry told me that he was moving to India. And I hadn't seen him or heard from him since, but we tried to get a gig at Slugs."

25. Slugs was located much farther east than the downtown New York City jazz clubs; it was in a drug-infested, poverty-stricken neighborhood, quite unlike the increasingly gentrified East Village of the twenty-first century.

26. Gluck 2014.

27. Photographer Dawoud Bey remembers a packed house at this performance. Interview by the author, December 20, 2013.

28. Jerome Cooper, interview by the author, July 19, 2012.

29. Sirone, quoted in Spann 2006, 85.

30. This and subsequent Jerome Cooper quotations through the end of the chapter are taken from an interview by the author, September 24, 2011.

31. Jerome Cooper recalls additional instruments: "Right before we broke up, we were in Munich, Germany, and Leroy played alto. I wrote a composition called 'Combination of Events.' I wrote it for Leroy playing alto, Sirone playing trombone, I'm playing piano. Leroy [had] played alto in high school, because there was no string section—in a concert band the strings section was the clarinet section, so Leroy played alto. But then we disbanded."

32. From the six- to ten-minute mark.

33. Part 2 opens with Leroy Jenkins's solo introduction, joined sparingly by Sirone at the one-minute mark. Soon, the bassist changes direction, crafting a highly active contrapuntal structure to supplement Jenkins. At 1:45, the trio is fully off and running in an intense, vibrant improvisation in which the three players build and shape a collective energy level. After a complex walking bass line, Sirone plays brief figures broken by pauses, followed by more intense ensemble work that is energetically charged by Cooper's rolls and combinations. At 2:20, Sirone creates a holding pattern with a dotted-note ostinato, which finds release after fifteen seconds, when the bassist shifts into a rapid walking pattern. The trio builds in intensity, Jenkins playing more fragmentary phrases as his cohorts charge ahead. The music then builds in intensity until Cooper lays out at the three-minute mark, and the remaining duo moves into a more pastoral section.

34. Sirone, quoted in Spann 2006, 81, 80.

35. Ibid., 81.

36. Lauren Wolman writes: "With his wife Veronika Nowag-Jones, Sirone was very active in German theater. Sirone served as musical director and actor in a production with the great Hungarian writer/director Georg Tabori at the famous Burgtheatre in Vienna. Sirone also created a play with his wife Veronika about homeless people in New York City. Together they played a homeless couple, with Sirone acting and playing the bass. They presented this piece in Germany, Austria, Switzerland, Atlanta, and New York. Excerpts of this production were shown on German television. Sirone also played and acted in many German television films. At Berliner Brecht, Sirone was the musical director and soloist for the Charlie Chaplin film version of 'Monsieur Verdoux.' German television has been producing a documentary film about the couple's extraordinary lives. In Berlin, Sirone led his own music ensemble called 'Concord.' They played many times in Berlin, and in Poland." "Sirone Memorial Concert at Saint Peter's Church, 2/25," http://www.broadwayworld .com/article/Sirone-Memorial-Concert-Held-at-Saint-Peters-Church-225-20100224. Accessed March 11, 2015.

Among Sirone's final performances as an actor was a role in *The Trojan Woman* at the University of Tennessee in October 2005.

37. Sirone, quoted in Spann 2006, 81.

Chapter Eight

1. Gluck 2012a.

2. Ibid., 173–75. Hancock found tremendous success subsequently with the more funk-oriented *Head Hunters* (1973).

3. Iain Anderson discusses the important role of federal (particularly the National Endowment for the Arts [NEA]), state, and private corporate grants in the support of jazz, including "free improvisers" during the economic decline of that music during the 1970s. This went on despite a bias toward "classical" art forms and better-known individual artists. Anderson 2006, 168–81. George Lewis addresses the role of Muhal Richard Abrams's advocacy in the broadening of NEA support beyond classical and idiomatic jazz musicians to African American musicians, such as members of the Association for the Advancement of Creative Musicians, which engaged in more experimentalist practices. Lewis (and Anderson) discuss A. B. Spellman's role through the NEA's Expansion Arts program, which reached out to minority community groups. G. Lewis 2008, 400–404.

4. Briefly in the early 1970s, the Art Ensemble of Chicago had a record contract with Atlantic Records, and in the late 1970s began recording on the ECM label, while otherwise adhering to the AACM value of self-determination. Steinbeck 2008b, 121–27 and 264–72, discusses how a commitment to administrative organization and continuity helped lead to its endurance as a group.

5. *Circle 1* and *Circle 2* were far more limited releases and remain largely unknown.

6. John Mars offers as an example the venues in Toronto: "The way those concerts were set up, it gave the music of people like Anthony Braxton, Roscoe Mitchell, and Cecil Taylor a first footing in this major North American city outside of NYC. An audience that was quite into all of this was always there, because the famous 'jazz' couple Bill and Chloe [Onari] Smith was such relentless promoters. A lot were presented at places like A Space, York University, and the Music Gallery, where I also often played with Stuart Broomer. The Smith connection with *Coda* magazine and Onari Records always gave Braxton and Mitchell a great venue in which to promote this new music. . . . [Prior] to that date, Braxton maybe hadn't had as much of a chance to put over his own music in concerts or on recordings like Dave [Holland] had, because he didn't have that name connection with a big, famous figure like Miles Davis. Interestingly, Dave had gone from playing for five hundred thousand with Miles at the Isle of Wight [Festival in England] to playing for probably fifty or so people with Anthony at A Space" (interview with the author, November 19, 2014).

7. William Lewis, quoted in *Cadence*, December 1990, 6–7; cited in G. Lewis 2008, 355.

8. Billy Higgins, quoted in Wilmer (1977) 1992, 220. Is it possible that Higgins couldn't imagine that the impulse to go electric came from Miles himself? The publication of Wilmer's book came on the heels of Ornette Coleman himself assembling an electric band, first documented on *Dancing in Your Head* (1976).

9. Barry Altschul, interview by the author, September 19, 2011. Altschul continues: "You can hear it on the Paris Concert. It was packed—and that was a big house. Europeans are, or were at that time, idealistic." He also found them critical of innovation: "If you were a jazz cat and you went to rock and roll, they reacted. It was different if you were trying to push the envelope, but to change [stylistically], I suppose they [would react negatively]." Altschul places the European response in context: "They booed Frank Sinatra, and they booed Ella Fitzgerald. In Germany, I remember we were playing the Berlin festival, and

Betty Carter was on the bill and she was very, very nervous, because they'd booed Ella. They booed if they felt like it. She just won the audience over; she was great."

10. *DownBeat* review, November 26, 1970, 37.

11. Feather 1971.

12. Litweiler 1967a, 1967b. The latter is a review of a concert of AACM-affiliated groups at the University of Chicago's Reynolds Club. Programmed as part of the university's 1967 annual Liberal Arts Conference, this was a double bill featuring the Anthony Braxton Quartet (with violinist Leroy Jenkins, bassist Charles Clark, and drummer Thurman Barker) and the (Alvin) Fielder Quartet (with pianist/clarinetist Richard Abrams—who had not yet taken on the name Muhal—tenor saxophonist Maurice McIntyre, bassist Lester Lashley, and drummer Alvin Fielder). Litweiler 1967b praises the Fielder Quartet and expresses appreciation for Anthony Braxton: "Braxton's lyricism is explosive, his musicianship sure," but then criticizes his group's performance as "formless" and characterizes Jenkins's playing as "muddy and repetitious."

13. Feather 1970a; review of a show at the Lighthouse in Hermosa Beach, California; to place this in context, Feather assessed the whole show as "alternately a fascinating, hypnotic experience and an enervating, chaotic drag."

What reviewers like Feather missed was the distinct logic in Anthony Braxton's sonic and formal approach, his consistent "tool kit" of melodic contours, patterns, and sound materials. One excellent example may be found in his solo in "Starp," recorded during the first sessions with Circle. Braxton's opening sustained note is followed by a lyrical phrase ending in an upward leap; the antecedent arrives after a pause, an angular, atonal gesture that ends in a three-note phrase, leaping down to a sustained note and then back up in a dotted rhythm, long-short-long, landing on another sustained note. What follows is even more angular and pointillistic—a growl and pause, followed by additional gestures. In one of these, Braxton alternates between two or three contiguous notes or short leaps, followed by an asymmetrical downward leap and another going back up, this time even higher. His phrases alternate between notes of long and short duration; often the melodic contour is more discernible than the exact notes played. Five- and seven-note tuplet figures abound. Throughout, Braxton is mindful of the relative rates of motion and degrees of angularity, amount of energy given to a trajectory, and sharp changes in direction. His saxophone articulations *highlighted* a sharp attack and a grainy sound. At points of heightened intensity, he made use of growls, screeches, and extended techniques. We can see how intentional his choices of articulations were by comparing those sounds with the bell-like timbre heard on the first track of "3 Compositions of New Jazz" and on his later Town Hall concert recording from May 1972. Some of these could just as easily be found in the playing of gutbucket saxophonists performing in bars as within European avant-garde settings.

Less than four years later, Braxton had the chance to pursue his eclectic approach buffered from the expectations of the jazz circuit. He embarked on the first of an eight-year stream of much-heralded recordings on the Arista Freedom label. Some of his music during this period continued to represent his very personal "take" on the jazz tradition, one of his many inheritances.

14. Corea: "I, for one, never read reviews or cared much about the opinions of the press. I don't think media criticism affected that group" (interview with the author, December 11, 2011). Barry Altschul, on the other hand, was "very" aware of what was being written: "There were a couple of reviews that some were hurt by. But angry? No, we knew that

was going to happen. We knew we would be 'guys from Miles Davis's band all of a sudden freaking, going out.' I knew there was going to be some shit, as far as critics were concerned. Especially where Anthony was concerned. Anthony got the most of the harshness and critical shit. And regardless of how one might know him, he's quite sensitive, so there were some things that were hurtful. There were some things that are said about him that are still hurtful. A lot of it has to be, I think, [because] they still placed us in the category that's called 'jazz.' And he's been saying for years and years and years that that's not his category. He's an improviser and a composer. And jazz music was a great influence on him. That's it, though" (interview by the author, September 19, 2011).

15. Denis Constant, quoted in Lehman 2005, 38.

16. French critics also may have found Braxton's ideological positions threatening. In the liner notes to one of his recordings made France, shortly before he joined Circle, Braxton wrote: "Since Ornette Coleman, the actual music, by the experience of 'jazz,' broke the western chains (by extension) which had victimized it and we can now perceive the appearance of a new art that has a lot of promise. While contemporary classical music is coming to acknowledge improvisation more and more, spontaneous improvisation has been an ancient art for jazz musicians (not to mention the rest of the world)." Liner notes to *Anthony Braxton*, actuel 6, 1969.

17. Lock 1999, 159–62.

18. Quoted in Belden 1998.

19. Atkins, quoted in ibid. Belden also quotes a *DownBeat* review lauding the band's show that week in London, observing: "This is the first time we'd heard Davis play in a style well in advance of anything he has recorded, and the impact he made was equaled in my experience only by John Coltrane."

20. J. Wilson 1970b.

21. Kort 2002, 121–22. One might also question the objectivity of an understandably proud father's recollections of this young singer. Yet an audience for Laura Nyro may have had difficulty bridging the aesthetic gap between the music of a singer-songwriter they came to hear and the high-volume abstraction of Miles Davis's electric band.

22. A phenomenon I personally experienced at several similar double bills in New York City, 1970–73. A case in point was the lack of interest shown Herbie Hancock's sextet at the Schaefer Music Festival in Central Park in late July 1970. In contrast, I recall rapt New York City audiences with a very similar demographic profile for John McLaughlin's Mahavishnu Orchestra in 1971–73. The audience, it seemed to me, perceived the performance aesthetically and socially as a rock show, not dissimilar, as I recall, from the reaction to Emerson, Lake and Palmer when they appeared at the Fillmore East in 1971.

23. In subsequent years, the band Weather Report found greater success among rock audiences. When Joe Zawinul was asked to identify Weather Report's genre, he responded: "I am always lost for an answer. Categorizing what we do has never really mattered to me. It's improvisational music. Even the pieces that sound very tightly arranged and orchestrated begin as improvisations—if they're my compositions, they often start with me playing around on the piano at home. I do feel that we're coming from jazz, that the music is inventive and very powerful rhythmically, which is what jazz is all about. The difference between what we do and what you might call straight-ahead jazz is, first, our rhythmic ideas are coming from everywhere, from all over the world, and second, that the energy of the rock age has affected us very positively." Quoted in Palmer 1982.

24. Davis opened for rock bands Neil Young and Crazy Horse, and the Steve Miller Band at the Fillmore East in March 1970.

25. Cuscuna 2014.

26. Albertson 1970, 12.

27. Davis with Troupe 1990, 330.

28. Moore 1970. The review continues: "Instances of subtlety and formal improvisational mastery come thick and fast. It is all so strange and new and yet so comfortable. Anyone who has listened to much jazz, popular and new classical music over the last decade will sense the roots of all that occurs here. But the Miles Davis synthesis is so ingenious and profound as to transform virtually each minute."

29. Goldman 1970.

30. Ibid. Yet, as noted above, these audiences might have felt greater affinity with the Mahavishnu Orchestra.

31. Welburn 1971, 148.

32. Tate 1992, 89.

Appendix Two

1. The sets continue with the ballads "I Fall in Love Too Easily" and "Sanctuary," concluding with "Bitches Brew," plus on "Saturday Miles," "Willie Nelson."

2. A topic discussed in Gluck 2012a, with respect to David Rubinson's work with the Mwandishi Band.

3. Szwed 2002, 298–99.

4. Airto Moreira describes the cuica as "a strange sounding instrument from Brazil which is a drum with a stick inside it. When you pull the stick it makes a kind of barking dog sound." Moreira 2014.

Appendix Three

1. The thematic material from "Return to Forever" appears at 3:07 to 5:03; we also hear the Corea tune "Sometime Ago" inserted at 5:03 to 5:50. The latter was subsequently recorded on Corea (1971) 1994 and as the opening section of a suite that continues with "La Fiesta" on Corea (1972) 1999.

2. Anthony Braxton, quoted in Heffley 1996, 362.

3. Ibid.

4. Barry Altschul, interview by the author, September 19, 2011.

5. Ibid., 365, citing Braxton's *Composition Notes, book A* (Edmonton, AB: Tree Frog Press, 1988), 62–66.

REFERENCES

Albertson, Chris. 1970. "Blood, Sweat & Tears: With Miles Davis." *Down-Beat*, September 17, p. 12.

Allen, Clifford. 2003. "Dave Holland's Opus." *All About Jazz*, November 11. http://www.allaboutjazz.com/dave-hollands-opus-dave-holland-by-clifford-allen.php#.U5tOTai7ngU. Accessed March 11, 2015.

Anderson, Iain. 2007. *This Is Our Music: Free Jazz, the Sixties, and American Culture*. Philadelphia: University of Pennsylvania Press.

Ashley, Richard. 2014. "Expressiveness in Funk." In *Expressiveness in Music Performance: Empirical Approaches across Styles and Cultures*, edited by Dorottya Fabian, Renee Timmers, and Emery Schubert, 154–69. New York: Oxford University Press.

Atterton, J. 1968. "Dave Holland at Home in Harlem (Miles Davis Quintet)." *Melody Maker*, September 7, p. 8.

Baraka, Amiri. 1968. *Black Music*. New York: William Morrow.

Bartok, Bela. (1940) 2004. *Mikrokosmos*. Vol. 5. London: Boosey and Hawkes.

Belden, Bob. 1998. "Session by Session Analysis." Liner notes to *Miles Davis: The Complete Bitches Brew Sessions*, 108–40. Sony.

Belden, Bob, and Michael Cuscuna. 1998. Discography and album index to *Miles Davis: The Complete Bitches Brew Sessions*, 141–45. Sony.

Bernstein, David W. 2006. "'Listening to the Sounds of the People': Frederic Rzewski and Musica Elettronica Viva (1966–1972)." *Contemporary Music Review* 25 (5–6): 535–50.

Bey, Amir. 2007. "THE NEW TIMES HOLLER! Interviews KUNLE MWANGA." July 20. http://thenewtimesholler.com/ARCHIVE/archivedisplay.kunle.html. Also at http://www.earthartproductions.com/Kunle.html. Both accessed March 11, 2015.

Brennan, Joseph, comp. Undated. "The Usenet Guide to Beatles Recording Variations." http://www.columbia.edu/~brennan/beatles/var-1962.html. Accessed March 11, 2015.

Brown, Anthony. 2011. "Jack DeJohnette NEA JAZZ Master interview." Transcript, Smithsonian Jazz Oral History Program, November 10–11. Archives Center, National Museum of American History, Washington, DC.

Butters, Rex. 2006. "Bennie Maupin: Miles Beyond." *All About Jazz*, September 12. http://www.allaboutjazz.com/php/article.php?id=22723. Accessed March 11, 2015.

Cage, John. (1961) 2011. *Silence*. Middletown, CT: Wesleyan University Press.

Carpenter, Brian. 2002. "William Parker: Mayor of the Lower East Side." Interview with William Parker. WZBC-FM, Boston College Radio. Aired January 21, 2002.

Carr, Ian. 1998. *Miles Davis: The Definitive Biography*. New York: Thunder's Mouth Press.

Chadabe, Joel. 1997. *Electric Sound: The Past and Promise of Electronic Music*. Upper Saddle River, NJ: Prentice Hall.

Chambers, Jack. (1983) 1985. *Milestones: The Music and Times of Miles Davis*. New York: Quill.

Chanan, Michael. 1995. *Repeated Takes: A Short History of Recording and Its Effects on Music*. New York: Verso.

Chénard, Marc. 2011. "Dave Holland: Basso Nobile." *La Scena Musicale*, May 20. http://www.scena.org/lsm/sm16-8/sm16-8_holland_en.html. Accessed March 11, 2015.

Cole, George. 2005. *The Last Miles: The Music of Miles Davis, 1980–1991*. Ann Arbor: University of Michigan Press.

Cook, Richard. 2005. *It's About That Time: Miles Davis On and Off Record*. New York: Oxford University Press.

Corea, Chick. 2013. "Interview with Chick Corea Talking about Miles Davis and *Live in Europe 1969: The Bootleg Series Vol. 2*." http://www.milesdavis.com/us/news/exclusive-interview-chick-corea-talks-about-miles-davis-and-live-europe-1969-bootleg-series-vol. Accessed March 11, 2015.

Coryell, Julie, and Laura Friedman. 1978. *Jazz-Rock Fusion: The People, the Music*. New York: Dell.

Cotter, Holland. 2006. "Allan Kaprow, Creator of Artistic 'Happenings,' Dies at 78." *New York Times*, April 6. http://www.nytimes.com/2006/04/10/arts/design/10kaprow.html?_r=0. Accessed March 11, 2015.

Crouch, Stanley. 1990. "Play the Right Thing." *New Republic*, February 12, pp. 30–37.

Curran, Alvin. 1995. "On Spontaneous Music," July 15–17. http://www.alvincurran.com/writings/spontaneous.html. Accessed March 11, 2015.

———. 2000. "Improvisationspraxis der Musica Elettronica Viva." *MusikTexte*, November. English translation: "From the Bottom of the Soundpool," http://www.alvincurran.com/writings/soundpool.html. Accessed March 11, 2015.

———. 2006. "On Spontaneous Music." *Contemporary Music Review* 25 (5–6): 483–90.

———. 2010. "From Via della Luce to the Road—a Short Story in Song Form." *Contemporary Music Review* 29 (6): 621–42.

Curran, Alvin, and Richard Teitelbaum. 1989. "Musica Elettronica Viva: Program Notes, New Music America Festival." Knitting Factory, New York City. http://www.alvincurran.com/writings/mev.html. Accessed March 11, 2015.

Cuscuna, Michael. 2014. Essay. Liner notes to *Miles at the Fillmore*. Columbia Legacy.

Davis, Miles, with Quincy Troupe. 1990. *Miles: The Autobiography*. New York: Simon and Schuster.

Davis, Peter G. 1970. "American Musicians from Rome Strive for Unusual Effect Here." *New York Times*, February 21.

Detheridge, D. 1968a. "Holland—the Man Miles Wants." *Melody Maker*, July 27.

———. 1968b. Dave Holland article. *Melody Maker*, October 26.

DeVeaux, Scott. 1997. *Bebop: A Social and Musical History*. Berkeley: University of California Press.

DownBeat. 1969. "Japanese Wreck Tour by Miles Davis Group." February 20, p. 10.

———. 1972. "Ad Lib: New York; Announcement of Performance by the Revolutionary Ensemble." March 30, p. 36.

Early, Gerald, ed. 2001. *Miles Davis and the American Culture*. St. Louis: Missouri Historical Society Press, distributed by University of Missouri Press.

Emmerson, Simon. 1998. "Aural Landscape: Musical Space." *Organized Sound* 3 (2): 135–40.

Ephland, John. 1989. "Tony Williams: Still the Rhythm Magician." *DownBeat*, May 1. http://www.downbeat.com/default.asp?sect=stories&subsect=story_detail&sid=981. Accessed March 11, 2015.

Ericson, Raymond. 1970. "Study of Noise Takes Art Form: Automation House Presents Ensemble of 'Happenings.'" *New York Times*, November 22.

Feather, Leonard. 1964. "Miles Davis: Blindfold Tests," part 1. *DownBeat*, June 18. In Kirchner 1997, 130–33.

———. 1968a. "Miles Davis: Blindfold Tests," part 1. *DownBeat*, June 13.

———. 1968b. "Dave Holland with Miles: Honorary Soul Brother from Wolverhampton." *Melody Maker*, October 26.

———. 1968c. "Miles Davis Plays in Concert at UCLA." *Los Angeles Times*, October 8.

———. 1970a. "Chick Corea Quartet Conducts Experiment." *Los Angeles Times*, October 2.

———. 1970b. Concert review. *Denver Post*, June 14.

———. 1971. Concert review of Circle. *Los Angeles Times*, July 30.

Fellezs, Kevin. 2011. *Birds of Fire: Jazz, Rock, Funk, and the Creation of Fusion*. Durham, NC: Duke University Press.

Floyd, Samuel A., Jr. 1995. *The Power of Black Music: Interpreting Its History from Africa to the United States*. New York: Oxford University Press.

Freeman, Philip. 2006. *Running the Voodoo Down: The Electric Music of Miles Davis*. Minneapolis: Backbeat Books, Hal Leonard Books.

Friendly, Alfred, Jr. 1970. "Expatriate Composers in Rome Using Audiences as Instrument." *New York Times*, February 7.

Gendron, Bernard. 2010. "Rzewski in New York (1971–1977)." *Contemporary Music Review* 29 (6): 557–74.

Glasser, Brian. 2001. *In a Silent Way: A Portrait of Joe Zawinul*. London: Sanctuary.

Gleason, Ralph. 1970. Program notes to Miles Davis, *Bitches Brew*. Columbia Records.

Gluck, Bob. 2012a. *You'll Know When You Get There: Herbie Hancock and the Mwandishi Band*. Chicago: University of Chicago Press.

———. 2012b. "Electric Circus, Electric Ear and the Intermedia Center in Late-1960s New York." *Leonardo* 45 (1): 50–56.

———. 2012c. "Nurturing Young Composers: Morton Subotnick's Late-1960s Studio in New York City." *Computer Music Journal* 36 (1): 65–80.

———. 2014. "Paul Bley and Live Synthesizer Performance." *Jazz Perspectives* 8 (1): 303–22.

Goddet, Laurent. 1979. Interview with Herbie Hancock. *Jazz Hot*, July–August, 363–64.

Goldberg, Joe. 1963. *Jazz Masters of the 50s*. New York: Macmillan.

Goldman, Albert. 1970. "So You Thought Jazz Was Dead." *New York Times*, June 21.

Goodman, Dave. 2011. "Tony Williams' Drumset Ideology to 1969: Synergistic Emergence from an Adaptive Modeling of Feel, Technique and Creativity as an Archetype for Cultivating Originality in Jazz Drumset Performance Studies." PhD diss., University of Sydney.

Goodwin, Jeremy D. 2012. "For Chick Corea and Gary Burton, It All Came Together in Boston." *Boston Globe*. October 18. http://bostonglobe.com/arts/2012/10/18 /for-chick-corea-and-gary-burton-all-came-together-boston/hhknhzxzgljzufcjc7jq0n /story.html. Accessed March 11, 2015.

Gourse, Leslie. 1989. "Dave Holland: Miles Ahead." *Jazz Times*, April, pp. 16, 18.

Griffin, Farah Jasmine, and Salim Washington. 2008. *Clawing at the Limits of Cool: Miles Davis, John Coltrane, and the Greatest Jazz Collaboration Ever*. New York: Thomas Dunne Books, St. Martin's Press.

Guardian. 2007. "Obituary: Leroy Jenkins, Bold Explorer of the Violin's Free Jazz Potential." *Guardian* (Manchester), March 15. http://www.theguardian.com/news/2007 /mar/16/guardianobituaries.jazz. Accessed March 11, 2015.

Hadlock, Dick. 1970. *Caught in the Act: University of California Jazz Festival* (Greek Theater, Berkeley). *DownBeat*, July 23, pp. 28, 30.

Hall, Greg. 1974. "Teo: The Man behind the Scene." *DownBeat*, July, pp. 13–15.

Harris, William. 2004. "'How You Sound??': Amiri Baraka Writes Jazz." In *Uptown Conversation: The New Jazz Studies*, edited by Robert G. O'Meally, Brent Hayes Edwards, and Farah Jasmine Griffin, 312–25. New York: Columbia University Press.

Heffley, Michael. 1996. *The Music of Anthony Braxton*. New York: Praeger.

Heller, Michael C. 2012. "Reconstructing We: History, Memory and Politics in a Loft Jazz Archive." PhD diss., Harvard University.

Henderson, David. (1978) 2008. *'Scuse Me while I Kiss the Sky: Jimi Hendrix, Voodoo Child*. New York: Atria.

Hermes, Will. 2012. *Love Goes to Buildings on Fire: Five Years in New York That Changed Music*. New York: Faber and Faber.

Holmes, Thom. (1985) 2012. *Electronic and Experimental Music: Technology, Music, and Culture*. New York: Routledge.

Hughes, Allen. 1969. "Moog Approves of Moog-Made Jazz: Synthesizers Perform in Museum Series 3,500 Throng." *New York Times*, August 29.

Jenkins, Leroy. 2006. "Leroy Jenkins, March 11, 1932–February 24, 2007, Pioneer of Creative String Improvisation." A biography submitted by Jenkins in 2006. http://www .jazzbows.com/leroyjenkins.html. Accessed March 11, 2015.

Jenkins, Willard. 2011. "Who Shot Miles?" *Independent Ear*, June 28. Reposted at the Open

Sky Jazz, http://www.openskyjazz.com/2011/06/who-shot-miles. Accessed March 11, 2015.

Johnson, Brooks. 1971. Interview with Herbie Hancock. *DownBeat*, January 21, pp. 14–15, 34.

Kart, Larry. 1969a. "Caught in the Act: Miles Davis, Plugged Nickel, Chicago." *DownBeat*, August 7, p. 28.

———. 1969b. "The Chick Corea File," *DownBeat*, April 3, pp. 21–22.

———. 1986. "Ornette Coleman Travels the Long Road, Making Up the Rules as He Goes Along." *Chicago Tribune*, May 11.

Keepnews, Peter. 1997. "The Lost Quintet." In *A Miles Davis Reader*, edited by Bill Kirchner, 184–89. Washington: Smithsonian Institution Press. Originally published as "Miles Davis at 60," *Village Voice* Jazz Supplement, August 1986, pp. 22–23.

Kelley, Robin D. G. 2001. "Miles Davis: The Chameleon of Cool; A Jazz Genius in the Guise of a Hustler." *New York Times*, May 13. http://www.nytimes.com/2001/05/13/arts/miles-davis-the-chameleon-of-cool-a-jazz-genius-in-the-guise-of-a-hustler.html. Accessed March 11, 2015.

———. 2009. *Thelonious Monk: The Life and Times of an American Original*. New York: Free Press.

Kemper, Mary B., writer and director. 2002. *120 Wooster Street*. Film. Island Sea Productions, Kemper Museum of Contemporary Art.

Kirby, Michael. 1965. *Happenings: An Illustrated Anthology; Scripts and Productions by Jim Dine, Red Grooms, Allan Kaprow, Claes Oldenburg, and Robert Whitman*. New York: E. P. Dutton.

Kirchner, Bill, ed. 1997. *A Miles Davis Reader*. Washington, DC: Smithsonian Institution Press.

Kisselgoff, Anna. 1972. "Unusual Arts Center Is Taking Shape." *New York Times*, February 10.

———. 1974. "Murray Louis Troupe in Premiere Here." *New York Times*, February 22.

Kofsky, Frank. 1970. *Black Nationalism and the Revolution in Music*. New York: Pathfinder.

Kort, Michele. 2002. *Soul Picnic: The Music and Passion of Laura Nyro*. New York: Thomas Dunne Books.

Lehman, Stephen. 2005. "I Love You with an Asterisk: African-American Experimental Music and the French Jazz Press, 1970–1980." *Critical Studies in Improvisation / Études critiques en improvisation* 1 (2): 38–53.

Lewis, George E. 1996. "Improvised Music after 1950: Afrological and Eurological Perspectives." *Black Music Research Journal* 16 (1): 91–122.

———. 2001/2002. "Experimental Music in Black and White: The AACM in New York, 1970–1985." *Current Musicology*, Spring, pp. 100–157. Also published in Robert G. O'Meally, Brent Hayes Edwards, and Farah Jasmine Griffin, eds., *Uptown Conversation: The New Jazz Studies*, 50–59 (New York: Columbia University Press, 2004).

———. 2007. "Leroy Jenkins: Reflections by George Lewis." *Institute for Studies in American Music Newsletter* 37 (1): 8, 15. Conservatory of Music, Brooklyn College of the City University of New York.

———. 2008. *A Power Stronger Than Itself: The AACM and American Experimental Music*. Chicago: University of Chicago Press.

Lewis, Joel. 1994. "Running the Voodoo Down." *Wire*, December, pp. 20–22, 24, 26, 79.

Lewis, Miles Marshall. (2006) 2010. *Sly and the Family Stone's There's a Riot Goin On*. New York: Continuum International.

Lewisohn, Mark. (1988) 2013. *The Beatles Recording Sessions: The Official Story of the Abbey Road Years 1962–1970*. New York: Sterling.

Liebman, Dave, with Lewis Porter. 2013. *What It Is: The Life of a Jazz Artist*. Lanham, MD: Scarecrow Press.

Litweiler, John. 1967a. "Caught in the Act." *DownBeat*, May 18, pp. 25–26.

———. 1967b. "Heard and Seen: Anthony Braxton." *Coda*, March, p. 28.

———. (1984) 1990. *The Freedom Principle: Jazz after 1958*. New York: Da Capo.

———. 1994. *Ornette Coleman: A Harmolodic Life*. New York: Da Capo.

Lock, Graham. 1988. *Forces in Motion: Anthony Braxton and the Meta-Reality of Creative Music; Interviews and Tour Notes*. London: Quartet Books.

———. 1999. *Blutopia: Visions of the Future and Revisions of the Past in the Work of Sun Ra, Duke Ellington, and Anthony Braxton*. Durham, NC: Duke University Press.

Looker, Benjamin. 2004. *Point from Which Creation Begins: The Black Artists' Group of St. Louis*. St. Louis: Missouri Historical Society Press, distributed by University of Missouri Press.

Lopez, Rick. 1997. *The Sam Rivers Sessionography*. http://www.bb10k.com/RIVERS.disc.html. Accessed March 11, 2015.

Losin, Peter. 2014. "Sessionography." Miles Ahead: A Miles Davis Website, http://www.plosin.com/milesAhead/Sessions.aspx. Accessed March 11, 2015.

Maconie, Robin. 1976. *The Works of Stockhausen*. London: Oxford University Press/Marion Boyars.

Mandel, Howard. 2008. *Miles, Ornette, Cecil: Jazz beyond Jazz*. New York: Routledge.

Marek, Piotr. 1996. *Jack DeJohnette Discography*. http://riad.pk.edu.pl/~pmj/dejohnette/discography.shtml. Accessed March 11, 2015.

Martin, Waldo E., Jr. 2001. "Miles Davis and the 1960s Avant-Garde." In Early 2001, 106–17.

McCormack, Ed. 1973. "New York Confidential." *Rolling Stone*, September 13, p. 16.

Mercer, Michelle. 2004. *Footprints: The Life and Work of Wayne Shorter*. New York: Penguin.

Merlin, Enrico. 1996. "Code MD: Coded Phrases in the First 'Electric Period.'" Paper presented at the conference "Miles Davis and American Culture II," Washington University, St. Louis, May 10–11. http://www.plosin.com/milesahead/CodeMD.html. Accessed March 11, 2015.

Milesdavis.com, the Official Miles Davis Community website. Undated. "Drummer Lenny White: Bitches Brew." http://www.milesdavis.com/us/drummer-lenny-white-bitches-brew. Accessed March 11, 2015.

Minsker, Marc. 2005. "Sam Rivers: A Giant among Us." Interview with Sam Rivers. *All About Jazz*, January 17. http://www.allaboutjazz.com/sam-rivers-a-giant-among-us-sam-rivers-by-marc-minsker.php#.U5cddS-7ngU. Accessed March 11, 2015.

MOMA 1969. Museum of Modern Art Archive. "Jazz in the Garden." Press release no. 73, June 5. https://www.moma.org/learn/resources/press_archives/1960s. Accessed March 11, 2015.

Monson, Ingrid. (2007) 2010. *Freedom Sounds: Jazz, Civil Rights, and Africa, 1950–1967*. New York: Oxford University Press.

Moog Archives. 2004. "Interview with Herb Deutsch." http://moogarchives.com/ivherb01.htm. [Interviews conducted October 2003 and February 2004.] Accessed March 11, 2015.

Moore, Carman. 1970. "The New Thing Meets Rock." *New York Times*, August 9.

Moreira, Airto. 2014. Personal narrative. http://www.airto.com/stories12.htm. Accessed March 11, 2015

Morgenstern, Dan. 1970. "Miles in Motion." *DownBeat.* September 3, p. 16.

Morgenstern, Dan, and Martin Williams. 1964. "The October Revolution: Two Views of the Avant Garde in Action." *DownBeat,* November 19, pp. 15, 32–33.

Munk, Erika. 1969. "Booking the Revolution: An Interview with Saul Gottlieb and Oda Jurges of the Radical Theatre Repertory." *Drama Review: TDR* 13 (4): 80–88. Cambridge, MA: MIT Press.

Myers, Marc. 2011. "Interview: Chick Corea (Part 1)." *JazzWax,* November 3. http://www.jazzwax.com/2011/10/interview-chick-corea-part-1.html. Accessed March 11, 2015.

Nemeyer, Eric. 2005. "Interview with Chick Corea." *Jazz Improv* 5 (3): 30–43. [Interviews conducted November 13, 2004, and January 31, 2005.]

———. 2012. "Interview with Dave Holland." *Jazz Inside,* December. http://jazzinsidemagazine.com/publications/guide/december-2012/download. Accessed March 11, 2015.

Ness, Bob. 1976. "Profile: Leo Smith." *DownBeat,* October 7. http://www.wadadaleosmith.com/pages/interviews_eng_3.html#profile. Accessed March xx11, 2015.

New Yorker. 1970. "Automation House." March 14, pp. 30–32.

New York Times. 1931. "Block Development Will Benefit City: Architect Sees Solution of Many Civic Problems in Large Scale Construction." February 22. Chelsea Reform Democratic Club website, http://crdcnyc.org/history [accessed March 11, 2015]; New Chelsea History Timeline, http://crdcnyc.org/Websites/CCtest/Images/History/New_Chelsea_History_Timelime.pdf [accessed March 11, 2015].

———. 1932. "Babe Ruth Is Santa at London Terrace, Distributes Gifts to Chelsea Children at Special Fete before Revealing Identity." December 25. Chelsea Reform Democratic Club website, http://crdcnyc.org/history [accessed March 11, 2015]; New Chelsea History Timeline, http://crdcnyc.org/Websites/CCtest/Images/History/New_Chelsea_History_Timelime.pdf [accessed March 11, 2015].

———. 1972. "Dissonants Hear Another Jazz." July 6.

Nicholson, Stuart. 1998. *Jazz Rock: A History.* New York: Schirmer Books.

Nisenson, Eric. 1996. "Bitches Brew and Art of Forgetting." Milestones: A Miles Davis Collector's Site. http://www.oakton.edu/user/4/larry/miles/nisenson.html. Accessed March 11, 2015.

Other Minds Festival. Undated. Leroy Jenkins biography. http://www.otherminds.org/shtml/Jenkins.shtml. Accessed March 11, 2015.

Ouellette, Dan. 1999. "Bitches Brew: The Making of the Most Revolutionary Jazz Album in History." *DownBeat,* December, pp. 32–34, 36–37.

Palmer, Robert. 1982. "Survivors in Jazz Rock Disclaim It." *New York Times,* June 11. http://www.nytimes.com/1982/06/11/arts/survivors-in-jazz-rock-disclaim-it.html. Accessed March 11, 2015.

Palombini, Carlos. 1993. "Technology and Pierre Schaeffer: Pierre Schaeffer's Arts-Relais, Walter Benjamin's technische Reproduzierbarkeit and Martin Heidegger's Ge-stell." *Organized Sound* 3 (1): 4.

Panken, Ted. 1993. Interview with Leroy Jenkins. WKCR-FM, Columbia University, New York. Aired October 12. http://www.jazzhouse.org/nlib/index.php3?read=panken17. Accessed March 11, 2015.

———. 1994. Interview with Kunle Mwanga. WKCR-FM, Columbia University, New York. Aired January 12. http://www.earthartproductions.com/KunleMwangaInterview2 .html. Accessed March 11, 2015.

———.1995. Interview with Anthony Braxton. WKCR-FM, Columbia University, New York. Aired February 5. Jazz Journalists Association Library, http://www.jazzhouse .org/library/?read=panken6. Accessed March 11, 2015.

———. 1997. "Ted Panken Interviews Sam Rivers." WKCR-FM, Columbia University, New York. Aired September 25. http://www.jazzhouse.org/library/index .php3?read=panken20. Accessed March 11, 2015.

———. 2008. Interview with Karl Berger. WKCR-FM, Columbia University, New York. Aired October 24. http://tedpanken.wordpress.com/2011/07/19/karl-berger-and -ingrid-berger-interviews. Accessed March 11, 2015.

———. 2009. "In Conversation with Jack DeJohnette." http://www.jazz.com/features -and-interviews/2009/6/15/in-conversation-with-jack-dejohnette. Accessed March 11, 2015.

Pareles, Jon. 1988. "Recordings; A Miles Davis Collection With Only Half the Story." *New York Times*, December 1. http://www.nytimes.com/1988/12/11/arts/recordings -a-miles-davis-collection-with-only-half-the-story.html?pagewanted=all&src=pm. Accessed March 11, 2015.

———.1990. "Sounds around Town: The Week's Jazz Album" [Miles Davis, *Pangaea* (Columbia)]. *New York Times*, June 22. http://www.nytimes.com/1990/06/22/arts /sounds-around-town-340090.html. Accessed March 11, 2015.

Piekut, Benjamin. 2009. "Race, Community, and Conflict in the Jazz Composers Guild." *Jazz Perspectives* 3 (3): 191–231.

Pond, Steven F. (2005) 2010. *Headhunters: The Making of Jazz's First Platinum Album*. Ann Arbor: University of Michigan Press.

Porter, Eric. 2001. "It's About That Time: The Response to Miles Davis's Electric Turn." In Early 2001, 130–47.

Porter, Lewis. 1999. *John Coltrane: His Life and Music*. Ann Arbor: University of Michigan Press.

Potter, Keith, and David Smith. 1976. "Interview with Philip Glass." *Contact*, Spring, cited in Radano1993, 161n.

Primack, Bret. 1978. "Leroy Jenkins: Gut-Plucking Revolutionary." *DownBeat*, November 16, pp. 23–24, 50–51.

Radano, Ronald M. 1981. "A Cultural and Musical Analysis of Avant-Garde Jazz." Master's thesis, University of Chicago.

———. 1993. *New Musical Figurations: Anthony Braxton's Cultural Critique*. Chicago: University of Chicago Press.

Ratliff, Ben. 2005. "Miles Davis 'The Cellar Door Sessions, 1970' (Sony Legacy)." *New York Times*, December 26. http://www.nytimes.com/2005/12/26/arts/music/26choi .html?_r=0. Accessed March 11, 2015.

———. 2006. "A Jazz Innovator during His Late Funky Phase." *New York Times*, March 13. http://www.nytimes.com/1997/08/03/arts/a-jazz-innovator-during-his-late-funky -phase.html. Accessed March 11, 2015.

———. 2007. "Leroy Jenkins, 74, Violinist Who Pushed Limits of Jazz, Dies." *New York*

Times, February 26. http://www.nytimes.com/2007/02/26/arts/music/26jenkins
.html?_r=0. Accessed March 11, 2015.

————. 2012. "Pete Cosey, Guitarist with Miles Davis, Dies at 68." *New York Times*, June 6.
http://www.nytimes.com/2012/06/06/arts/music/pete-cosey-guitarist-with-miles
-davis-dies-at-68.html?_r=0. Accessed March 11, 2015.

Riggins, Roger. 1972. "Caught in the Act: The Revolutionary Ensemble." *DownBeat*, October 26, p. 34.

Robson, Britt. 2012. "Interview: Jack DeJohnette." *Wondering Sound*, February 17. http://
www.wonderingsound.com/interview/interview-jack-dejohnette. Accessed March 11, 2015.

Rockwell, John. 1974. "Face of Jazz Is Changing Visibly." *New York Times*, June 4.

Rivers, Sam. 1995. "New American Music, Volume 1: New York Section, Composers of the 1970's." Program notes to *Shadows*. Smithsonian Folkways Records, stereo LP.

Rusch, Bob. 1990. Interview with William Parker. *Cadence* 16 (12): 6.

Rzewski, Frederic. 2006. "On Improvisation." *Contemporary Music Review* 25 (5–6): 491–95.

Sharpe, John. Undated. "Ted Daniel: *Tapestry* and the Loft Years." http://www.allaboutjazz
.com/php/article.php?id=33172. Accessed March 11, 2015.

Shipton, Alyn. 2007. *A New History of Jazz*. New York: Continuum.

Skilbrigt, Borge. (2001) 2013. "Graham Bond." http://grahambond.org/biography.html. Accessed March 11, 2015.

Smith, Bill. 1973. Interview with Dave Holland. http://vancouverjazz.com/bsmith
/2006/01/dave-holland-interviews-1973-1989.html. Accessed March 11, 2015.

Smith, [Wadada] Leo. 1973. "notes (8 pieces) | source | a new | world | music: creative music." Excerpts posted at http://www.wadadaleosmith.com/pages/philos.html. Accessed March 11, 2015.

Spann, Michael. 2006. "Interview with Sirone." *Xochi* 23 (2): 77–92.

Spellman, A. B. 1965. "Jazz at the Judson." *Nation*, February 8, p. 149.

————. 1985. *Black Music: Four Lives in the Bebop Business*. New York: Limelight Editions, Hal Leonard Books.

Stanleigh, Bertram. 1969. "Moog Jazz in the Garden." *Audio*, November.

Steinbeck, Paul. 2008a. "'Area by Area the Machine Unfolds': The Improvisational Performance Practice of the Art Ensemble of Chicago." *Journal of the Society for American Music* 2 (3): 397–427.

————. 2008b. "Urban Magic: The Art Ensemble of Chicago's Great Black Music." PhD diss., Columbia University.

Stephenson, Sam. 2009. *The Jazz Loft Project: Photographs and Tapes of W. Eugene Smith from 821 Sixth Avenue, 1957–1965*. New York: Alfred A. Knopf. Project website at Center for Documentary Studies, Duke University: http://www.jazzloftproject.org/. Accessed March 11, 2015.

Stern, Chip. 1978. "Jack DeJohnette: South Side to Woodstock." *DownBeat*, November, pp. 23–26, 51–52, 54.

Sterne, Jonathan. 2003. *The Audible Past: Cultural Origins of Sound Reproduction*. Chapel Hill, NC: Duke University Press.

Stockhausen, Karlheinz. 1978. "Weltmusik" (1973). In *Texte zur Musik*, 4:468–76. Co-

logne: Verlag M. DuMont Schauberg. Translation available at https://ojs.library.dal.ca
    /dalhousiereview/article/viewFile/dr693stockhausen/3070. Accessed March 11, 2015.
Svorinich, Victor. 2015. *Listen to This: Miles Davis and Bitches Brew*. Jackson: University
    Press of Mississippi.
Szantor, Jim. 1970. "Bitches Brew." *DownBeat*, June 11, pp. 20–21. In Kirchner 1997, 254.
Szwed, John. 2002. *So What: The Life of Miles Davis*. New York: Simon and Schuster.
Tate, Greg. 1992. *Flyboy in the Buttermilk: Essays on Contemporary America*. New York:
    Simon and Schuster.
Teltsch, Kathleen. 1993. "M. McClelland, 53; Helped Experiments in Theater and Arts."
    New York Times, September 22. http://www.nytimes.com/1993/09/22/obituaries
    /m-mcclelland-53-helped-experiments-in-theater-and-arts.html. Accessed March 11,
    2015.
Tingen, Paul. 2001a. *Miles Beyond: The Electric Explorations of Miles Davis, 1967–1991*. New
    York: Billboard Books.
———. 2001b. "Miles Davis and the Making of *Bitches Brew*: Sorcerer's Brew." *Jazz Times*,
    May. http://jazztimes.com/articles/20243-miles-davis-and-the-making-of-bitches
    -brew-sorcerer-s-brew. Accessed March 11, 2015.
Togashi, Nobuaki, Kohji "Shaolin" Matsubayashi, and Masayuki Hatta. (2001) 2014. Jazz
    Discography Project. http://www.jazzdisco.org. Accessed March 11, 2015.
Tomlinson, Gary. 1991. "Miles Davis, Musical Dialogician." *Black Music Research Journal* 11
    (2): 249–64. In Kirchner 1997, 234–49.
Toner, John. 1974. "Chick Corea." *DownBeat*, March 28, pp. 14–16.
Troupe, Quincy. (1998) 2004. "Overview Essay—Bitches Brew." Liner notes to *The Com-
    plete Bitches Brew Sessions*. Sony Records.
Veal, Michael. 2002. "Miles Davis and the Unfinished Project of Electric Jazz." *Raritan*
    (Summer): 153–63.
———. 2009. Review of Miles Davis, *The Complete "On the Corner" Sessions*. *Jazz Perspec-
    tives* 3 (3): 265–73.
Waters, Keith. 2011. *The Studio Recordings of the Miles Davis Quintet, 1965–68*. New York:
    Oxford University Press.
Wein, George, Nate Chinen, and Bill Cosby. 2004. *Myself among Others*. New York: Da
    Capo Press.
Welburn, Ron. 1971. "The Black Aesthetic Imperative." In *The Black Aesthetic*, edited by
    Addison Gayle Jr., 126–42. New York: Doubleday.
Welch, Jane. 1970. "Europe's Answer to Woodstock: The First Actuel Paris Music Festival."
    DownBeat. January 22, pp. 16–17, 31.
Williams, Richard. 1970. "What Made Miles Davis Go Pop? (Richard Williams Talks to
    Bassist Dave Holland in New York)." *Melody Maker*, June 13, p. 21.
Wilmer, Valerie. 1971. "Musicians Talking: Anthony Braxton." *Jazz & Blues*, May, pp. 27–28.
———. (1977) 1992. *As Serious as Your Life: John Coltrane and Beyond*. London: Serpent's
    Tale.
Wilson, John S. 1968. "Herbie Hancock, Pianist, Establishes New Sextet; Leaves Miles
    Davis Quartet after Five-Year Tenure." *New York Times*, September 16.
———. 1970a. "Hyman, at Museum, Gives Moog Synthesizer Concert." *New York Times*,
    August 20.

———. 1970b. "Miles Davis's New Group Cuts Deeper into Rock at the Fillmore." *New York Times*, June 19.

———. 1972. "Folklore Center Switches to Jazz: Abdullah, an Avant-Garde Group, Is Effective." *New York Times*, June 11.

Wilson, Olly. 1983. "Black Music as an Art Form." *Black Music Research Journal* 3:1–22.

———. 1992. "The Heterogeneous Sound Ideal in African-American Music." In *New Perspectives on Music: Essays in Honor of Eileen Southern*, edited by Josephine Wright, 327–38. Warren, MI: Harmonie Park Press.

Winner, Langdon. 1970. "Bitches Brew" (album review). *Rolling Stone*, May 28. http://www.rollingstone.com/music/albumreviews/bitches-brew-19700528. Accessed March 11, 2015.

Young, Ben. 1993. Interview with James Duboise. WKCR-FM, Columbia University, New York. Aired December 6.

———.1998. *Dixonia: A Bio-Discography of Bill Dixon*. Westport, CT: Greenwood Press.

Zak, Albin J., III. 2010. *I Don't Sound Like Nobody: Remaking Music in 1950s America*. Ann Arbor: University of Michigan Press.

DISCOGRAPHY

Art Ensemble of Chicago. 1969. *Message to Our Folks*. BYG/actuel, audio LP.
———. 1969. *The Paris Session*. Freedom, audio LP.
———. 1969. *People in Sorrow*. Nessa, audio LP.
———. 1974. *Fanfare for the Warriors*. Atlantic Records, audio LP 1999;
    Koch Records, audio compact disc.
———. (1979) 1991. *Nice Guys*. ECM, audio compact disc.
Braxton, Anthony. 1968/1993. *3 Compositions of New Jazz*. Delmark Records,
    audio compact disc.
———. (1969) 2002. *B-X0 NO-47A*. BYG/Fuel 2000, audio compact disc.
———. (1970) 2000. *For Alto*. Delmark Records, audio compact disc.
———. 2011. *Town Hall Concert* (1972). hatOLOGY, audio compact disc.
Brown, Marion. 1970. *Afternoon of a Georgia Faun*. ECM, audio LP.
Burton, Gary. 1967. *Duster*. RCA, audio LP.
———. 1969. *Throb*. Atlantic Records, audio compact disc.
Circle. (1971) 2004. *Circle 1: Live in Germany*. CBS/Sony, Uni audio com-
    pact disc.
———. (1971) 1997. *Circle 2: The Gathering*. CBS/Sony, Uni audio com-
    pact disc.
———. (1971) 2001. *The Paris Concert*. ECM Records, audio compact disc.

Coleman, Ornette. (1959) 1990. *The Shape of Jazz to Come*. Atlantic Records. audio compact disc.

———. (1960) 1992. *Change of the Century*. Atlantic Records, audio compact disc.

———. (1960) 2008. *Free Jazz*. Atlantic Records, audio compact disc.

———. (1969) 2000. *Crisis*. Impulse Records, audio compact disc.

———. (1970) 2013. *Friends and Neighbors: Ornette Live at Prince Street*. Flying Dutchman/Beat Goes Public, audio compact disc.

———. (1971) 2000. *Science Fiction*. Columbia Records, audio compact disc.

Coltrane, John. 1961/1998. *Live at the Village Vanguard*. Impulse Records, audio compact disc.

———. (1964) 2003. *A Love Supreme*. Impulse! Records, audio compact disc.

———. (1965) 2000. *Ascension*. [Impulse! Records] Polygram Records, audio compact disc.

———. (1965) 2012. *Live in Seattle*. [Impulse! Records] Grp Records, audio compact disc.

———. (1974) 2000. *Interstellar Space* (1967). Impulse Records, audio compact disc.

Corea, Chick. (1966) 2004. *Tones for Joan's Bones*. Vortex, audio compact disc.

———. (1968) 2002. *Now He Sings, Now He Sobs*. Solid State Records, audio compact disc.

———. (1969) 2002. *Is*. Blue Note Records, audio compact disc.

———. (1969) 2006. *Sundance*. Groove Merchant, audio compact disc.

———. (1970) 2004. *The Song of Singing*. Blue Note Records, audio compact disc.

———. (1971) 2000. *A.R.C.* ECM Records, audio compact disc.

———. (1971) 1994. *Piano Improvisations Volume 1*. ECM Records, audio compact disc.

———. (1972) 2000. *Piano Improvisations Volume 2*. ECM Records/Polydor Records, audio compact disc.

———. (1972) 1999. *Return to Forever*. Polydor Records, LP.

———. 1975. *Circling In*. Blue Note Records, LP.

———. 1978. *Circulus*. Blue Note Records, LP.

———. 2008. *Early Circle*. 2008. Capitol, audio compact disc.

Creative Construction Company. 1976. *CCC (Muhal)*. Muse Records, LP.

———. 1976. *CCC, Volume 2*. Muse Records, LP.

Davis, Miles. (1959) 2000. *Kind of Blue*. [Columbia Records] Sony, audio compact disc.

———. (1965) 1998. *E.S.P.* [Columbia Records] Sony, audio compact disc.

———. (1967) 1998. *Miles Smiles*. [Columbia Records] Sony, audio compact disc.

———. (1967) 1998. *Nefertiti*. [Columbia Records] Sony, audio compact disc.

———. (1967) 2008. *Sorcerer*. [Columbia Records] Sbme Special Mkts, audio compact disc.

———. (1968) 2008. *Filles de Kilimanjaro*. [Columbia Records] Sbme Special Mkts, audio compact disc.

———. (1968) 2008. *Miles in the Sky*. [Columbia Records] Sbme Special Mkts, audio compact disc.

———. (1969) 2002. *In a Silent Way*. [Columbia Records] Sony, audio compact disc.

———. (1970) 2010. *Bitches Brew*. [Columbia Records] Sony Legacy, audio compact disc.

———. (1970) 1997. *Black Beauty: Miles Davis at Fillmore West*. [Columbia Records] Sony, audio compact disc.

———. (1970) 1997. *Get Up with It*. [Columbia Records] Sony, audio compact disc.

———. (1970) 1997. *Live-Evil*. [Columbia Records] Sony, audio compact disc.

———. (1970) 1997. *Miles Davis at Fillmore: Live at the Fillmore East.* [Columbia] Sony, audio compact disc.

———. (1971) 2000. *A Tribute to Jack Johnson.* [Columbia Records] Sony, audio compact disc.

———. (1972) 1997. *Miles Davis in Concert: Recorded Live at Philharmonic Hall, New York.* [Columbia Records] Sony, audio compact disc.

———. (1972) 2010. *On the Corner.* [Columbia Records] Sony, audio compact disc.

———. (1974) 2010. *Big Fun.* [Columbia Records] Sony, audio compact disc.

———. (1974) 1997. *Dark Magus.* [Columbia Records] Sony, audio compact disc.

———. (1975) 2009. *Agharta.* [Columbia Records] Sony, audio compact disc.

———. (1975) 1990. *Pangaea.* [Columbia Records] Sony, audio compact disc.

———. (1976) 2002. *Water Babies.* [Columbia Records] Sony, audio compact disc.

———. (1979) 1990. *Circle in the Round.* [Columbia Records] Sony, audio compact disc.

———. (1981) 2001. *Directions.* [Columbia Records] Sony, audio compact disc.

———. (1982) 1995. *The Complete Live at the Plugged Nickel,* vol. 1. Columbia Records/ Columbia Legacy, audio compact disc.

———. (1996) 2004. *The Complete Miles Davis-Gil Evans Studio Recordings.* Columbia/ Legacy CXK 67397; Sony, audio compact disc.

———. 1997. *Live at the Fillmore East, March 7, 1970: It's About That Time.* Sony, audio compact disc.

———. (1998) 2004. *The Complete "Bitches Brew" Sessions.* Sony, audio compact disc.

———. (1998) 2004. *Miles Davis Quintet, 1965–'68.* Sony, audio compact disc.

———. 2001. *The Complete "In a Silent Way" Sessions.* Sony, audio compact disc.

———. 2005. *The Cellar Door Sessions 1970.* Sony, audio compact disc.

———. 2005. *The Complete "Jack Johnson" Sessions.* Sony, audio compact disc.

———. 2007. *The Complete "On the Corner" Sessions.* Sony, audio compact disc.

———. 2010. *Bitches Brew: 40th Anniversary Collectors Edition.* Sony, audio compact disc and LP box set.

———. 2011. *Bitches Brew Live.* Sony Legacy, audio compact disc.

———. 2011. *Miles Davis Quintet: Live in Europe 1967a.* The Bootleg Series, vol. 1. Sony, audio compact disc.

———. 2013. *Miles Davis Quintet: Live in Europe 1967a.* The Bootleg Series, vol. 2. Sony, audio compact disc.

———. 2014. *Miles at the Fillmore.* The Bootleg Series, vol. 3. Sony, audio compact disc.

DeJohnette, Jack. (1969) 2006. *The Jack DeJohnette Complex.* Milestone, audio compact disc.

———. 1970. *Have You Heard?* Milestone, LP [1998, Sony, Japan, audio compact disc].

Dibb, Mike. 2001. *The Miles Davis Story: The Definitive Look at the Man and His Music; A Film by Mike Dibb for Channel 4 Television.* Sony, DVD.

Evans, Bill. (1969) 1998. *At the Montreux Jazz Festival.* Verve Records, audio compact disc.

The Free Spirits. 1967. *Out of Sight and Sound.* ABC Records, LP.

Getz, Stan. 1969. *The Song Is You.* LRC Records, LP.

Hancock, Herbie. (1970) 2001. *Fat Albert Rotunda.* Warner Brothers, audio compact disc.

———. (1971) 2003. *Mwandishi.* Warner Brothers, audio compact disc.

———. (1972) 2001. *Crossings.* Warner Brothers, audio compact disc.

———. (1973) 2008. *Sextant.* [Columbia Records] Columbia Legacy, audio compact disc.

———. 1973. *The Spook Who Sat by the Door—Original Motion Picture Soundtrack*. United Artists Records, audio LP.

———. (1974) 1997. *Head Hunters*. [Columbia Records] Sony, audio compact disc.

———. (1974) 1998. *Thrust*. Columbia Records. [Columbia Records] Sony, audio compact disc.

———. (1977) 2007. *V.S.O.P.* [Columbia Records] Sony / Bmg Japan, audio compact disc.

———. (1994) 2014. *Mwandishi: The Complete Warner Brothers Recordings*. Warner Brothers, audio compact disc.

Hendrix, Jimi. (1967) 2013. *Are You Experienced*. MCA, audio compact disc.

———. (1968) 2013. *Axis Bold as Love*. Sony Legacy, audio compact disc.

———. (1969) 2013. *Electric Ladyland*. Sony Legacy, audio compact disc.

———. (1970) 1998. *Band of Gypsies*. Capitol/Experience Hendrix, audio compact disc.

Holland, Dave. (1972) 2013. *Conference of the Birds*. ECM Records, audio compact disc.

Lerner, Murray, dir. 2004. *Miles Electric: A Different Kind of Blue*. Eagle Rock, DVD.

Mahaffay, Mike, prod. 2009. *Free Life Loft Jazz: Snapshot of a Movement*, vol. 1. Privately released recording of a January 15, 1970, live radio broadcast from the WBAI Free Music Studio. Mahaffay's Musical Archives LLC, compact audio disc.

Mingus, Charles. (1956) 2001. *Pithecanthropus Erectus*. Atlantic Records.

Monk, Thelonious. (1957) 1991. *Monk's Music*. (Riverside) Ojc, audio compact disc.

———. 2006. *Live in '66*. Reeling in the Years Productions, Jazz Icons series, DVD.

Musica Elettronica Viva. 1969. *Friday*. Polydor, LP.

———. 1970. *Leave the City*. BYG, LP.

———. 1970. *The Sound Pool*. BYG. LP.

———. 2008. *Musica Elettronica Viva: MEV 40*. New World Records. 4-CD

Musica Elettronica Viva/AAM. 1970/2009. *Live Electronic Music Improvised*. Mainstream Records/Wergo. LP.

Powell, Bud. (1956) 1988. *Bud Powell: Jazz Giant*. Verve, audio compact disc.

———. (1958) 1990. *The Amazing Bud Powell, Time Waits*. Capitol Records, audio compact disc.

The Revolutionary Ensemble. 1973. *Manhattan Cycles*. India Navigation, LP.

———. (1972) 2009. *Vietnam 1 and 2*. ESP-Disk, audio compact disc.

———. 1975. *The Psyche*. RE Records, LP.

———. 1976. *The People's Republic*. A&M Records, LP.

———. 1977. *Revolutionary Ensemble*. Enja, LP.

———. 2004. *And Now . . .* Mutable Music, audio compact disc.

———. 2008. *Beyond the Boundary of Time*. Mutable Music, audio compact disc

Rivers, Sam. (1965) 2004. *Contours*. Blue Note Records, audio compact disc.

Sandor, Gyorgy. 2003. *Bartok: Complete Solo Piano Music*. Vox, audio compact disc. *Mikrokosmos* vol. 5 is on disc 2, track 2.

Schaeffer, Pierre. (1990) 2010. "Etudes aux Chemins de Fer" (1948). *L'Oeuvre Musicale*. EMF Media/Ina-GRM, audio compact disc.

Shorter, Wayne. 1959. *Introducing Wayne Shorter*. Vee-Jay records. Also released as *Shorter Moments*.

———. (1969) 1990. *Super Nova*. Blue Note Records, audio compact disc.

———. (1970) 2013. *Moto Grosso Feio*. (Blue Note Records) EMI Japan, audio compact disc.

————. (1970) 2008. *Odyssey of Iska*. Blue Note Records/Capitol, audio compact disc.

Stockhausen, Karlheinz. 1991. *Gesang der Jüngling* (1956). *Elektronische Musik 1952–1960*. Stockhausen-Verlag, audio compact disc.

————. 1995. *Mikrophonie I, Mikrophonie II, Telemusik*. Stockhausen-Verlag, audio compact disc.

————. 2010. *Plus-Minus*. Ives Ensemble. Hat Hut, audio compact disc.

Sun Ra. 1956. *Supersonic Jazz*. Saturn Records, LP [1992, Evidence, audio compact disc].

Taylor, Cecil. 1956. *Jazz Advance*. Transition, LP [2008, Fresh Sounds Spain, audio compact disc].

Tony Williams Lifetime. (1969) 1997. *Emergency*. Polygram, audio compact disc.

————. (1971) 1999. *Ego*. PolyGram, audio compact disc.

Tyner, McCoy. (1972) 1996. *Extensions*. Blue Note Records, audio compact disc.

Vitous, Miroslav. 1970. *Purple*. CBS/Sony Records, LP.

————. 1972. *Mountain in the Clouds*. Atlantic, audio LP. Also released as *Infinite Search* ([Embryo 1974] Rhino Atlantic 2004, audio compact disc).

Weather Report. (1971) 2009. *Weather Report*. [Columbia Records] Columbia Legacy, audio compact disc.

————. (1972) 1990. *I Sing the Body Electric*. [Columbia Records] Sony, audio compact disc.

————. (1972) 1998. *Weather Report: Live in Tokyo*. [Sony Japan] Columbia Europe, audio compact disc.

Williams, Anthony. (1964) 1999. *Lifetime*. Blue Note Records, audio compact disc.

————. (1965) 2009. *Spring!* Blue Note Records, audio compact disc.

Zappa, Frank. (1991) 1995. *The Best Band You Never Heard in Your Life*. Zappa Records, audio compact disc.

Zawinul, Josef. (1970) 2007. *Zawinul*. [Atlantic Records] Mosaic, audio compact disc.

INDEX

Curran, Alvin: concert at Antioch College, 74–75; concert at BAM, 210n72; meeting Anthony Braxton, Leo Smith, and Leroy Jenkins, 62; MEV American tour, 69–75

Davis, Miles: *Birth of the Cool*, 83; *Bitches Brew*, 35–40; *Black Beauty: Miles Davis at Fillmore West*, 189n2; *The Cellar Door Sessions*, 221n26; comparative economics of the jazz business and Davis's unique place within it, 157–59, 163; comparing the Lost Quintet with other 1970s bands, 109–11; *Dark Magus, Agharta*, and *Pangaea*, 13, 108–9; and Dave Holland, 16; electric direction, 192n28; electric piano, 219n7; *Filles de Kilimanjaro*, 16; *In a Silent Way*, 13, 22, 31, 42, 50, 105, 172–81; influence of James Brown and Sly and the Family Stone, 13; influence of Karlheinz Stockhausen, 107–8, 221n31, 222n32; influence of Stravinsky, 199n4; and Jack DeJohnette, 24; leadership style, 14, 53–55, 133, 189n7; *Miles Davis: In Concert: Recorded Live at Philharmonic Hall, New York*, 108; Miles Davis Quintet, 1960s, 10, 12–13–16, 21; Monterey Jazz Festival, 8; Michael Henderson–Keith Jarrett–John DeJohnette band, at the Cellar Door, 1970–71, 105–7, 126, 221n27; "Nefertiti," as recorded with the 1960s Quintet, 225; *On the Corner*, 107–8, 159, 221n31; and Ornette Coleman, 3, 9–11, 190–91nn9–10; and Pete Cosey, 108; playing with wah-wah, deeper rhythmic pocket, 106–7; postproduction of *Bitches Brew*, 40–43; preferences for accompaniment, 52; shooting incident, 198n121; solos on the studio version of *Bitches Brew*, 45; structuring live performances of "Bitches Brew," 47; *A Tribute to Jack Johnson*, 13, 50, 101, 106, 203n47, 218n63; use of "coded phrases" as segue between tunes, 49–50. *See also* Miles Davis Lost Quintet

DeJohnette, Jack: AACM, 22–23; and Anthony Braxton, 3, 23, 60; attending Peace Church concert, 78; with Bill Evans, 16, 24; at the Cellar Door, 221n27; collaborat-

ing with Airto Moreira, 100; developing musical affinity with Chick Corea, 29–31; drum duos with Chick Corea, 55; as drummer, 196n101; early career in Chicago, 22, 57; at the Fillmore East, March 1970, 97; at the Fillmore West, April 1970, 102; first recording, 104; influence of other drummers, 24; at the Isle of Wight, 105; and John McLaughlin, 18; with Karl Berger at the Creative Music Studio, 130; and Keith Jarrett, 101, 222n40; July 1969 performances, 52–53; with the Lost Quintet, 32–33; the Michael Henderson–Keith Jarrett–John DeJohnette band, 109–11, 126; and Miles Davis, 2, 13, 16, 22, 24–25, 107; in New York City, 23–24; *On the Corner*, 107–8; performing "Bitches Brew" live, 48–49; recording *Bitches Brew*, 37–38; recording Corea's *The Sun*, 126; at Ronnie Scott's club, 193

democratic principle in music, 1; "harmolodic," 191; (Waddada) Leo Smith, 78. *See also* Coleman, Ornette

DePietro, Tom: Upsurge Studio, 83, 95, 115, 117, 127, 223n12, 226n34

Deutsch, Herb, and his New York Improvisation Quartet, 99

Emerson, Keith: Moog synthesizer, 99–100

Free Life Communication: black participants, 217n45; influence of John Coltrane's *Ascension*, 84; organization, 84, 215–16n36; origins, 82–84; philosophical differences with AACM, 84–85; public events, 86, 158, 216n44, 231–32n16; at Space for Innovative Development, 86, 216n37; WBAI Free Music Store concert, 85–86

Grossman, Steve: at Dave Liebman's loft, 83, 219n12; departure from Free Life Communication, 86; with Miles Davis, 86, 94, 104; recording Corea's *The Sun*, 126; WBAI Free Music Store concert with Free Life Communication, 85–86

Hancock, Herbie, 8; collective improvisation, 189–90n7, 193n49, 197n111; electric

piano, 97–98; *Head Hunters*, 234n2;
Joseph Zawinul's *Zawinul*, 219–20n13;
with the Miles Davis Quintet, 16, 101;
on Miles Davis's leadership style, 14; and
Mwandishi Band, ix, 88, 107, 148, 153,
157, 189–90n7, 237n2; "Nefertiti" with
Miles Davis, 225n30; *A Tribute to Jack
Johnson*, 218n63
Henderson, Michael (bassist): at the Cellar
Door, 221n27; the Michael Henderson–
Keith Jarrett–John DeJohnette band,
109–11, 126; with Miles Davis, 50, 105–
7; *On the Corner*, 107–8
Hendrix, Jimi, 53, 63, 108, 197n116, 218n61
Holland, Dave, 11; acoustic duo with Chick
Corea, 80; with Barry Altschul in the
Sam Rivers Trio and Anthony Braxton
Quartet, 129–30, 229n53; with Circle,
113–17, 118–39, 184, 223n8; on *The
Complete Braxton*, 126; *Conference of the
Birds*, 129, 158, 184, 225n24, 229n53;
and Dave Liebman, 80–81; decision to
leave Miles Davis, 87–90; early career,
17–18; eclectic style, 53; electric bass, 25,
47; and exploratory music, 13; final dates
with Miles Davis, 105, 115; final days of
Circle, 127–31; July 1969 performances,
52–53; with Karl Berger, 130, 229n55;
with the Miles Davis Quintet, 2, 16;
with Miles Davis at the Fillmore East,
March 1970, 97; musical affinity with
Chick Corea, 31–33, 79–80; performing
"Bitches Brew" live, 48–49; playing with
Jimi Hendrix (and John McLaughlin),
197n116; playing "Nefertiti" in the early
Lost Quintet repertoire, 225n30; playing
on Wayne Shorter's *Moto Grosso Feio*,
219n13; recording *Bitches Brew*, 37–38;
recording Corea's *The Sun*, 126; at Ronnie
Scott's club, 193; trio with Chick Corea
and Barry Altschul, 2, 86–87, 89–90, 95,
105, 113–15, 140; wah-wah electric bass
at the Fillmore West, 102, 105

Jarrett, Keith: at the Cellar Door, 221n27;
with Charles Lloyd, 24; early career
development, 101; and Jack DeJohnette,
24, 101, 222n40; with Miles Davis band

in September 1970, 106–7, 108–11, 126,
221n25; RMI electric piano, 102–3;
as second electric keyboard with Miles
Davis, 47, 52, 79, 101
Jenkins, Leroy, 2; as an AACM member 2,
216n44; cofounding the Revolutionary
Ensemble, 57; death of, 148; early career,
58; forming the Revolutionary Ensemble,
134; Gordon Mumma's "Communication in a Noisy Environment," 126,
168, 227n37; and Jerome Cooper, 134;
meeting MEV at Festival Actuel, 62–63;
meeting Muhal Richard Abrams in Chicago, 59; meeting with Free Life Communication, 84–85; move to New York City,
59, 68, 207n47; move to Paris in 1969, 58,
59; playing alto saxophone, 233n33. *See
also* Revolutionary Ensemble

Liebman, Dave, 86; influence of John Coltrane, 212n3; meeting Dave Holland in
London, 80–81; Nineteenth Street loft,
82–84; with Ten Wheel Drive, 87, 158;
WBAI Free Music Store concert with
Free Life Communication, 85–86
lofts (jazz lofts), x, 4, 67–69, 80–87, 90, 95,
114–15, 136–38, 139, 158, 161–62, 166,
167, 213n13, 214n18, 215n29, 216n44,
219n12, 229n53, 230n10, 231nn15–16,
231n18, 231n23; New York Musicians
Jazz Festival, 231n15

Macero, Teo: creating a musical structure for
"Bitches Brew," 46; editor of *Bitches Brew*
and *Miles Davis at Fillmore: Live at the Fillmore East* (1970), 171; electronic effects
in the studio, 47; live in Paris and Berlin,
48–49; producer David Rubinson's view
of Macero's role, 42; recording *Bitches
Brew*, 36, 38; role in postproduction of
Bitches Brew, 40–43
Maupin, Bennie: performing on Chick Corea's
Is, 198n120; recording *Bitches Brew*, 36,
45–46, 220n22; and Sirone, 136
McCall, Steve, 23; leading the AACM exodus
to Paris, 58; quartet with Anthony
Braxton, Leroy Jenkins, and Leo Smith,
58, 61, 134